Michael S. Owen

AFTER IKE: ON THE TRAIL OF THE CENTURY-OLD JOURNEY THAT CHANGED AMERICA

First published by Dog Ear Publishing
8888 Keystone Crossing
Suite 1300
Indianapolis, IN 46240
www.dogearpublishing.net

ISBN: 978-145757-042-1

This book is printed on acid-free paper.
Printed in the United States of America

for Annerieke

INTRODUCTION

Just to the south of Washington's White House, in a spot favored by tourists for its myriad photographic possibilities, stands an unassuming four-foot granite obelisk. The view to the north of the obelisk offers a prime opportunity for selfies with the White House in the background. To the south towers the Washington Monument, and just beyond, visible through the pruned oaks and cherry blossom trees, are the Tidal Basin and Jefferson Memorial. Most tourists pay little attention to the obelisk, but those who take the time to examine it can read two inscriptions. On the parallel face: "Point for the measurement of distances from Washington on highways of the United States." And on the west face: "Starting point of first transcontinental motor Convoy over the Lincoln Highway VII.JUL.MCMXIX."

The transcontinental expedition comprised some eighty-one military vehicles ranging from ten-ton Mack trucks to Harley-Davidson motorcycles, manned by thirty-seven officers and 258 enlisted personnel. The expedition's commanding officer was Lieutenant Colonel Charles McClure, and one of its stated objectives was to traverse the 3,200-plus miles from Washington to San Francisco in order to assess the feasibility of rapid cross-country transport by military vehicles. Such a trek had never before been attempted, and many doubted it could succeed. Convoy member Captain William C. Greany, waxing poetic, wrote: "The Convoy possessed an historic significance, it being the first motor Convoy to cross the American Continent, comparable in its sphere to the first ox-team prairie-schooner trek; the first steam railroad train, and the first airplane flight across the vast expanses of fertile valleys, rolling prairies, rugged mountains, and the desolate wilderness that lie between the Atlantic and Pacific Oceans." In the words of Secretary of War Newton Baker, who waved the Convoy off on that morning of July 7, "This is the beginning of a new era."

The Convoy was huge national news. Thousands of people all across the nation lined the route to cheer the Convoy on as it passed, and its arrival made front-page headlines in the newspapers of towns all along the way. Best estimates are that over 3.5 million people saw the Convoy, which at that time was about 3.5 percent of the US population. Henry Ostermann, field secretary of the recently formed Lincoln Highway Association, led the way. He had driven the route several times and, fortunately, could steer the Convoy through all the nuances and challenges that lay ahead. Dr. S. M. Johnson of the National Highways Association, and chief proponent of the American Good Roads Movement, also accompanied, and he rarely missed an opportunity to make speeches or press statements to promote improved roads.

One of the Convoy's officers was a twenty-eight-year-old, six-foot-two lieutenant colonel named Dwight D. Eisenhower. (Ike had been catapulted into the lieutenant colonel rank by the needs of the war, but he would soon be demoted back to his previous rank of captain). In his final trip report at journey's end, submitted on November 3, 1919, Ike wrote that the Convoy was "well received at all points along the route. It seemed that there was a great deal of sentiment for the improving of highways." Years later, of course, Ike was the driving force behind the construction of the interstate highway system, the world's largest-ever civil engineering project, and an undertaking that continues to transform America even today.

Cross-country road trips have held a particular fascination for Americans throughout our nation's history. In 1806, President Thomas Jefferson ordered the construction of a "National Road" stretching from Cumberland, Maryland, to Ohio in order to facilitate settlement of the Midwest. Walt Whitman extolled the joys of cross-country travel in "Song of the Open Road" long before automobiles existed. Authors ranging from Jack Kerouac to John Steinbeck to William Least Heat Moon have authored American literary classics about cross-country trips. There were several individual transcontinental motor trips completed and documented well before the military's 1919 expedition. In 1903 Horatio Nelson Jackson won a fifty-dollar bet by driving with his invaluable mechanic, Sewall Crocker, and trusty pit bull, Bud, from San Francisco to New York in sixty-three grueling days. Jackson's trip was the first documented motorized cross-country trip, and it's been chronicled in Ken Burns' film, *Horatio's Drive: America's First Road Trip.* Jackson's car, a 1903 Winton without roof or windshield, is on display in the Smithsonian's Museum of American History, along with related paraphernalia down to a life-sized model of Bud, who sported specially fitted goggles throughout the trip because the road dust irritated his eyes.

In 1909 twenty-two-year-old Alice Ramsey led the first all-female transcontinental journey, and in 1916 Nell Richardson and Alice Burke drove their yellow Saxon touring car back and forth across the country, logging more than 10,000 miles to highlight the Women's Suffrage Movement. Perhaps the unlikeliest such pioneer is etiquette guru Emily Post, who, in 1915, crossed the country from New York to San Francisco via portions of the still mostly aspirational Lincoln Highway. Her son and cousin appear to have slogged through most of the tiresome driving while Post reclined comfortably in the back seat. Post later published an account of the trip entitled, *By Motor to the Golden Gate*, which offered up such helpful tips as "recommended attire: an orange-colored chiffon veil for the woman who minds getting sunburnt." At one point out West she got annoyed with the roads and hopped on a train instead.

I have spent forty-plus years living and traveling in Europe, Africa, and Asia, so I was especially attracted by the allure of an American cross-country trip, and I found the 1919 military Convoy that Ike joined to be particularly fascinating. Although other motorists preceded this expedition, the military Convoy was by far the largest and best documented of trips up to that time, coming at the very dawn of the automobile age. Its subsequent impacts on Ike and on our entire country make this expedition unique. I longed to retrace the Convoy's exact route, not only for the curiosity of seeing what it looks like today, but also to witness firsthand the changes that have been wrought across this particular swath of America in the century since Ike's trip, many of them a result of Ike's trip. And so it was that I set out on a breezy April morning from the modest obelisk south of the White House to follow in Ike's footsteps and see all that came after him.

DISTRICT OF COLUMBIA

Washington DC in 1919 was a sleepy but growing town of a little over 400,000 inhabitants. Large areas of the District of Columbia were still heavily forested or cleared farmland. Not too many years earlier, sheep had grazed on what is today the National Mall, and the area where the State Department and Kennedy Center now stand was a boggy morass. Even today that drained area of Washington bears the apt name of Foggy Bottom. The most popular song of 1919 was the post-World War I hit "How Ya Gonna Keep 'Em Down on the Farm, After They've Seen Paree." Henry Ford had recently made history by introducing the first minimum wage: five dollars per day. Oregon had become the first state to impose a gasoline tax: one cent per gallon. Women did not yet have the right to vote, and a few years earlier Teddy Roosevelt's daughter Alice had shocked Washingtonians by daring to ride in a car with men and to smoke a cigarette in public.

Automobiles were quickly becoming popular but were still a relative rarity on Washington's roads in 1919. So the appearance of an 81-vehicle military Convoy was instantly noteworthy. The vehicles assembled at Camp Meigs on Florida Avenue, a short distance northeast of the Capitol building. Different accounts of the trip report differing numbers of vehicles, in part because at various times other non-official vehicles joined the Convoy. But the official report on the Convoy, filed by Lieutenant Elwell Jackson, lists eighty-one vehicles, including thirty-four heavy trucks, twenty-six light trucks, two Cadillac passenger cars for officers, a Cadillac searchlight vehicle, a pontoon trailer, two kitchen trailers, and several Harley-Davidson motorcycles. By the time the first vehicles in the Convoy reached the starting point south of the White House, there were still vehicles waiting at Camp Meigs. When the Convoy finally got out onto open roads, it stretched out for well over three miles, and, lumbering along at less than 10 miles per hour, often took over three hours to pass through towns.

At the Opening Ceremony, politicians, as always, pounced on the opportunity to deliver speeches. President Woodrow Wilson was on a ship heading back to the US from Paris, but the proceedings were attended by Secretary of War Newton

Baker, senators, members of Congress, and senior military brass. The remarks droned on for over an hour, delaying the Convoy's departure. Ike, in a testimonial to the old writer's adage, "incident reveals character," managed to come up with an excuse to miss the opening ceremony and joined the Convoy later in Maryland. Ike later wrote "My luck was running; we missed the ceremony."

The July 6 edition of the *Washington Post*, the day before the Convoy got underway, headlined

60 Trucks Will Cross Continent!
Monument Will Be Placed on Ellipse Tomorrow to Mark Start

And the accompanying article noted, "Ceremonies on the north side of the Ellipse. . .will be held at 10 o'clock tomorrow morning to mark the start for a motor Convoy of 60 trucks and other vehicles for San Francisco, the first transcontinental trip of its kind ever undertaken. . .A small monument will be erected at the starting point as the Zero Milestone of the national highway system. The monument is designed to be the milestone from which, as from the golden milestone in Rome, all road distances will be reckoned."

Several people have written about the history of the first trans-continental Convoy. Perhaps the best account is Pete Davies's excellent *American Road*. Of the Convoy's send-off Davies writes, "As (the speeches) finished, the men of the Convoy bent their backs to the weighty business of cranking 46 truck engines. This was a job that called for care; if one of these brutes backfired, it could easily break an arm." At around eleven o'clock, the Convoy finally got underway.

In his final trip report of October 1919, Elwell Jackson articulates the War Department's four specific purposes of the trip:

a) The War Department's contribution to the Good Roads movement for the purpose of encouraging the construction of through-route and transcontinental highways as a military and economic asset.

b) The procurement of recruits for the enlisted personnel of the Motor Transport Corps, or any other branch of the US Army. . .

c) An exhibition to the general public, either through actual contact or resulting channels of publicity, of the development of the motor vehicle for military purposes, which is conceded to be one of the principal factors contributing to the winning of the World War.

d) An extensive study and observation of the terrain and standard army motor vehicles by certain branches of the army. . .

The nascent Good Roads Movement, as well as the Lincoln Highway Association, were enthusiastic boosters of the trip, and at various times members of the two organizations drove along with the Convoy. Henry Ostermann, Field Secretary of the Lincoln Highway Association, had driven the route previously, and he led the way for the entire trip. Henry Joy, President of Packard and ardent member of both organizations, also accompanied for long stretches in his Packard convertible, and never missed an opportunity to deliver a rousing speech urging support for good roads.

At that time one of the few major roads that headed northwest from the White House toward Maryland was Wisconsin Avenue, one of several state-named major arteries envisioned in Pierre L'Enfant's original 1791 master plan for Washington. To reach Wisconsin Avenue, the Convoy passed around the White House and by the imposing presence of what is today the Eisenhower Executive Office Building, built in 1888 to house the Departments of State, War, and Navy. Some ten years after the Convoy, Ike would be working inside that building as Executive Officer to Assistant Secretary of War General George V. Mosely, and in 1955, Ike held the first-ever televised presidential press conference there. The building was named after Ike in 1999.

Just beyond lay Lafayette Square, Decatur House, and Blair House, all of which were there in 1919 and still stand today. Blair House has served as the official residence for visiting heads of state and other dignitaries since it was purchased by the government in 1942, but it was originally the residence of the Blair family, whose patriarch, Francis Preston Blair, was a member of Andrew Jackson's original "kitchen cabinet." Lafayette Square has long been a prime Washington staging ground for demonstrations in support of causes ranging from the urgent to the incoherent.

In the first irony of my trip, the spot where the historic motor Convoy began is no longer accessible to motorized vehicles. In the aftermath of the terrorist attacks of September 11, 2001, most streets around the White House are now closed to vehicular traffic, and open only to pass-holding employees of the White House or adjacent Eisenhower Executive Office Building. So my own trip in my little Chevy sedan started up on 16th Street, just north of Lafayette Square: Andrew Jackson, right up in the middle, tipping his Admiral's hat while expertly handling a rearing horse surrounded by cannons. The Convoy—minus Ike—passed right by.

To reach my car I walked through Lafayette Square, where I briefly paused to chronicle the day's demonstrations. There was a lone man sweltering outside a pup tent fashioned from clear plastic sheeting, surrounded by signs reading: "No more Chernobyls!" "No more Fukushimas!" "Ban nukes!" "Honor Indigenous Treaties!" Nearby a small troupe was assembling with signs denouncing the Trans-Pacific Partnership Treaty. And then arrived a tall man in a dark suit wearing a Donald Trump mask and voluminous orange-blonde wig. He paraded through the crowd, waving his hands high and shouting, "It's gonna be great, folks! You won't believe it!"

I stopped briefly in the Decatur House to check out an exhibit on "the President's Neighborhood." Built in 1818 by naval hero Commodore Stephen Decatur, the house was the first private residence on Lafayette Square. After Decatur's death in a duel, the house was occupied by a succession of Washington notables, including Henry Clay and Martin Van Buren, and today houses the White House Historical Association. The survival today of so many historic buildings around Lafayette Square owes a great deal to First Lady Jackie Kennedy, who in 1961 spearheaded a historic preservation movement that stymied congressional ambitions to "modernize" the area.

A bit farther north on 16th Street, the Convoy rumbled around Scott Circle and took a left onto Massachusetts Avenue. Scott Circle, like so many circles in central DC, is named for a war hero, in this case Winfield Scott. Scott somehow earned the nickname "Old Fuss and Feathers" and is still the longest-serving general in US military history. The circle that's named for him has a statue of him in the middle, and he too is astride a horse, with his right hand on his hip, gazing assertively into the distance. The monument, made out of cannons Scott captured during the Mexican-American War, was installed in 1874, so the Convoy passed right by.

A short distance beyond is Dupont Circle, one of L'Enfant's most prominent planned features and, at the time of the Convoy, still a fashionable residential area just beginning the transition to commercial enterprises. A century later, Dupont Circle is a bohemian, artistic neighborhood favored by Washington's gay community. The annual High Heel Race, featuring dozens of drag queens racing three blocks down 17th Street, has since its inception in 1986 been a hugely popular Washington event attracting thousands of spectators. Just beyond is Embassy Row, with dozens of embassies scattered among posh houses built near the turn of the twentieth century.

The Convoy turned northward where Massachusetts Avenue intersects Wisconsin Avenue near the National Cathedral. Construction of the cathedral began in 1907, with President Teddy Roosevelt in attendance for the laying of the cornerstone, so it was already far along when the Convoy passed by. The full structure was finally completed in 1990, and nowadays it's the second largest church in the US (New York's Cathedral of Saint John is largest). Even today, work on details continues. Numerous stone masons from Italy were brought in during the early 1900s to work on the cathedral, and many of them mentored their children to continue the task. Ike lay in repose in the cathedral after his death in 1969, and Martin Luther King delivered his final sermon there in March 1968.

In 1919 almost the entire length of Wisconsin Avenue to the Maryland line was two narrow lanes, just adequate to accommodate the heaviest trucks of the Convoy. Marching orders for the Convoy were to be as self-sufficient as possible, so there were numerous trucks weighing in at ten tons or more, that carried cargo ranging from machine spare parts, to a full blacksmith shop, to mobile machine shops, to 1,500 gallons of gasoline. Creeping up Wisconsin Avenue were also a caterpillar tractor, a pontoon trailer, and a specialized four-ton vehicle labelled as an "artillery wheeled vehicle," otherwise known as the Militor, designed to winch out other vehicles that had broken down or gotten stuck. As it turned out, if the Convoy had designated a Most Valuable Player award, the Militor would have won, hands down.

Although no specifics are available, a phalanx of such monstrous bulky vehicles like this would surely have caused substantial damage to Wisconsin Avenue on the way out of town. As automobiles became more popular in the first decades of the twentieth century, there were corresponding improvements in road conditions, particularly in the East. Up to the early twentieth century most roads, even in major cities, were dirt or gravel, but road technology was improving rapidly. Washington in 1919 had numerous roads paved with bricks, crushed stone, asphalt, or concrete. But paving practices were nowhere near the exacting standards of today, and Wisconsin Avenue was surely the worse for wear once the Convoy had passed. And Washington DC at that time was considered to have the best roads of any US city—reflective members of the Convoy must have wondered about what lay ahead in the West, where dirt tracks were still the norm.

Wisconsin Avenue today is one of the major commuter arteries into central Washington, used by thousands of motorists every day. It is now mostly six lanes of almost constant hubbub, and there are usually parked vehicles on both sides, narrowing everything to four lanes. As I drove up through clogged, cacophonous traffic beyond Rock Creek, past the Naval Observatory and the cathedral, bicyclists swerved in and out and taxis careened through precipitous lane changes, horns blaring from all directions. A U-Haul van made an abrupt monstrous U-turn from the far right lane, brakes squealing all around.

I motored on and fantasized briefly about driving a four-ton winch truck right through the midst of it all, asphalt chunks spewing up in my wake.

The Convoy rolled by just a bit west of the National Zoological Gardens, which in 1919 had already been open for almost thirty years and drew enthusiastic crowds to view such exotic species as elephants, crocodiles, and bison. The zoo was the brainchild of William Temple Hornaday, official taxidermist of the Smithsonian Institution in the late nineteenth century. In his zeal for authenticity, Hornaday had collected some 185 wild animals to serve as models for his work. They grazed, mostly peaceably, on the national mall near the Smithsonian castle. But on a late-1880s trip out west, Hornaday was shocked by the near decimation of beaver, bison, and other species and became committed to the idea of a national zoological park in Washington. With avid Smithsonian support, the zoo, designed by noted landscape architect Frederick Law Olmstead, became a reality and opened its gates to visitors in 1891. Hornaday's 185 original model animals were its first residents. By the time the Convoy rolled nearby in 1919, the zoo was already hugely popular, with over 2 million visitors per year.

Past Cleveland Park I motored northwest through still dense, shrilling traffic. Past high-rise condominiums ranging from the ornate to the austere, office blocks, commercial strip malls. Starbucks, Baskin-Robbins, Burger King. A hair salon with the sign "Discover the True You!." And then a large liquor store with the sign:

Beer, Wine, Spirits!
Open 7 Days a Week!
We Deliver!

Almost all of it was farmland or forest at the time of the Convoy. On upper Wisconsin Avenue I resisted the temptation to detour over to the east for a stop at Politics and Prose, one of the best bookstores in the US. Instead, I negotiated my way around traffic-clogged Tenleytown, past Coffee Nature: Chill café with Korean grub, past the Joy of Motion dance studio, and finally passed over the District of Columbia boundary line and into Maryland.

MARYLAND

"Travelling leaves you speechless, then turns you into
a storyteller. Travelling offers you a hundred roads to
adventure, and gives your heart wings. Travelling gives
you home in a thousand strange places, then leaves you
a stranger in your own land."

–Ibn Battuta

I churned on up through the maelstrom of traffic that defined Wisconsin
Avenue, through Chevy Chase and Bethesda, traffic clogged on all sides,
even early in the morning.

Chevy Chase, Maryland, was first developed in the 1890s by the Chevy
Chase Land Company. The company was partly owned by Senator Francis
Newlands of Nevada, who evidently generously supplemented his senator's
salary with active off-line real estate dealings in the Washington area. The first
houses began appearing in the late 1890s, and by the time the Convoy passed
through in 1919, Chevy Chase was a lively suburban settlement of upscale
housing. Newlands was an avowed racist who ran his 1912 presidential bid
on a proposed constitutional amendment to disenfranchise black men and
limit all immigration to whites only. Chevy Chase remained all-white until
well after World War II.

The Convoy continued up what is today Maryland State Highway 355
through the town of Friendship Heights. At the time of the Convoy, 355 was
known as Rockville Pike, an extension of Wisconsin Avenue. This stretch
of road dates way back to colonial times and was used as an escape route
for Washingtonians fleeing the capital during the War of 1812. I followed
it northward, alternately through leafy residential areas and towering office
blocks, toward Frederick.

Downtown Bethesda nowadays is a mélange of high-rise office buildings, apartments, and honking traffic. And a string of interesting-sounding
shops as well: Massage Envy, Seoul Spice, Red Bandana Bakery, Shangri-La

Indian-Nepali Cuisine. The Villain and Saint: Drink, Dine, Music. That name alone made me want to stop in, but alas, it was early morning and it wasn't open yet. There's also the classic old Bethesda Cinema, now featuring live entertainment, and a couple of nineteenth-century stone buildings that Ike and the Convoy would have passed right by. But also this: six-story buildings being clobbered down into rubble, to make room for even taller structures. I wondered how many generations of buildings have lined this portion of the Convoy's route, and what they saw when they passed.

North of Bethesda, on through Rockville and Gaithersburg. In my Rand-McNally Atlas these are all shown as distinct towns, but I could never tell were one stopped and the other started, amidst the relentless suburban sprawl. Sushi Bars and Pizza Huts. CVS Open 24 Hours! Popeye's, Taco Bell, Wendy's. Gas stations and acres-wide car dealerships.

The only true respite through all of this was the beautiful campus of the National Institutes of Health. NIH was founded back in the 1870s, and its primary campus is in Bethesda and Rockville. It's the US government agency with the chief responsibility for biomedical and public research, and is today the largest biomedical research institution in the world. The current site was not utilized until the late 1930s, so when the Convoy passed through Bethesda and Rockville, the NIH campus was open farmland.

A short distance beyond the Maryland state line, at the Washington beltway, I-270 begins, just to the west of the Convoy's route. Up to ten lanes of hurtling traffic. Mercifully, I did not have to drive it, but in Gaithersburg I detoured over slightly just for a short look. Trucks, cars, and campers barreled forward at 80 mph-plus in all lanes. The freeway is lined with new bedroom commuter communities, squarish dark office buildings, and still more automobile dealerships. A large sign announcing "I-270 high-tech corridor!" loomed up. All ten lanes rampant with traffic but still whizzing by at 80 mph-plus. And then a huge billboard for a politician running for office: "Time to widen 270 now!!" I quickly retreated to the relative tranquility of Rockville Pike and pressed onwards.

I have groused from time to time about slow Washington traffic, but I've had work colleagues who commuted into downtown Washington from Frederick and environs every day, and it was rare that I failed to hear a word from at least one of them about the abysmal traffic. "Everything was totally clogged!" "Took me an hour and a half to get here!" "There were times when we were only going 15 miles per hour!" But consider this: on the Convoy's first day of travel from the White House to Frederick,

Elwell Jackson's trusty daily log of the trip reports that a trail mobile kitchen broke a coupling, a fan belt broke on an observation car, and a broken magneto coupling on a cargo truck meant the truck had to be towed into camp. Nonetheless, Jackson's log notes, "Roads excellent. Made 46 miles in 7.5 hours." That's an average speed of a little over six miles per hour for the entire day, and this on some of the best roads the Convoy would encounter for the entire trip.

Just beyond Gaithersburg I turned off northward on Highway 27, following the Convoy's route, and was suddenly liberated from suburban sprawl. Open countryside, passing through little towns with sonorous names like Cedar Grove, Damascus, Friendship. Ancient lightning-scarred sycamores; old clapboard churches; spreading orchards, the trees aligned as perfectly as marching soldiers. There were crumbling lonely houses boarded up and for sale, and on some even the "For Sale" signs were crumbling. But there were also picturesque old white farmhouses, set way back from the road on rolling green hillsides, with gingerbread lattice work on the front porches, where rocking chairs stood waiting.

Near Damascus I stopped to walk through a cemetery with gravestones dating from the 1890s. Names like Burdette, Watkins, Brown, Moxley. The Convoy passed right by. I eventually visited several cemeteries all along the route, and always wondered if the Convoy's members had relatives buried in any of those cemeteries. With 300 men from all over the US, it seemed entirely possible. Did they ever stop to visit a grave site? No record.

Just south of Friendship I pulled over and got out, just to stand and look. Not another car in sight, just the open countryside, and I thought, for the first time since I pushed off from the White House, "Yes. This is what they saw, what they passed through." A century ago.

I turned back west on Highway 144, which is also the Old National Pike. The National Pike was the nation's first federally funded highway, begun in 1811. It ran from the Potomac River at Cumberland, Maryland, out to central Illinois, and was intended to "open up the West." Much like the original Lincoln Highway, large portions of the original National Pike are now long abandoned, but I drove this portion all the way into Frederick. Through more beautiful open countryside: goats and chickens rooting down by an ancient red barn, "Farm Market Apples," "Firewood for Sale," and then the Full Gospel Church. I passed through the exquisite main street of New Market, lined with nineteenth-century buildings and antique shops galore. The Convoy passed right through this as well. And approaching Frederick, the Blue Sky Bar and Grill—another place I couldn't visit in the early morn-ing, before opening time.

At Frederick, I turned off the highway into the serenity of Jefferson Street, right up through Patrick Street and the middle of a beautiful downtown, exactly where the Convoy had passed in 1919. First settled by German col-onists in the 1740s, Frederick's natural beauty has long been celebrated by writers. In his Civil War poem, "Barbara Fritchie," John Greenleaf Whittier writes: "The clustered spires of Frederick stand, green-walled by the hills of Maryland." I walked along the Carroll Creek Promenade and then chatted with a very helpful assistant named Maria in the Frederick Visitor Center. I asked her about the Emmitsburg covered bridge, which was damaged by the Convoy. According to Elwell Jackson's journal: "Unsafe covered wooden bridge, one mile south of Emmitsburg. . . . .two hours delay . . . . .necessitat-ing detours and fording. Mack Machine Shop #5 damaged top of low bridge."

Maria told me that the original Emmitsburg Road Bridge that the Convoy had passed through and smashed up had eventually been torn down and replaced by a concrete bridge in 1923. Only three covered bridges still remained in all of Frederick County, she said, and two could be visited. "The other one was damaged a few weeks ago," she said, "when a truck that was too big tried to pass through it." Even after a century of driving, some mistakes persist.

But at least the Convoy had some semblance of a bridge in this case. Drake Hokanson writes that in the early days of the Lincoln Highway, "Bridges were another problem. . .No matter how steep the sides, no matter how rough the streambed, a dry arroyo or stream was seldom honored with a bridge."

At the Frederick Public Library, I read the July 8, 1919, edition of the *Frederick Register,* which had a front-page story: "America's Heaviest War Truck Unit Ever Assembled in Motion." The article begins with "Into this little town through which the wagon trains of Lee's defeated Army crawled southwards 56 years ago. . . yesterday rolled the . . . United States Motor Transport Corps on the first leg of its ocean to ocean run. The great carriers travelled from Washington to Frederick on Maryland's unexcelled highways." Union Pride and Civic Boosterism!

I drove out along Patrick Street to the east and stopped at the fairgrounds where the Convoy spent the first night of their trip. This is where Ike and his pal Sereno Brett joined the team after skipping out on the speeches at the opening ceremony.

Frederick has a long and fascinating African American history. In the nineteenth and early twentieth centuries, the crowded All Saints Street neighborhood was a hive of activity for African Americans throughout Frederick County. During a time of systematic discrimination, All Saints Street was a thriving and completely self-contained neighborhood, with shops, banking, medical care, and a lively entertainment scene on weekend nights. Just one example: Ulysses Grant Bourne came to Frederick in 1903 and practiced medicine there for half a century. He founded the Maryland Negro Medical Society, was the first African American on the staff of the Frederick Memorial Hospital, and co-founded the Frederick branch of the NAACP. His practice was going strong when the Convoy passed through.

I followed the Convoy's route up Highway 15 to the north of Frederick, through more rolling green countryside filled with cattle and, to my surprise, the occasional llama. Just to the west of Thurmont lies Catoctin Mountain Park, some 6,000 acres of gorgeous hiking trails through dense, steep oak and pine forest, and more importantly, the site of the 120-acre Camp David compound. Franklin Roosevelt first made this a presidential retreat in 1942, and named it Shangri-La, but Ike subsequently named it Camp David after his father and grandson. Ike was the first-ever president to convene a cabinet meeting at Camp David, in November 1955, and it's been a regular presidential getaway ever since. For security reasons Camp David's precise location is secret, but there's a large empty area on the Catoctin Mountain Park map that gives you a pretty good idea. In late 1919, just a few months after Ike and the Convoy passed through, Prohibition became the law of the land, and all of Catoctin Mountain, including today's Camp David, became a bootlegging hub.

I paused briefly in Emmitsburg to visit the site of the covered bridge over Tom's Creek that the Convoy damaged and then repaired. Elwell Jackson reported in his log that the Convoy suffered a two-hour delay due to "unsafe covered bridge," and that the Convoy's "engineers rendered valuable work in bridge inspection." Always looking on the bright side, Jackson wrote at the day's end, "Roads excellent with exception of two detours on account of unsafe bridge and repairs. Made 62 miles in 10.5 hours." According to the May 6, 1922, edition of the *Frederick News*, a county commissioner deemed the covered bridge "faulty and dangerous to traffic" and recommended its replacement "as soon as possible." By late 1923 the covered bridge had been demolished and replaced by a modern concrete structure.

I continued onward along the path of the Convoy and passed into Pennsylvania just south of Gettysburg.

PENNSYLVANIA

"The road stretching over the horizon has represented a
sense of possibility and freedom, discovery, and escape,
a place to get lost and find yourself."

–David Campany

Crossing over into Pennsylvania on Highway 15. Right away a hand-written sign:

Farm fresh eggs!
Laid by Happy Chickens!

I meandered on through beautiful green countryside: pastures and cattle and no-doubt many happy chickens. White farmhouses set back neatly on flowing hillsides, and red barns gleaming in the sunlight. A pig-tailed blonde girl riding a tricycle next to a white clapboard house and carefully trimmed hedges.

Crossing into Pennsylvania the Militor was already proving its mettle. Elwell Jackson writes: "Militor pulled Class B Machine Shop (ten tons) out of mud. . .after two Macks in tandem had failed. . .Militor made Piney Mountain on 3rd speed, with tow. Class Bs had to use 2nd speed. Mack trucks had difficulty making this grade in low gear. Packards also lazy on hills." The Militor was in the command of Edward Reis, the only civilian driver in the official Convoy, and he quickly earned the respect of everyone for his tireless efforts all along the route. But it was most frequently driven by Sergeant T. E Wood, who did yeoman's work.

Highway 15 intersects Highway 30, the Lincoln Highway, at the main square in downtown Gettysburg. An historic spot: the nearby Gettysburg Train Station was where Lincoln arrived on the evening of November 18, 1863, and the David Wills House on the square was where he spent the night and polished his renowned speech before delivery the next day. Ike and the Convoy drove past here on July 8, 1919, but, much to the regret of Gettysburg citizens, did not stop for the night. The Convoy instead pushed on to Chambersburg, some 30 miles to the West. The ensuing July 9 headline in the *Gettysburg Times* read, "Military Convoy Did Not Stop Here—Efforts of Citizens Wasted."

Gettysburg and environs are replete with historic markers, signs, and souvenir shops marking the historic battle. A short distance west of downtown's square on the Lincoln Highway, through gorgeous open countryside with perfectly zig-zagging split-rail fences, I discovered a particularly noteworthy marker at McPherson Ridge: The Union Second Brigade horse artillery, Battery A, with a grand total of six three-inch cannons, under the command of Lieutenant John Calef, here fired the first Union shot of the decisive battle of the Civil War. Calef and his brigade had arrived from Emmitsburg the evening of June 30, 1863. So they had followed exactly the same route that I followed and Ike and the Convoy had followed some fifty-six years after the battle. Through the same Emmitsburg covered bridge, the same Route 15 dirt road to Gettysburg. Ike followed the same route, past the first shot, not far from his future one and only house, the house where he lived and died after his presidency.

Ike yearned desperately to see action in Europe during World War I, but instead he was assigned to Camp Colt at Gettysburg, in charge of training of the army's nascent tank corps. He chafed at what he considered a hum-drum domestic assignment, and at war's end wrote, "I was mad, disappointed, and resented the fact that the war had passed me by. At times I was tempted, at least faintly, to try my luck as a civilian again." After the war Ike was reassigned to Camp Meade in Washington DC. There was no housing for families there, so Mamie and their one-year-old son, Icky, had to move out to Denver to live with her parents, the Douds. Ike had to pack out of the Gettysburg house by himself, and Mamie would not see any of their possessions for years. When she finally unpacked them years later, she discovered the coffee percolator was still full of coffee grounds.

But then the fateful moment came. Ike: "Major Sereno Brett and I heard about a truck Convoy that was to cross the country from coast to coast, and we were immediately excited. In those days, we were not sure it could be accomplished at all. Nothing of the sort had ever been attempted. . . .I promptly reported that I would be glad to make the trip." So it must have been with some satisfaction that on July 9, 1919, Ike could gaze out at his former training site of Camp Colt as the Convoy proceeded westward, toward San Francisco, on a route that was adventurous and highly uncertain to say the least.

Ike and Mamie, because of or in spite of their experiences, loved Gettysburg. Ike had first visited in 1915 when he was a cadet at West Point. And so it was that they bought a farm and house there and settled down after retirement from the White House. It is the only house they ever owned. During renovation of their house, a Confederate body was found buried in the back yard. When I walked through the premises, I noted the impressive gifts given by heads of state over the years. But they struck me as being of secondary importance for Ike and Mamie. Tabriz rugs, lacquer inlay boxes, etc. were on display in the living room, but the TV, painting easel, and card decks were out on the back porch, where Ike and Mamie actually lived. It was a thoroughly comfortable and unassuming residence for them both in retirement. To quote the guide brochure about Ike's den: "The Civil War pike and musket above the fireplace, the red lamp decorated with fishing flies, and the art books in the bookcase reflect Ike's interests." In 1963, just a few years before his death, Ike delivered the commemorative speech on the centennial of Lincoln's Gettysburg Address.

A few words here on the Lincoln Highway: At the very dawn of the automobile age, car enthusiasts came up with the idea of a national highway from Atlantic to Pacific. The first major proponent was Carl Fisher, who socked away millions by manufacturing bicycles, carbide headlights, and later developing Miami Beach. He used much of it to support modern cars and roads. Despite his own physical frailties, Fisher fearlessly drove test cars throughout the 1910s, and was the motivating force behind the creation of the Indianapolis 500.

Fisher and others advocated fiercely for a national coast-to-coast highway, and eventually teamed up to support the Lincoln Highway. Today's Lincoln Highway is more or less the modern Highway 30 from Philadelphia all the way through to southwestern Wyoming, and then Highway 50 to California, but large portions of the original 1913 version run more or less parallel nearby, often weed-infested crumbling concrete or pure dirt. But with some persistence you can still track it down and can, in many cases, still drive it. Fisher told his followers: "A road across the United States! Let's build it before we're too old to enjoy it!" Fellow enthusiast Henry Joy, who was CEO of Packard, quickly contributed some $300,000 to the effort. Joy was a motoring enthusiast and had driven extensively out west long before the idea of the Lincoln Highway surfaced. But once the idea arose, he pioneered and sought out the best route for the Lincoln Highway and was thus a guiding force in determining the highway's exact alignment. He served as the first president of the Lincoln Highway Association and drove the route many times coast to coast. Frank Seiberling, CEO of Goodyear and second president of the association, strongly supported the Convoy also.

But back in the early twentieth century, it was up to every state to pave their portion of highway. Out in the West the "Lincoln Highway" was often not much more than a cartographer's scribbled line on a paper map, patched together from an amalgam of old wagon roads and Pony Express trails. Henry Joy had some serious misadventures on his first trips, and he wrote that west of Omaha, the road was "nothing but two ruts across the prairie." It was something the Convoy would also discover, sometimes very painfully.

Nowadays the Lincoln Highway is a highly recognized historic route with a large following of road enthusiasts. Distinctive red, white, and blue "L" signs mark the entire length of the Lincoln Highway, and they are a godsend for rookie travelers like me, scrabbling to find the way. The many concrete pillars were placed by the Boy Scouts back in 1928. The Lincoln Highway Association (of which I am a proud member) was formed in 1913, and President Woodrow Wilson promptly mailed in his five-dollar membership fee and became Member Number One. The LHA has a superb website, professional staff, and gung-ho members. A multitude of events, festivals, jubilees, etc. are held along the Lincoln Highway every year, at which vintage century-old vehicles are a common sight.

Plenty of authors have written about various portions of the Lincoln Highway. Drake Hokanson's book, *Lincoln Highway: Main Street Across America*, sparked a renewed interest in the Lincoln Highway and spurred the re-establishment of the Lincoln Highway Association in 1987. Hokanson writes in his Introduction: "The Lincoln Highway was an expression of the national desire to bind the country from east to west." Brian Butko was one of the original board members of the revived LHA and has written several books about the highway, including *Greetings from the Lincoln Highway* and *Lincoln Highway Companion*. For anyone interested in the Lincoln Highway, Hokanson and Butko are the two go-to sources.

Back in 1919, the first Lincoln Highway Association President, Henry Joy, sent a message to Convoy Commander Colonel McClure: "The sending of the Convoy of motor trucks by the Motor Transport Corps to the Pacific Ocean via the Lincoln Highway is the realization of the vision of the highway's founders. . .the commercial and military needs of such a main artery highway were paramount in the minds of the originators. . .I am very proud of the connection I and my company had with the inception of the Lincoln

Highway idea. For several years prior to 1913, the year the Lincoln route was established, I sent all experimental motor cars on testing trips for the Packard Company westward in search of the best route to the Pacific. I drove various routes myself and studied the general topography. The final location of the highway became a matter of the simplest decisions logically forcing itself by the accumulated data as to its feasibility. Your truck train run should be an object lesson, which will lead to the wise location of other main artery routes and the building of them as fast as the ways and means can be provided."

With few or no alternatives, it was inevitable that the Convoy would choose to follow—with a handful of minor detours—the Lincoln Highway all the way from Gettysburg to San Francisco, and in following the Convoy's route, I too was primarily on the old Lincoln Highway from Gettysburg all the way to the Pacific Ocean. The old Lincoln Highway is not the same as the current Lincoln Highway for much of the way across the country, due to numerous re-directions, straightening of curves, and by-passing of towns by the more modern highway. But with some diligence it's still possible to follow the old route that the Convoy took back in 1919, which led right through the middle of every town on the route, and regularly took me out to delightful old dirt roads traversing lonely countryside.

All across the country, along the Convoy's route through small towns, I noticed everywhere America's penchant for superlatives: biggest, oldest, first, fastest, best. Capital of This, Home of That. Is this part of our national character? In all my world travels I've never seen these superlatives anywhere else to the extent that we Americans celebrate them. They all celebrate, in one way or another: We made a bigger one, a better one, a new and unique one, or made more of it than anybody else. That constant striving for the best seems to me to be a laudable American characteristic, and I saw it repeatedly all across the country.

I drove on past scattered battlefield sites, just like Ike and the Convoy back in 1919. Rolling verdant farmland and tight pockets of oak, birch, and maple. Past Mister Ed's Elephant Museum and Candy Emporium, an unmissable site offering some 12,000 elephant models, a 1903 peanut roaster, jellybeans, Fireballs, Root Beer Barrels, and delicious homemade fudge. Out in the garden are huge Crayola crayon models hanging from the trees, life-size models of Snow White and company, toilet bowls overflowing with plants, and a host of other sights. Mr. Ed has welcomed famous guests for decades, and also hosts an annual 6,000-egg Easter egg hunt. I have no idea why he built this garish spectacle, but he must have had a ball doing so. He created it all in the 1950s, long after Ike and the Convoy passed right by the same site.

I passed through Chambersburg where the Convoy spent their second night on the road. Past historic buildings that were already old when Ike passed through. Cozy inviting shops: Boswells Pipes and Cigars, a barber shop with the pole already revolving even before sunrise. Past the Courthouse, the only building with a queue before 8:00 a.m. Handwritten signs on the outskirts:

"Ice cream Sandwiches and Mini-Golf!"
"Egg Roll Queen: Eat In or Take Out!"

The *Chambersburg Public Opinion* of Wednesday, July 9, 1919, has the headline "Truck Train in Camp is Visited by Many People; Soldiers are Living Real Field Life; Band Gives Concert." The accompanying article relates, "scores of town's people were attracted to the grounds by the presence of the Motor Convoy which left Washington on Monday on its trip to the Pacific. . .Those who went to the lot found plenty to interest them."

Elsewhere on the *Public Opinion's* front page is another headline: "Wets Filibuster in House; Drys Have the Votes." Prohibition was looming.

The Convoy departed Chambersburg early and stopped for lunch in McConnellsburg. After that, Lieutenant Jackson wrote, "Encountered heavy grades and altitudes exceeding 2200." But happily, "No losses or damages. Excellent driving for untrained personnel. Enthusiastic reception in Bedford. Camp attendance 2,000. Band concert and street dances." Even today the grades are exceptionally steep, and the original Lincoln Highway in this area is still arrow-straight. Because the road avoids switchbacks and plows straight up steep hillsides, it is treacherous in slippery or foggy weather. All along this stretch of the route nowadays are signs: "Caution! Trucks Avoid Using Highway 30!"

The little town/intersection of Breezewood is nowadays an appalling entanglement of perpetually clogged and honking traffic. When I passed through I thought I might have just come on a bad day, but NO! Everybody I asked corrected me on that one. "It's terrible," said an Indian-American lady named Lakshmi at a nearby gas station. "They did not link up Interstate 70 with the Turnpike, so everybody must get off, drive through downtown, and get back on."

"Is there a plan to fix that?" I asked. It seemed remarkably simple.

"I am not thinking so," she shrugged, and gave a firm head waggle. "The politicians, they start arguing? There is being no end to it, no?"

I stopped off at the 1788 Inn just west of Breezewood and spoke to the owner and manager, retired Colonel Scott Lloyd. The Inn does indeed date from 1788 and has been in more or less continuous operation since then, so Ike and the Convoy passed right by it in 1919. Although I was not a paying guest, Scott nonetheless graciously took the time to give me a full tour. The building and premises had fallen into some disrepair when Scott and his wife Cathy purchased the property and lovingly restored it a little over a decade ago. Exquisite original features, working fireplaces all around, period antiques, and gorgeous porches where you can nurse a cool drink with a great view. Ike passed right by in 1919, but there's no evidence that he stopped.

Scott showed me up into the attic as well, which he and Cathy had not yet fully renovated. "This is where all the stagecoach drivers slept. Can you imagine the stories they would have told?" There was no fireplace in the attic; there would have been just straw scattered on the floor where all the drivers slept huddled up and trying to stay warm. But I already knew: if I'd been around back in 1788, I'd have happily forgone a cozy private heated room and instead hunkered down in the attic, listening to all those stories the entire night long.

Whenever I discovered such inviting spots along the entire route, I always wondered if Ike didn't look at them and, at least for a moment, yearn to sit in a comfortable rocking chair on the front porch, slowly sip a frosty drink, gaze out over the gorgeous scenery, and briefly escape from the constant grinding hubbub of 300 men and 81 vehicles, always in a churn. There were so many beautiful old inns along the route: the Golden Eagle Inn, the Cashtown Inn, the Jean Bonnet Tavern: Ike and the Convoy passed right by each one of them. Many of them had welcomed stagecoaches decades before automobiles came along. Perhaps Ike wished he could stop for a pleasant little respite, but there is no evidence that he ever took action, apart from his delayed arrival at the beginning of the Convoy.

In addition to showing me around his Inn, Scott also told me about local Rails to Trails projects, as well as a special Pike to Hike project. Rails to Trails is a national program that has successfully converted hundreds of miles of abandoned rail lines into beautiful and now heavily-used hiking and biking trails. But Pike to Hike? Scott told me to park at a particular place, clamber up a steep hill, turn left at the top, and I would see what he meant. I did so, and discovered an abandoned portion of the Pennsylvania Turnpike, deeply wooded all around and overgrown with brush, but set up to be a terrific hiking or biking trail.

A lone bicyclist whizzed by as I wandered otherwise all alone on the narrow asphalt, through the thick forest, contemplating this: a path through the forest, no doubt a Native American path. Then a settler's path, then a wagon trail. Stagecoaches and then cars. Then Pennsylvania Turnpike. Cars, trucks, buses— all 80 mph. Then an improved PA Turnpike on a straighter stretch half a mile over to the side, and an abandoned stretch returning to nature. Pike to Hike.

I hiked along for some distance but stopped and turned around at the entrance to an ominously forbidding dark tunnel. I later learned that this very tunnel and stretch of road figured menacingly in the 2013 movie, *The Road*, based on Cormac McCarthy's novel of the same name. A spot where, after a global apocalypse, a father and young son fled ravaging marauders. Good time to turn back.

The very moving memorial to 2001's Flight 93 near Shanksville draws lots of visitors. I stopped by early on a Tuesday morning and had difficulty finding a parking place. Not just tour buses but also scads of individual cars. It's a tastefully done memorial, and many visitors cry when they read the story of 9/11, see the extensive running video footage, and particularly when they read about the bravery of the 40 passengers and crew of Flight 93, which crashed at the site of the memorial. *"Let's roll!"* A group of passengers overwhelmed the hijackers, but not in time to take control of the plane, and it went plummeting down into a field at over 500 mph. Their efforts almost certainly saved the US Capitol Building, by most accounts the intended target. For several years the memorial had a golden retriever named Happy who offered solace to grief-stricken visitors. But alas, Happy passed away in early 2018.

I drove on a short distance from the Flight 93 Memorial and came across an automobile junkyard near Stoystown. I parked and wandered around for a while, seeing everything from flattened Mercedes to crushed Chevy pickups. All lined up perfectly in precise rows, like a military exercise. Amazing the infinite diversity of calamities and variety of distortions an automobile can suffer. Head-on collisions, rear-ends, T-bones, skittering multiple smash-ups. For almost every one, I couldn't help wondering, "Who got out alive?"

I took a few photos, and after a while a man came ambling up and asked if he could help me.

"I'm just looking around," I said. "Fascinating to look at all these wrecked cars."

"Yep. Got over fifty acres of cars now. Company started out with just six acres, over fifty years ago. We're still family-owned after all those years."

"So, do you sell many of these?" I asked.

"Mostly just spare parts. We got a computerized inventory system that can pinpoint any part somebody's looking for. You'd be amazed the number of people who come from all over, looking for that one particular part they need for the car they're fixing up."

Automobile junkyards did not exist, of course, until automobiles were invented. The first-ever junkyard was reportedly the Old Car City, opened in 1931 just north of Atlanta. Nowadays it's home to over 4,500 junked cars and covers 34 acres. There are some 8,200 others with about 12.6 million junked cars all across the country, covering many square miles of land. It's a $22 billion business, and still growing. Wrecked or decommissioned vehicles are often taken apart and still usable components sold. Car fanatics are frequent customers of junkyards, combing about in search of, for example, that unique 1964 Mustang left taillight to complete their re-make. Leftover scrap is often sold to China.

I drove on slowly, toward Bedford, along the open and thinly travelled Lincoln Highway. Thinking about the history of the highway, of highways in general, and then into my brain from an unexpected direction careened road songs. So many classic road songs: Chuck Berry's "Maybelline," the Beatles' "Baby You Can Drive My Car," Willie Nelson's "On the Road Again." I was humming, shuffling through all of them like a classic old jukebox. Wilson Pickett's "Mustang Sally." And the Beach Boys "Fun, Fun, Fun," but then, alas, her daddy took the T-Bird away.

I wandered around in the picturesque and historic town of Bedford, where Ike and the Convoy spent the night of July 9. Past a 30-foot high monument of a coffee pot, right next to the fairgrounds where Ike and the Convoy stayed overnight. Also past a classically maintained 1930's Gulf gas station. I eventually discovered that President James Buchanan, who immediately preceded President Lincoln, made his summer retreat from Washington here. And so it was that on August 15, 1858, Queen Victoria sent the first-ever trans-Atlantic telegraph cable from Buckingham Palace, London, to President Buchanan's summer cottage in Bedford. The first trans-Atlantic cable to tiny Bedford, only sixty-one years before the Convoy passed through.

While digesting this fact, I visited the Bedford Fort Museum and encountered a startlingly moving exhibit: an ordinary small oak antique dining table with this text: "On a chilly April morning in 1856, six-year old George Cox and his five-year-old brother Joseph leaped up from breakfast at this table and chased their barking dog into the forest. They were never seen again." This only sixty-odd years before the Convoy passed through.

The Convoy enjoyed a warm welcome from the entire population of Bedford, as reported in the *Bedford Inquirer*: "Army Convoy Stopped in Bedford—Soldiers Given Welcome—Interesting Speeches Made!" The accompanying article notes, "The warrior fighters, proceeding in the heaviest unit ever organized under the flag of any nation, represented every make of truck used in the American Army overseas, and included all types of motor vehicles such as engineer units, rolling kitchens, ambulances, repair shops, baggage cars, and officers' cars." Bedford went all out and provided a banquet with some esoteric entertainment that evening. According to *the Inquirer*: "At eight o'clock the Bedford band gave a concert. During the rendition of one of the pieces, Miss Helen Corboy drew two crayon sketches."

Elsewhere top of the front page, the *Inquirer* featured a two-column-wide "Personal and Local News" feature, with scintillating tell-all items like, "Miss Edith Foster of Johnstown spent the weekend with relatives and friends in Bedford." Front-page news.

In 1919 Bedford was already a two-newspaper town, and the *Inquirer's* competitor, *The Bedford Gazette*, was not to be outdone. Its front-page headline in its July 16 issue was "Cross Country Tour is Greeted Royally— Information Collected Vital to All Auto Users." The article states: "This first Atlantic to Pacific military trip will be a significant illustration of the tremendous possibilities of highway transportation. Furthermore, it will demonstrate the practicability of long-distance freight haulage and the urgent necessity of linking up interstate highway routes and presenting the people with a unified system of national roads."

Of the day's progress, Elwell Jackson wrote, "Encountered heavy grades and altitudes exceeding 2200. No losses or damages (although he did report that one needle valve had become eccentric). Excellent driving. . .enthusiastic reception in Bedford. Roads very good. Made 57 miles in 11.5 hours."

Ike had his own particular view of Elwell Jackson's perpetually sunny renditions of the Convoy's progress, as well as of the banquet. Ike wrote, "Despite the lieutenant's (Jackson's) good cheer, we had, in three days if my addition is correct, spent twenty-nine hours on the road and moved 165 miles. This was an average hourly speed of about five and two-thirds miles per hour—not quite so good as even the slowest troop train. Before we were through, however, there were times when the pace of our first three days would seem headlong and the four speeches at Bedford only a slight taste of the hot air ahead."

The Convoy departed Bedford at 6:30 a.m. on July 10, and they had a rough day ahead. Just a sampling of Elwell Jackson's litany for the day: "Class B down with loose valve tappet. . .(other) Class B stalled account too rich mixture. . .(other) brakes dragging and motor overheats. . .(other) stalled with magneto trouble. . .(other) impulse coupling stuck, hole in distributor block. . .Garford burns out engine bearings. . .Dodge delivery van ran into stretcher trailer on downgrade and stove large hole in radiator. . .Militor towing disabled Garford and Dodge, also kitchen trailer." And then, as if all of this wasn't enough, a bolt of lightning struck a truck, the driver lost control, and: "GMC skidded off road and down mountain side damaged beyond hope of repair by Convoy." The driver was uninjured, but the vehicle totaled, the first casualty of the trip. There was still a long way to go, over far worse roads, and many in the Convoy must have been thinking there would be more such calamities, but remarkably, there were few: by my count only one ambulance, one pontoon trailer, and one kitchen trailer. Given what most of the men thought about the food, the latter may have been cause for celebration. The Convoy finally struggled into Greensburg at 11:00 p.m. that evening. Elwell Jackson again: "Heavy rains all day. Roads very slippery. Made 63 miles in 16.5 hours." That works out to about 3.8 miles per hour, not much faster than a brisk walk.

I woke up early one morning in Bedford, refreshed and ready for a leisurely new day. I looked forward to cruising slowly along lonely country roads, making random last-minute decisions on which way to go, enjoying the evolving landscape at a tranquil 30 mph pace, meandering westward along the Convoy's route but taking side detours as well. In the bright slanting early morning sunlight, I set off. Within moments, after a rapid-fire succession of regrettable decisions, I somehow found myself on the Pennsylvania Turnpike.

As turnpikes go, this one was not too bad. Perfect pavement, wide shoulders, great signage. But it was, nonetheless, a turnpike. I was by now used to tooling along at 30 mph and just pulling over any time I liked, getting out and poking around at a moment's notice. But such was not possible on the super-efficient Pennsylvania Turnpike, with cars and trucks alike thundering past at 85 mph. I took the first available exit and groped my way back to recognizable territory.

But before proceeding, a few words about the Pennsylvania Turnpike: Planned during the 1930s as a route through Pennsylvania's Allegheny Mountains that would avoid those treacherous steep grades, the turnpike's first phase from Irwin to Carlisle was opened in 1940. This made it the first-ever long-distance controlled access highway in the country. First ever. The PA Turnpike was soon lengthened to run from New Jersey to Ohio, and quickly became the model of the type of highway that would comprise the interstate highway system. It didn't exist when Ike and the Convoy passed through in 1919, but Ike drove it during the 1940s and 1950s, and he no doubt compared its smooth, solid efficiency with the slovenly unpredictability of the roads on his earlier trip.

Meandering around in western Pennsylvania, back on the original Lincoln Highway and the Convoy's route. Fog and misty clouds shrouding the green forested hillsides in the early morning. Beautiful rolling hills and hand-written signs everywhere: "Fresh Goat's Milk Over Here!" "The Lost Sock Laundromat" "This Wall 4 Rent!" on a shambling ruin of a barn. "Flea Market This Weekend! Y'all Cum On In!" Scooter's Mountainside Tavern: "Scoot On In!"

In Ligonier, the Convoy took the original Lincoln Highway up and along a scenic and winding mountainside lane that stands up above the current Highway 30. I parked and walked along the route for a while: winding lanes up to expensive hillside houses on one side, and Ligonier's little downtown on the other side. While in nearby Latrobe I also stopped by the Lincoln Highway Experience, an information center and museum in a 200-year-old building that Ike and the Convoy passed right by. Today it's dedicated to conservation and promotion of the Lincoln Highway in Western Pennsylvania. I talked for quite a while with Kristin Poerschke, who was a font of information.

"There are a lot of different routes," she said. "They've straightened out long stretches and paved bypasses around towns. You have to search a little bit to track down the original route." Kristin knew about the trip of Ike and the Convoy, and gave me some helpful tips, as well as contact info for other Lincoln Highway aficionados in Pennsylvania who would be knowledgeable. "But you really need to talk to Brian Butko. Up in Pittsburgh. He's the real expert."

Ligonier is the birthplace of the legendary golfer Arnold Palmer, who grew up playing on the nearby Latrobe Country Club course. Ike later became a great friend of Arnie; they first met in Latrobe in 1958, and they began playing together regularly after Ike left the White House. But even before this, Ike was an obsessive golfer, and played some 800 rounds while he was president, about 100 rounds per year. He had a putting green built on the south lawn of the White House, and he often dictated letters in his office while practicing his swing. Some of the floorboards in the Oval Office are reportedly pockmarked with golf-shoe spike marks, thanks to Ike.

Henry Ostermann, who was the Field Secretary of the Lincoln Highway Association back in 1919, was at the head of the Convoy the entire route, driving a gaudy red, white, and blue Packard Twin Six convertible. Ostermann, who had driven the route by himself several times before, probably knew the way better than anyone alive, and his guidance was particularly crucial in the western states where the route was anything but clear.

Ostermann was reportedly born in Indiana in 1876, but the details of his early life are lost to history—the first known fact about him is that he was selling newspapers on the streets of New York at the age of six and living in a newsboy's home. He later became a bellboy in a hotel, a cigar clerk, and then enrolled in the US Navy at the age of 14. After discharge at age 17 he drifted around the West, traveled with Buffalo Bill's Wild West Show, and ranched for a while in Montana and North Dakota. Still later he was a conductor on the Illinois Central Railroad and ran an automobile business in Deadwood, South Dakota. The Deadwood Chamber of Commerce feted him for his civic and business efforts. Such was the man who became the first Field Secretary of the fledgling Lincoln Highway Association, who drove the route alone numerous times to promote the idea of a national highway, and who led and guided the Convoy over 1919's often-obscure route.

It was no trivial matter to find the correct route in those early days of auto travel. Alice Ramsey dutifully followed the *Official Automobile Blue Book*, first published in 1901 and known as the *Standard Road Guide of America*. At one point she and her traveling companions were following the *Blue Book* instructions in Ohio: "At 11.6 miles yellow house and barn on right. Turn left." But, as she relates the story:

> We looked in vain for a yellow house.
>
> "I don't see any yellow house. Do you?" I inquired.
>
> We found a woman working in the front yard of a house, which was not yellow either. I called out to her.
>
> "Will you please tell me if that road goes to Cleveland?"
>
> "Oh, no," said the woman. "That road is a mile back."
>
> "By the green house?" I asked.
>
> "That's right."
>
> "But the *Blue Book* says to turn by a yellow house."

"Yes, I know," she said. "Last year the man wanted to paint his house and barn. He's agin' automobiles. So he said, 'Now you watch! We'll have some fun with them automobile drivers.'"

After arriving so late the preceding night, the Convoy delayed official departure from Greensburg until 7:00 a.m. Once again, one mechanical issue after another: "carburetor trouble," "broken clutch disc," "fouled spark plugs," "broken fan belt." Eventually, one of the two-wheeled kitchen trailers broke down and was shipped back to Fort Meigs. But the ever-sunny Elwell Jackson seemed to consider it a successful day: "Lunch and reception in Pittsburgh. Fair and cool. Roads excellent. Made 48 miles in 10 hours." Speed ramping up by a full one mph from the previous day. The Convoy set up camp for the night in Sewickley, a suburb northwest of Pittsburgh, at 5:00 p.m.

The July 11 *Greensburg Daily Tribune* headlined, "Motor Transport Corps, Huge Convoy Train Arrived in Greensburg Last Night." The article quoted at length a speech delivered in the wee hours of July 10 by Henry Ostermann. "Pennsylvania right now doesn't need to take a back seat in the union in the matter of highways." All along the Convoy's route, Ostermann, along with S. M. Johnson and other Convoy speakers, was a consistent booster for good roads, cheering on road-building efforts but not hesitating to point out deficiencies.

Along the way, I passed a huge billboard, advertising toilet bowl seats: "King of Thrones!"

Another smaller handwritten sign advertising a Volunteer Fire Department's upcoming soup sale.

In between the original Lincoln Highway and the nowadays Highway 30 Lincoln Highway, a go-cart track, with helmeted kids careening around.

I made a brief detour northward from Greensburg to visit Vandergrift, the nation's first-ever entirely planned industrial town. Designed by Frederick Law Olmstead, it was intended to be fully owned by workers, and was dubbed "The Working Man's Paradise." It boasted wide roads, comfortable houses set back from the streets with plenty of pleasant, Olmsteadean landscaping, and attractive open spaces. The management of the Apollo Iron and Steel Company came up with the original idea, in an attempt to ward off labor unrest and build a trustworthy work force. They hired Olmstead to design the town in early 1895, and most of Vandergrift was complete by late 1896. Management's goal of creating a happy and loyal workforce proved to be unexpectedly prescient: Apollo's workers were so loyal they were used to break the first-ever strike against US Steel a few years later.

Vandergrift was in its heyday when Ike and the Convoy passed by in 1919, although there is no record that anyone from the Convoy actually made the short detour north for a visit. The town annexed an outlying area just before the first World War, and the steel mill prospered during the war. The population peaked at well over 10,000 in 1940, but today is less than half that figure, and the steel industry has long since departed for sunnier shores. When I walked around the central part of Vandergrift, I admired Olmstead's design. Almost all the original buildings are still intact and in ostensibly good condition. Towering century-old trees are everywhere. But there was something eerie about Vandergrift's emptiness. In my forty-five minutes of wandering around, I did not encounter a single other pedestrian, and the two cars that passed by in that time seemed like major events. Perhaps this lonely eeriness is why Vandergrift was chosen as the location to film the science fiction movie, *I Am Number Four*, in 2011.

Back on the route, I passed through Irwin, home to the McDonald's Big Mac museum. It's there amid the sense-numbing urban sprawl just west of the Pennsylvania Turnpike, the McDonald's surrounded by the likes of Denny's, Wendy's, Pizza Hut, Taco Bell. Bob Evans close by. But inside, there's a normal McDonald's, and on top of that, all along the walls, a whole series of exhibits on the very first Big Mac, which was served in nearby Uniontown back in 1967. There's also a 14-foot tall Big Mac, standing on a pedestal over by the window. The wall exhibits looked interesting, but I had to lean in intrusively over booths full of squirming kids and annoyed parents, so I didn't stay long. But I did inspect a Big Mac Sauce Gun, and a Big Mac toaster from back in the 1970s.

Fast food restaurants are yet another creation made possible by the automobile age. The first McDonalds was opened near Los Angeles by brothers Richard and Maurice McDonald in 1937. They initially featured drive-in car-side service by carhops on roller skates, and offered up hot dogs, hamburgers, and all-you-can drink orange juice for a nickel. They didn't really take off until after World War II, when the brothers eliminated the carhops, and focused on hamburgers, cheeseburgers, and fries. Business grew exponentially, McDonalds became a franchise, and is today, of course, the world's most recognizable fast-food eatery. Nowadays there are over 35,000 McDonalds operating in over 100 countries. According to some sources, there are over seventeen Big Macs served per second just in the US alone.

Back on the Convoy's route, I followed the Lincoln Highway through ponderous suburbs, a few pockets of shabbiness, and into the center of Pittsburgh.

Near the corner of Baum and St. Clair Street, I found the historic marker at the site of the first gas station in the US, opened in 1913. Right across the street from the Pittsburgh Institute of Mortuary Science. According to fueleconomy.gov, today there are some 168,000 gas stations in the US that pump over 140 billion gallons of gasoline per year. Ike and the Convoy passed close by the lonely first-ever station in that summer of 1919. Yet another first-ever for Pennsylvania. There is no record that the Convoy actually stopped to fill 'er up. The Convoy was supposed to be entirely self-sufficient, and with 81 vehicles and a 1,500-gallon fuel tanker a fill-up from a commercial gas station would have been a tall order.

The *Pittsburgh Chronicle Telegraph* of July 11 headlines, "Army Motor Train Thunders Into the City on Coast Run – Thousands Cheer Men Running Giant Machines as They Parade Downtown," along with three accompanying photos of the Convoy. The competing *Pittsburgh Gazette* headlines "Motor Transport Train Three Miles in Length to Pass Through City Today." Both the *Gazette* and the *Chronicle Telegraph* ran extra "Transport Day" sections highlighting the Convoy but also cheering on the Good Roads Movement.

I stopped off at Carnegie-Mellon's Department of Electrical and Computer Engineering – Collaborative Innovation Center – to talk with Professor Raj Rajkumar, who has been consistently in the forefront in developing self-driving cars, known officially as autonomous vehicles (AVs). Raj painted an optimistic but cautious picture of the future of AVs and outlined their many advantages: elimination of human error, which is the cause of 94 percent of all road accidents, greater access for the elderly and handicapped who are otherwise unable to drive, and a more efficient use of time. He said that the average car spends thirty-five hours per year running but just idling, and many more hours just parked and unused. Uber-type AVs could be in service and on-call 24/7 and could motor along with minimal headways between cars since vehicles would be communicating with one another. This would greatly reduce congestion and could be quickly introduced in the agriculture, mining, and construction sectors within a couple of years. Much of the necessary technology for AVs has already been developed, he said, but fine tuning to develop higher reliability was still ongoing. He expected gradual introduction of AV technology with fully autonomous vehicles available to the public within about five years.

This would require some work, however, to sort out all the regulations governing usage of automobiles, since most of those regulations are now state or local. And quite a bit of time to transition because there are now some

250 million vehicles on USA roads, with about 17 million sold every year. Retiring that fleet will take several years. But the usage of ride-sharing AVs in particular he expected to spread quickly in many urban areas, perhaps even within five years. The abandonment of car ownership would save consumers millions of dollars, but might well be opposed staunchly by automakers, the steel industry, auto parts manufacturers and other vested interests. Raj noted that in some cases rides on AVs might even be transactional—for example, a free ride in exchange for the purchase of a Starbucks latte.

I asked Raj about the fact that some peopled loved to drive and would not easily give up driving in exchange for an AV. He had clearly already thought about this and said there could be car ranches for such people, a place where they could drive all they wanted safely removed from the AV-controlled public roads. I had never considered such an option, but I could immediately see its allure: a place where enthusiastic drivers could strap themselves behind the wheel of the most up-to-date race cars and then, after signing no doubt prodigious quantities of waiver forms, careen around a track at absurdly dangerous speeds to their heart's content. Carl Fisher would be smiling in his grave.

I also dropped by to visit Brian Butko at the Heinz History center. I had been in touch with Brian by email before the start of my trip and found him to be an unending source of helpful information on the Lincoln Highway. He told me there would be several stretches where the original highway would be difficult to follow, and said some states were better marked than others. "Modern-day Highway 30 is easy to follow, but if you want the original road, the one the Convoy would have followed, that really varies from state to state. Iowa is great," he said. "Nebraska too. But there are some stretches where the old road is abandoned or way off the beaten track, and it takes some riding around to find." He gave some tips and the names of lots of Lincoln Highway experts all across the west. These folks, and Brian's books proved invaluable, and I was delighted that I could in fact follow the Convoy's route all the way to San Francisco. Even many of those portions long abandoned and now overgrown with weeds I was often able to track down, and when I strolled along them, in windblown solitude, I sometimes thought of Brian, Drake Hokanson, Carl Fisher, Henry Joy, Henry Ostermann, and all the others who are lasting parts of the Lincoln Highway lore.

I crisscrossed through a lot of streets in downtown Pittsburgh, and finally drove northwestward on Pennsylvania Avenue, following Ike's route. I found myself wondering if there was a Pittsburgh 1600 Pennsylvania Avenue address equivalent to the White House, and if so, what was there. I had already seen the numbering system would make 1600 on my left-hand side just before 16th street. I edged on through the traffic: 33rd, 32nd, 31st. When I reached 17th Street, I eagerly looked down to the left at 1600 to see the Pittsburgh White House equivalent and it was. . .Yikes! McDonalds!

No, false alarm. Tucked in just beyond the McDonalds at presumably 1600 was an attractive church building, which on closer inspection proved to be the current headquarters of the ATM Payment Alliance International Company, with an adjacent square windowless block of a building right at the corner. So McDonalds was presumably 1602 Pennsylvania Avenue. I say presumably because as I had so often seen, neither had a street number and were recognizable only by their symbols. Perhaps two of the most recognizable symbols across the country: the church steeple and the golden arches. Across the street at presumably 1601 Pennsylvania Avenue, was an appealing Argentinian Gaucho restaurant with a large handwritten sign on the side door:

"We Need Cooks!"

I crossed the Ohio River over the 6th Street Bridge (nowadays named the Roberto Clemente bridge), the same bridge the Convoy passed over, and drove by the Pittsburgh Pirates huge PNC stadium, heading northwest along the north bank of the Ohio. Eventually, I came onto Beaver Road through the middle of Sewickley, a gorgeous lane of towering oaks and million-dollar-plus houses. The Convoy camped all along the road here for the night on July 11, 1919, and I found myself wondering what would happen if I decided to pull over and sleep in my car here on Beaver Road for the night. Even the corner street signs were works of art. The first-ever Convoy of eighty-one military vehicles was no doubt a lark of a major event for the residents, but one lonely guy in a raggedy Chevy would have given a very different impression. I could envision worried 911 calls, muddled middle-of-the-night explanations to skeptical police officers. So I pressed on, up highway 65, sun setting out through the oaks in front of me and the Ohio River glinting down below to my left. With nightfall approaching, I crossed into Ohio.

OHIO

A riddle from my primary school days, decades ago: Which state is round at both ends, and high in the middle? OHIO! Okay, moving right along. . .

The Convoy generally followed the path of the Lincoln Highway all the way to San Francisco, but there were several detours. One was in the crossover from Pennsylvania to Ohio, where the Convoy veered northward toward East Palestine, Ohio, in order to accept a luncheon invitation from Harvey Firestone in nearby Columbiana. But the reception in East Palestine was noteworthy too. Elwell Jackson writes, "Factory whistles blown and church bells rung. City elaborately decorated. Dinner to officers at the Rubber Club." But all was not rosy. "All tools furnished with trucks are of inferior quality and construction. . .Roads chucky." The next day – a Sunday rest day – the Red Cross set up a canteen at the campsite, at which – according to Davies – they served "seventy gallons of lemonade, thirty-five of ice cream, four hundred chocolate bars, and five hundred packs of cigarettes."

About the Firestone dinner on July 13, Elwell Jackson's always laconic description goes as follows: "At 11:30 a.m. entire command was taken in private automobiles to homestead of Mr. H. S. Firestone, 6 miles west at Columbiana. Here a fine chicken dinner was served to over 400 guests in a large assembly tent. Music was furnished by a band, several soloists, and a male trio. Addresses were made. . ..Dr. Howley showed his Bureau of Economics moving pictures."

Nowadays, not far from the site of that 1919 gala dinner, is the Firestone Farm Tire Testing Center (FFTTC). I tried mightily, but could never obtain permission to enter, so this is all from their website. This 400-acre facility lies well-protected behind a high chain link fence with barbed wire on the top. Inside, according to their website, "is the only facility in the world fully dedicated to the testing of agricultural tires." The facility operates 24 hours per day, 365 days per year, and tests the entire line of Firestone farm tires, as well as competing products. At the core of the facility is the "mean machine," described as a "one of a kind 30-ton behemoth that can exert more than 34,000 pounds of pull."

The Convoy had been strongly supported by Frank Seiberling, CEO of Goodyear and second president of the Lincoln Highway Association (following Henry Joy), and now had been feted by Harvey Firestone. One can imagine that both men may have taken satisfaction from this note from Elwell Jackson's diary of July 14: "Seventeen miles out (from East Palestine) Dodge had puncture in Goodrich tire." Seiberling remained a lifelong enthusiastic supporter of Good Roads and the Lincoln Highway, and a portion of the route out West is named for him.

Early wagon wheels were made of wood and then of steel. It wasn't until the late nineteenth century that rubber tires came along: John Dunlop invented the first, for his little boy's tricycle. The first automobile tires were of solid rubber and had, to say the least, a few issues. But then along came Goodyear and Firestone, pneumatic tires, and the automobile age was off to the races.

The *Columbiana Ledger* dutifully reported:

> The big Army truck train which set out for the Pacific coast from Washington passed through town Monday. It had camped on the fairground on Sunday and left that place on Monday. East Palestine was all decorated for the occasion and gave the boys a rousing reception. The boys in charge of the trucks were bronzed and business-like and showed already the effects of the trip, though all were alert and gave no indication of being tired of their job.
>
> A most enjoyable feature of the trip for the boys was the chicken dinner given Sunday by H. E. Firestone of Akron at the Firestone homestead east of town. Ladies of the Grace Reformed Church made the noodles for the dinner. Entertainers from Akron performed for the benefit of the company, and speeches were made by a number of prominent citizens of the county.

The *Ledger* of that date also contained an advertisement for the latest model Oldsmobile: "Model 37 – six $1,295. Touring or Roadster!"

The Convoy enjoyed the lavish hospitality of Firestone, but Frank Seiberling, CEO of Goodyear, was not to be outdone. So he dispatched the official Goodyear traveling band, in their own small truck, to accompany the Convoy all the way from Ohio to San Francisco. The Goodyear band truck drove out in front of the Convoy, so in every town along the way, no matter what hour or what weather, the arriving Convoy was greeted by melodic tunes from the Goodyear band. Townspeople along the way loved it, and Goodyear band concerts often featured prominently in local press coverage of the Convoy's passage.

With seventy-three vehicles, eight trailers, and mostly untrained drivers, the whole Convoy was a work in progress. One truck had apparently been stalling out constantly all the way from the White House. Near East Palestine there was this discovery: the driver didn't understand the clutch and had never used it. In his after-action report, Ike wrote, "The vehicles had not been properly tested and adjusted before starting the trip. This occasioned many short halts on the part of individual trucks, to adjust carburetors, clean spark plugs, adjust brake bands. . .and make minor repairs of this nature. It was evident though that many of these difficulties were caused by inefficient handling of the vehicle by the driver."

The Convoy was progressing across country during the midst of the most catastrophic influenza pandemic in modern history. The H1N1 virus first infected humans in January 1918, and it wasn't fully contained until late 1920. It was a global pandemic, with cases reported on remote Pacific islands and in the Arctic. It infected 500 million people altogether, and between and 50 and 100 million died as a result, between three and five percent of the globe's population. But there's no evidence that anyone on the Convoy was impacted by the flu.

In the breezy early morning sunlight I walked around through the center of East Palestine. It's a small town, and the central business street showed some signs of tough times; several stores were closed. But there was nonetheless a vibrancy about East Palestine that I sensed almost immediately. Almost every shop window—even some that were closed—had a photo of an East Palestine High School varsity football player and/or a cheerleader, with their names and GO BULLDOGS! There were Bulldog footprints all along the sidewalks. I noticed signs that read "Sign Up for Apple Butter Making!" and further along three young girls were selling homemade muffins from a folding card table on the sidewalk. I bought a blueberry muffin and asked them about the apple butter. They said that every October, when the apple harvest is in, everybody gets together and makes lots of apple butter. "Pretty much everybody in town turns out," said one of the girls. "They have some antique cars too."

Walking along, I noticed two beautiful wall murals on the sides of two-story brick buildings that were next to vacant lots. Farther along, I met a thirtyish blonde woman high up on a ladder painting the side of another building white, obviously preparing to start another mural. I asked her if she had painted the other murals, and she said that she had. I complimented her on her artistry and asked what this mural was going to be. "Don't know exactly," she said. "I don't have it all blocked out yet. But there's gonna be rolling farmland, some nice farmhouses spaced out over the land, nice grove of trees in the background, deep blue sky with some puffy white clouds. And the American flag." She didn't stop painting while she talked, but just kept on going, high up on that skinny ladder leaning against the side of the building.

I went away from East Palestine thinking that it was a town that had taken some tough knocks, but East Palestinians weren't the sort of people to take tough knocks lying down. Later, I sometimes reflected back on East Palestine, and I wished I could have been there for apple butter days and a hometown Bulldogs football game. Bite 'Em Bulldogs!

I drove on through flattening farmland, the transition from the Allegheny mountains into the wide, fertile Midwest. Beautiful flowing fields of young corn, and farmhouses set back from the road with breezy front porches, American flags ruffling overhead. Past signboards: "Vital Vittles!" "Chainsaw Sharpening!" "We Buy Barns!" I continued, wondering exactly what I would do if I were suddenly to become the proud owner of a secondhand barn.

All across my route I came across roadkill, ranging from bulky to tiny: deer, raccoons, cats, dogs, beavers, rats. On the positive side, I never saw a roadkill turtle, the slowest off all animals, which led me to conclude that turtles must be clever enough not to cross the road until the coast was exceedingly clear. Wikipedia notes that in the early twentieth century, the dawn of the automobile age, roadkill was known as "highway pizza." *Animal People Newsletter* estimates that every year some 41 million squirrels, 22 million cats, 19 million opossums, 15 million raccoons, 6 million dogs, and 350,000 deer are wiped out in road accidents. Sounds awful, but buzzards and crows are not complaining.

In Canton I stopped off at the Pro Football Hall of Fame for a brief visit. The entire surroundings ooze football: even the nearby utility poles are in the shape of goal posts. There is a stadium next door where NFL preseason games are played, and an open-air artificial turf field right by the Hall's entrance where some ten-year-old boys were having an enthusiastic game of flag football when I arrived. "Grady! Go long!" "Post pattern—right!" "Cut back! Cut back!" "Aw c'mon man! That was pass interference!"

The Hall, which opened in 1963, was located in Canton because that was where the original American Professional Football Association (later the NFL) was founded, and because the Canton Bulldogs were an early pro football powerhouse. The Bulldogs star player was the legendary Native-American running back Jim Thorpe—more on him later. Emblazoned in large letters on the wall by the entrance to the Hall is the following credo:

Honor the Heroes of the Game;
Preserve its History
Promote its Values;
Celebrate Excellence Everywhere

The Hall struggled in its early years. Staff members were often dispatched to show NFL highlight reels in remote towns in order to drum up interest. But in the ensuing years the Hall has had four major renovations/enlargements, and its total floor space has sextupled in size. Annual visitors now exceed 200,000, and revenue is well over $20 million. As I walked around inside I saw lots of families, fathers with young boys but plenty of young girls too. And a substantial number of huge, bulky, graying men with gimpy knees—many walked with the aid of a cane. I pegged them all as former NFL players, coming back to relive some memories. They quickly gathered into groups, pointing at photos, gesticulating, laughing, and hooting among themselves.

Ike was an enthusiastic athlete and later wrote, "Not making the baseball team at West Point was one the greatest disappointments of my life, maybe the greatest." But Ike did make the varsity football team at West Point in his freshman year. In those days everyone played both offense and defense, so Ike was a running back and a linebacker. In writing about his play as a running back, he does not use the words "run" or "rush," but instead offers up "plunge," indicative of the close-quarters style of play in Ike's West Point days. And so it was that in the fall of 1912, while playing linebacker in a hotly-contested game against the Carlisle Indians, Ike made a rare singlehanded open field tackle of the legendary Jim Thorpe. Alas, later in the same game, during a plunge, Ike suffered a debilitating knee injury that ended his football career.

Ike was throughout his life a generous person. In 1952, when he heard that Thorpe was in poor health and low on money, Ike sent—through a third party—a check "intended for use in whatever fashion you may consider of benefit to Thorpe." Ike insisted that his gift remain anonymous and confidential.

But football and sports in general had a profound, lasting influence on Ike. He later wrote, "I noted with real satisfaction how well ex-footballers seemed to have leadership qualifications. . ..I believe that football, perhaps more than any other sport, tends to instill in men the feeling that victory comes through hard—almost slavish—work, team play, self-confidence, and an enthusiasm that amounts to dedication."

While in Canton I also stopped at the Canton Classic Car Museum, featuring some 40-plus classic automobiles in pristine condition, plus countless memorabilia. The cars are beautifully displayed and range from a 1901 Oldsmobile to a classic 1966 Ford Mustang. The memorabilia are not just car-related: they also include many examples of classic road advertising and even a portrait of Franklin Roosevelt made solely with a manual typewriter. There's a sign posted near the entrance: "Do not touch cars. Bob (the manager) shoots every 10th toucher, and the 9th one just left."

I drove on westward, following the Convoy's route through gorgeous farmland and picturesque small towns, and into Mansfield. There, I stopped by a downtown tavern and sat at the bar by a very large fortyish man who told me his name was Roy. When I told Roy I was from the East Coast he seemed a little reticent, but after a while he opened up. He told me he had grown up near Mansfield and was a star on his high school football team. "Back then, lots of us played both ways. I was a tight end and a middle linebacker. I stomped some butt back in those days. Rung a lotta peoples' bells."

I asked him what he did after he finished high school, and if he had played college ball.

"Nah, I never even finished high school. Back then I was just thinkin' about football, nothin' else, and once that senior season was over, I didn't see any reason to hang around. I'd always been good at repairin' cars, and I got me a job offer from a garage right away. Chance to make some money, build up something. So I just quit school and started workin'. Saved up enough in three years to buy me a house trailer. Still livin' in that same damn broke-ass trailer."

I wanted to keep him talking, so I was asking questions. "Do you have family here in Mansfield?"

He talked a while, and then all of a sudden, abruptly, there it was: "My sister died last year. OD. Not but 39 years old, with two little kids. Oxycontin."

I expressed sympathy, and he said, "It happens. She's sure not the only one."

And then, "You know, you go through life, and I guess I just always thought everything would keep on gettin' better. Never thought maybe I'd already passed my best years. That football team, my senior year—we were damned good. I guess that was the best time of my life."

I tried to buy a beer for Roy, but he wouldn't accept, and so I said farewell and left. Thinking mightily about what I'd just heard. Oxycontin OD for a mother of two small kids—I'd read about so many others. But also Roy's disappointment in his own life, the despair, and the way that could give rise to a powerful resentment. Seething down inside him—how many others were like that? I drove on westward, thus thinking.

Over the years the Lincoln Highway has been widened, straightened, rerouted, and diverted around towns so often that it is sometimes difficult to find the original Lincoln Highway that the Convoy traversed in 1919. In many cases the original Lincoln Highway has been long bypassed entirely and is now overgrown with weeds. I spent a good deal of time consulting Hokanson, Butko, and other experts and trekking through grassy fields and up stony hillsides in search of abandoned portions, which were always fascinating. It was where Ike and the Convoy had driven, a century ago. But I also enjoyed groping around for portions of the original Lincoln that were still in use but distinctly separate from by-passes or modernization, and found the Lincoln Highway Association road markers invaluable in this effort. These excursions were always rewarding in seeing parts of our country that most cross-continent motorists would inevitably miss, but that Ike and the Convoy passed along. All those years ago.

One such example is the portion of the original highway that cuts right through the middle of Dalton, Ohio, just a bit west of Massillon. Dalton is a tiny but gorgeous town with a long picturesque entrance featuring towering oaks spreading out over the two-lane road from both sides, creating a fairy-tale type canopy. This entrance stretches on for at least a mile, with solid old clapboard and shingled houses along both sides, front porches festooned with hanging ferns and, more often than not, American flags flapping in the breeze. In the small downtown there were solid brick century-old buildings lining the street, some boarded up but others with hopeful signs in the windows: "Re-opening Soon!" All across the country, tableaus such as these gave me the sudden powerful feeling: *This is it. This is the real Lincoln Highway that Ike and the Convoy saw.*

If the Convoy of vehicles had been a sports team, the Militor would have won most valuable player, hands down. Virtually every day of Elwell Jackson's diary contains heroic exploits of the Militor towing other wayward vehicles out of ditches, mudholes, hillsides, and other assorted trouble and into camp. But what about the driver of the Militor, Sergeant first class T. E. Wood Jr.? On July 16, Elwell Jackson writes that Sergeant Wood, "drove Militor from 8 a.m. July 15th until 2:50 a.m. July 16th without sleep or food, no rations having been sent back to him." I sure hope Sergeant Wood got a promotion at the end of the trip.

I stopped and walked around for a while in downtown Bucyrus (the Bratwurst capital of America—another superlative). There is a mural on the main square that's a Lincoln Highway classic: "The Great American

Crossroads," painted in 1999 by Eric Grohe. It depicts the view down Main Street Bucyrus, also the Lincoln Highway, as it would have been in 1917, thus at the time of the Convoy. There's a panorama of life underway: boys peering in from the corners to see pedestrians all over the place; men and women along the sidewalks, going into shops, chatting on street corners, gawking at the traffic. But back in a far corner, there's a man in an Army uniform, his back to the canvas, talking to a civilian. According to Grohe's explanation, the uniformed man is Ike during the 1919 trip, asking to borrow a dime from a pedestrian so he could telephone Mamie while he was in Bucyrus.

Just south of Galion is the Mid-Ohio sports car course, which I stopped by to see. Built in 1962 and improved several times, the main course is 2.4 miles with several precipitous turns. The course is used for races by stock cars, IndyCars, vintage sports cars, motorcycles, and Karts. I talked to a young man named Ken, who told me that "lots of people" come out to watch races, and that they had a special space set up for campers and motor homes.

Almost from the moment automobiles were invented, men have felt an overpowering compulsion to race them at ridiculous speeds. Despite several injuries suffered in crashes, Carl Fisher loved racing, and he established and financed the Indianapolis 500 way back in 1909 to provide a fixed venue for racing. Those early years of the Indy 500 saw several calamitous crashes that were fatal for both drivers and spectators, but Fisher quickly began establishing safety measures, such as banked curves, improved all-brick pavement, and solid concrete boundary walls. The race became an annual event in 1911, and on May 31, 1919, just about five weeks before the Convoy got underway, Howdy Wilkes won the Indy 500 with an average speed of about 84 miles per hour. Today of course the Indy 500 draws an annual attendance of around 300,000 plus millions of TV viewers, and average speeds top 200 miles per hour.

Stock car racing sponsored by the National Association of Stock Car Racing (NASCAR) is also a wildly popular sport that attracts millions of fans and TV viewers every year. Most NASCAR experts contend that stock car racing got its start in bootleggers trying to outrace police and revenuers during and after Prohibition. Bootleggers would soup up their cars to attain top speeds on winding mountain roads, and the combination of tinkering with cars and then driving them at breakneck speeds proved to be irresistible. Today NASCAR annual attendance is just under 4 million, and revenue exceeds $3 billion. One can imagine what Ike and the Convoy members would think, as they tooled along at six miles per hour.

I stopped off at the birthplace of the twenty-ninth US president, Warren Harding. It was a small country house set amidst rolling farmland near the town of Blooming Grove. Ike and the Convoy passed close by here in 1919, and the following year Harding was elected president. I got out and walked around. The house was closed, and there were no other people in sight. It was so quiet, I heard only the faint breeze whispering over the soft hills of young corn and soybeans, dotted in places with groves of oak or elm. There were apple trees in the front yard.

What must it have been like to grow up in such a gorgeous, peaceful spot, and years later land in the White House as president. Thick fescue spotted with dandelions, oaks, spruces, and crepe myrtles on the sides. There was a solitary flag luffing in the steady easterly breeze. A fallow field across the tiny road, with a distant line of trees, dogwoods spotted in, and a small red barn up on the ridge. Farther away still a sturdy-looking white clapboard house with a silo behind. I got back into my Chevy and drove on with the windows down, feeling the wind. Suddenly from out of nowhere came a spotted terrier who chased my car, barking ferociously, for a long time before pulling up and loping across an open field.

As president, Harding was to play a significant role in the history of automobiles. In 1921 he signed into law the second Federal Highway Act that provided additional money to states to improve roads. This act, unlike the 1916 act signed by President Wilson, specifically mandated that states should target the money to focus on major roads. In addition, earlier that same year Harding became the first president to ride to his inauguration in an automobile instead of a horse-drawn carriage.

We lament the air pollution emitted by automotive traffic today, but one often-overlooked fact is the game-changing role that cars had in greatly reducing another type of pollution in the early twentieth century. In 1900 there were more than 3 million horse-drawn delivery wagons in US cities, which produced more than 30,000 tons of manure per day. Per day. And that's not including passenger and personal wagons. Emily Post would have quickly noted that flip-flops were not recommended attire for pedestrians in those days. Harding's choice of an automobile over a horse-drawn carriage was emblematic of the change that brought the virtual elimination of horse manure on city streets in just a couple of decades.

Sherwood Anderson's novel, *Winesburg Ohio*, was published in 1919, the year of the Convoy, but the events depicted happened some fifteen years earlier. The fictitious town of Winesburg was based closely on Anderson's actual hometown of Clyde, Ohio. There is only one mention of automobiles in the book—modes of transportation are horse-drawn wagons, the train, and that old standby—walking. Trains pass by Winesburg with regularity every day, and the train whistle invariably sets the town's dogs barking and yowling. Everyone hears all of this in the summer months because everyone's windows are open and there is no television. Entertainment consists of going out walking in the evening, and the big event of the year is the town fair, over at the fairgrounds, which were frequent bivouac sites for the Convoy through-out the East and Midwest. In Winesburg, young couples out on a date who wanted some privacy would invariably go out for a long, leisurely walk in the countryside. Ambitious young people chafe at the town's limitations, and just beneath the town's polite veneer, scandalous behavior lurks of course, but Anderson depicts a bucolic setting that is classically American. But by the time of the book's publication, the prolific spread of the automobile was already wrenching the country toward a vastly different reality, and the idyllic vision of towns like Winesburg would rapidly become objects of nostalgia.

Registered Trucks in the USA:

1910	410
1914	80,000
1920	1,000,000

On my trusty Rand-McNally Road Atlas, I noted a spot marked "Ghost Town" a bit northwest of Upper Sandusky, near Findlay, and I couldn't resist making a brief detour to investigate. This ghost town turned out to be an assemblage of mostly nineteenth-century buildings and accessories, some-what deteriorating, now arranged in the form of a small town. A sign by the parking lot advertised it: "Visit the Haunted Ghost Town!" Although it was closed, I walked around a bit and eventually met the owner and manager, Kevin, who very generously offered to give me a tour.

Kevin explained that he loved restoring and displaying old buildings and furniture but needed to find a way to earn some revenue doing so. This led him to establish the Haunted Ghost Town, which was open for adventurous thrill-seeking visitors every weekend evening. While the facades of the build-ings were a late nineteenth-century post office, livery stable, blacksmith shop, general store, and so on, if you walked into the vaguely lighted interiors you were confronted by a creative variety of ghosts, witches, suddenly-leaping-to-life corpses, and deranged men toting large blood-dripping axes.

I asked him how business was and who his customers were, and he immediately replied, "Best customers are high school girls. They go into some of these buildings and come screaming right out of there, shrieking like crazy. Then they come right back and do it all over again the next weekend." But Kevin said the main point of it all was to preserve and restore the building facades and all the assorted accessories that came with them. "This is all part of our history, of who we were, and it pains me to see it all go to ruin and get torn down." He said he is always on the lookout for old buildings he can buy or just haul away, and is hoping to continue expanding the Haunted Ghost Town. I wondered if any of the facades had been on the nearby Lincoln Highway, and if the Convoy members might have seen any in their original location.

I passed close by the town of Lima, which is home to the annual 4-Wheel Motor Truck Jamboree, and then made a brief detour to the south to visit the Neil Armstrong Air and Space Museum in Wapakoneta. Armstrong grew up in Wapakoneta, and the museum honoring his exploits opened in 1972 with Armstrong and President Richard Nixon's daughter Tricia as honored guests. The small but well-organized museum features exhibits such as Armstrong's Gemini and Apollo spacesuits, a moon rock, the Gemini 8 spacecraft, and two airplanes that Armstrong flew.

In 1919, at the time of the Convoy, flight was still in its infancy. The first-ever nonstop flight across the Atlantic—from Newfoundland to Ireland—had just been completed June 14–15 of that same year by John Alcock and Arthur Brown. Just three weeks before the Convoy's departure from Washington. As President Ike played a pivotal role in the nascent space program, signing the law creating NASA, and another law providing the first substantial federal funding for higher math and science education. Explorer I, the first US satellite, was launched during Ike's presidency. Armstrong walked on the moon in July 1969, exactly 50 years after the Convoy's trip and Alcock and Brown's flight. Sadly, Ike passed away in March of 1969 and did not witness Armstrong's walk, which might have seemed to him a remarkable half-century bookend to the beginnings of vehicular and air travel he had lived through.

Of the Convoy's drive from Bucyrus to Delphos, their last full day in Ohio, Elwell Jackson wrote,

> No maintenance difficulties of any consequence. Escorted through Upper Sandusky and into Delphos by Mayors and Reception Committee. Mayor of Delphos made address of welcome and presented the key of the city (water hydrant key) to the Exp. Commander. Every phase of the Convoy is functioning

better as experience is accumulating. Fair and warm. Excellent roads generally. Made 70 miles in 9 hours.

Just under a whopping eight miles per hour!

The front page of the *Delphos Herald* of July 17, 1919, screamed: "Delphos Thrown Wide Open to Soldier Boys." And the town did indeed go all out, with food, soft drinks, two dance halls, and music all set up expressly for the Convoy. The *Herald* article noted that this was "one of the largest and most successful affairs ever conducted in this city." The entire town seems to have turned out, with multiple entertainment venues. Over at the Knights of Columbus Hall, "aesthetic dances were given" by a group of ladies, and "the whistling of Jeanne Roth. . .won the approval of the audience."

The front-page article notes also that the arrival of the Convoy "brought with it all the romance and color of the old transcontinental expeditions to the California gold mines." And that the Convoy "takes hold of one's imagination and makes one wish to go along on the great ocean-to-ocean trip. The fact that it is a pioneer venture makes the idea all the more alluring."

Elsewhere in the same edition of *the Herald* one finds the article, "Chinese Girl Given War Stamp Medal: Sets Good Example for Ohio Boys and Girls." The article goes on to relate that Ping Wong , "a Chinese Miss of 13 years," was the champion War Stamp salesperson among those of foreign parentage in Ohio.

Halfway between Delphos and Van Wert is the Van-Del drive-in movie theater, the name a compromise between the two neighboring towns. It was still going strong when I passed by, so I got out to walk around for a while at midday. Rows of speakers up on steel posts, tracks cut through each row. A huge towering screen, and the grass mowed down low. A couple of sandwich wrappers scattered around, and then a used condom, down in the grass.

Drive-in movie theaters were, of course, another creation made possible by the automobile. There weren't any drive-ins yet when Ike and the Convoy crossed the country in 1919—the first full-fledged drive-in movie theater was opened by Industrial magnate Richard Hollingshead in Camden, New Jersey, in 1933. That first drive-in featured a 40-by-50-foot screen and parking slots for 400 cars. Hollingshead got a patent for his invention and advertised, "The whole family is welcome, regardless of how noisy the children are." Hollingshead sold out a few years later, but the idea then quickly caught on, and it was off to the races. By World War II there were fifteen open nationwide.

Drive-ins flourished through the 1950s and 1960s, and at one time there were over 4,000 operating in the US. They prospered in small towns and rural areas where traditional indoor movie theaters were few and far between. Mom and Dad could take the rowdy kids without disrupting the entire theater, and for teens who could manage to get the family car keys, they were a prime make-out spot. Many drive-ins featured elaborate snack bars, and their signboards out front were often works of art. But color TV, the VCR, and eventually the Internet spelled the doom of the drive-in. As of 2014 there were only about 350 remaining in the US. I saw plenty as I drove over the Convoy's route cross-country, but not many were still operating like Van-Del Theater.

On July 17 Elwell Jackson wrote, "Departed Delphos 6:30 a.m. Some difficulty in starting several motors on account of low gravity gasoline secured." Widely fluctuating product standards were a serious problem confronting motorists in the early days of automobile travel and would cause headaches for the Convoy on several occasions. Fortunately, I had no such problems, and cruised on northwest along the Lincoln Highway, through Van Wert, and on into Indiana.

INDIANA

"The automobile is the only really new significant art form of the twentieth century."

–Stanley Wanlass

From Van Wert I crossed into Indiana and drove on up the Lincoln Highway and into Fort Wayne, where the Convoy spent its first night in Indiana. Elwell Jackson wrote, "Convoy met and escorted thru Fort Wayne to campsite in Lawton Park by Mayor. . .Postmaster. . .Secretary Chamber of Commerce. . .Army Recruiting Officer. . .and Reception Committee. Local Motor Service Corps and Red Cross delivered and served lunch."

They arrived and set up camp in Fort Wayne already at 12:30, but there was evidently work to be done. Elwell Jackson: "Meeting of enlisted personnel, conducted by Captains McMahon, Greany & Lt. Bissell, to discuss matters of operations, maintenance, records, and general conduct." This matches Ike's observation: "At the beginning of the trip, discipline among the enlisted personnel. . .was almost unknown. . .This lack of discipline was largely due to inexperience, and poor type of officers. It resulted in excessive speeding of trucks, unauthorized halts, unseemly conduct, and poor handling of truck in the Convoy." Later, Ike added "It is not believed that the enlisted men were inferior in type to any other body of soldiers, but they lacked training and good officers."

The front page of the *Fort Wayne Journal Gazette* of July 18 reports that many of the enlisted men went to the local swimming hole in the afternoon, but "owing to the fact that but few of the men had bathing suits, the good offices of the Wolf Tent and Awning Company were called upon by the local committee and in a short time the entire pool was surrounded by a wall of canvas so that the visiting soldiers could revert to the good old swimmin' hole costume with perfect propriety."

Elsewhere on the front page of the same edition, the *Journal Gazette* reports on the speeches delivered at the dinner that evening for Convoy officers and city luminaries. The article notes "the Convoy is in reality a big publicity move in the interest of good roads," and goes on to quote S. M. Johnson as saying that "the long cross-country run of the motor Convoy (is) a demonstration of the possibilities of overland transportation with motor vehicles." Johnson went on to say, "It is the purpose of the war department . . .to direct public opinion toward appreciation of the necessity for placing our highways in shape to be used a means of national defense or, in times of peace, for commercial purposes. . .the construction of wide roads is necessary."

Billboard near Fort Wayne:

Live Exotic Dancers!

With a silhouette of a curvaceous woman. But underneath a smaller sign:

Now Hiring: Exotic Dancers

I wandered around for a while in Lawton Park, where the Convoy bivouacked for the night. It's in an attractive setting, on the north bank of the St. Mary's River, and there were plenty of people out on a sunny weekend afternoon. Kids throwing frisbees, other kids getting a pick-up softball game underway, a few couples strolling along the riverside—all on the spot where eighty-one vehicles and some three hundred soldiers were camped a century earlier.

Near the Convoy's route through Fort Wayne is the gravesite of Johnny Appleseed. John Chapman was born in 1774 and earned the nickname "Johnny Appleseed" because of his generosity during his wide-ranging travels across the Midwest. Details vary, but it is universally agreed that Chapman spread apple seeds all over the place. He planted dozens of nurseries and came back regularly to nurture them. Native Americans respected him greatly. To say he lived simply is a gross understatement: he was always barefoot, even in the middle of winter, wore a tin pot on his head, and slept outdoors or on church floors. Nowadays the Fort Wayne minor league baseball team is called the Tin Caps in his honor. Boil 'em, Tin Caps!

Johnny Appleseed died in 1845 and was already an American legend during his lifetime. He was certainly well known when Ike and the Convoy passed not far from his gravesite. It's a lovely spot, up on a small hilltop, with the grave fenced off by iron railing, and flowering apple trees all around.

The Convoy departed Fort Wayne at 6:30 on July 18, but Elwell Jackson reports, "At 8 a.m. halted by request in Churubusco, Ind. for 10 min., while refreshments were served by local Red Cross Canteen Service." This entry highlights something that happened everywhere. The Convoy was a huge story all across the country. Everywhere I looked, in every single town, the Convoy's passing through was front-page news the next day. In every town hundreds of citizens lined the streets to cheer them on, even if the Convoy was just passing through for a few brief minutes. Captain William Greany, in his after-action report, writes that "approximately 3,250,000 persons" personally witnessed the Convoy, in over 350 towns along the route. He further estimates that "about 33,000,000 persons, or nearly one-third of the population of the entire country," learned about the Convoy through friends, family, or newspaper accounts. The ever-faithful Red Cross Canteen or other volunteer organizations were always there to serve up refreshments, and most towns rigged up some sort of system for showers for 300 men. All the while celebrating. The Convoy was the Apollo moon landing of 1919.

I stayed for two nights in a delightful B&B in a small town, managed by a thirtyish woman I'll call Laura. She asked me not to divulge her name, or that of her five-room B&B. Both mornings Laura presented scrumptious, complicated breakfasts. So, on the second morning when I was the only guest, I asked her why she didn't open a restaurant. "You're a great cook, and you obviously enjoy cooking," I said.

"Can't get any help," she replied. "I can manage the B&B by myself, but a restaurant? I'd need some help. Around here, all the young people, when they graduate high school, they go off to Ohio State, IU, Notre Dame, someplace, and then they never come back." (How Ya Gonna Keep 'Em Down on the Farm, After They've Seen South Bend?)

Auburn, just north of Fort Wayne and a few miles off the Convoy's route, is a small town with a dizzying array of transportation museums. There's the Cord-Duesenberg Automobile Museum, the Hoosier Air Museum, the National Auto and Truck Museum, the National Military History & Automotive Museum, the Early Ford V-8 Museum, and let's not forget: the DeKalb County Draft Animal Museum, honoring all those anonymous donkeys, mules, and oxen who slogged us along into the twentieth century. DeKalb County understandably calls itself the "Hub of Transportation Heritage."

I visited the Cord-Duesenberg auto museum, in part because I had never heard of Cord-Duesenberg automobiles. As I learned, in the early days of the automobile age, dozens of manufacturers were rolling out custom-crafted cars, many with uniquely innovative and elegant designs. Cord-Duesenberg was one of them. The early Cord-Duesenbergs featured streamlined fenders, elegant gleaming fixtures, and efficient motors that allowed them to dominate the Indianapolis 500 in its early years. But alas, in the end, the brutal cold efficiency of the Ford assembly line wiped them out, and Cord-Duesenbergs were relegated to museums by the 1930s. And they are a wonder to behold: sleek curves, astounding attention to detail. Even the spare tire holders were intricate works of art.

Auburn loves its classic cars, and it celebrates that fact every Labor Day weekend with the Auburn Cord-Duesenberg Festival, billed as the "World's Greatest Classic Car Show and Festival." Vintage automobiles of every era and style are on display, culminating in a "Parade of Classics" featuring some 200 cars, and the "Cruise-in" with over 600 vintage autos. Auburn's tourist brochure says these events "will exceed your wildest imagination," and evidently plenty of auto enthusiasts agree. Little Auburn (population 13,000), welcomes over 100,000 people every year for the festival.

To get up to Auburn from Fort Wayne, I got onto I-69 for a mercifully brief period—the first interstate I'd driven since departing Washington, except for my wayward escapade on the Pennsylvania Turnpike.

Ike, of course, is renowned for having shepherded the Interstate Highway System Act through Congress and into fruition, and there are many interstate segments all across the country that are named for him. It was not an easy task, and as president he had to argue that such a system was vital to the national defense. During World War II he had seen the German autobahns and was greatly impressed, and this experience, combined with the memories of the 1919 trip, convinced him. As the most honored military officer on the planet, his national defense argument carried lots of weight, and the Interstate Highway Act was finally passed by the Senate on an 89-1 vote in 1956. But even then there were restrictions. States had to contribute funding, and the total mileage of the entire system could not exceed 41,000. Even today, the total mileage of the system is just a bit over 47,000. Ike had wished for extensive use of toll roads, but Congress by and large did not go along with that.

Portable sign in front of a gas station:

Jesus Saves!
Oil and Lube $24.95

I stopped in Kendallville to visit the Mid-America Windmill Museum. Windmills played a vastly underappreciated role in the early settlement of the west. Wind power was essential to pump out the water vital for the first farming or ranching. Even railroads were dependent on windmills to pump water because steam engines needed to replenish their water at virtually every station along the way. The Windmill Museum has some fifty-three working windmills of every conceivable size and shape, and it was fun walking among them and hearing the constant whoosh they all made together. Crossing the country nowadays, I saw plenty of lonesome windmills out there on the prairie, still pumping water, but there were far more generating electric power. In 2015, windmills in the US generated some 191 terawatt hours of energy, or just under 5 percent of all electric energy. Nowadays, modern windmills are omnipresent all along the Convoy's route (more on this later).

Just south of Churubusco I tracked down another original and abandoned stretch of the Lincoln Highway, a portion the Convoy would have driven over in 1919. Later iterations straightened out many portions of the original route, and this was another such forlorn curve of crumbling asphalt, weeds growing up through the cracks and down the middle, within sight of the current, straighter Lincoln Highway/US Highway 30.

I walked around for a while in Goshen on a breezy sunny morning. Near Shanklin Park I noticed a parked Oldsmobile with the bumper sticker "If you think I drive bad, you should see me putt." Bumper stickers: yet another creation that emerged because of the automobile. Early bumper signs were painted on metal plates and wired to bumpers, much like license plates; it wasn't until after World War II that the current version of stickers came into use. Anybody who visited the highly touted Rock City in Lookout Mountain, Tennessee, back in the 1950s, probably remembers that while they were enjoying the view, employees were out there scampering around the parking lot, busily slapping "See Rock City!" stickers to bumpers front and rear. It took razor blades and hours of tedious work to remove them. Professor William Szemklo of Colorado State University has found that aggressive driving is directly correlated with the number of bumper stickers the driver has on his/her car. Back in 1952, Ike and Adlai Stevenson were the first presidential candidates to utilize bumper stickers in their campaigns.

The Convoy passed through Elkhart, where today more than 65 percent of all the recreational vehicles or motor homes (RV/MH) in the US are manufactured. I stopped off at Elkhart's RV/MH museum to take a look. Currently some 9 million US households—roughly 8.5 percent of all households—own an RV/MH. And sales are booming: Manufacturers shipped a record 450,000 RVs in 2017, which was a substantial increase over 2016, also a record year. Sales are being driven in large part by younger purchasers, many of whom are in their twenties or thirties.

The motor home dates back to 1910, when Pierce-Arrow unveiled a touring model home at an automobile show in Madison Square Garden. The first RV/MHs were designed for campers and were manufactured sporadically during the 1920s and 30s. After a hiatus during World War II, production ramped up quickly in the 1950s, as more Americans took to the road. The Elkhart museum was full of beautiful models from over the years, with sleek stylish curves and gleaming chrome finish. Airstream, Winnebago, Spartan, others I'd never heard of. There's even a Chevrolet Housecar that was once owned by Mae West.

The Midwest Museum of American Art in downtown Elkhart is an underappreciated trove of beautiful American art from the nineteenth and twentieth centuries. I wandered around there for over an hour, and since I was the only visitor on a rainy Tuesday afternoon, the man at the entrance came over and showed me around. There's a superb collection of Norman Rockwell lithographs, and many excellent landscapes by artists I'd never heard of. The museum is in a former bank building, and they have a portion of their permanent collection displayed back in the bank vault, with the original hulking, round, tons-heavy door still there.

"Do you get many visitors?" I asked my guide.

"Not really," he said. "Most people who come here know something about American art and have sorta sought us out. We don't get many people just wandering in."

"You have a great collection," I said.

"Yeah. We're kinda flying under the radar, I guess."

The Convoy was welcomed into South Bend by the mayor, the chief of police, the fire chief, the secretary of the Chamber of Commerce, a reception committee of "prominent citizens," three fire companies, and two bands furnished by the Chamber of Commerce and the Goodrich Company. It was the sort of welcome the Convoy was beginning to get used to.

All the way across Indiana, Elwell Jackson notes the dusty road conditions. July 17: "Considerable inconvenience caused by road dust," and July 18: "Dust caused considerable inconvenience." I thought back to Bud the bulldog, with his handy custom-made goggles to combat road dust. There is no indication that anyone in the Convoy had goggles unless they purchased them themselves. And as unpleasant as the dust was, heavy rains would have made portions of the road into a muddy morass that would have slowed the lumbering trucks to a crawl.

Amid the hospitality and warm welcomes the Convoy received all along the route, it's easy to lose sight of the difficulty and danger involved in the trip. For the entire trip, some twenty-one men dropped out because of injury, illness, or other reasons. Take July 19, for example. Here's what Elwell Jackson had to say:

> Kitchen trailer drops range and stack in the road, due to 4 bolts thru frame shearing off. . .Riker stops with bad choke valve in carburetor. . .a railroad watchman named Miller was run down by a Dodge Light Delivery, and suffered a fractured collar-bone. . .Garford blew out petcock on account poor material which broke through ball. . .Ambulance ran off road and overturned in ditch on account careless driving. . .frame kinked in several places. . .planking on small steel bridge gave way.

Despite all this, Jackson reports that the Convoy "made 80 miles in 8 ¾ hours" for one of the fastest paces thus far in the trip.

The *South Bend News-Times* of July 19 reports: "The first Convoy of Uncle Sam's mammoth motor trucks to tour across the United States in behalf of better roads. . .departed South Bend at 6:30 o'clock this morning." The article notes that the Convoy had been met by a large welcoming committee and long parade the preceding afternoon and all the men given sandwiches along with cigars and cigarettes. And to top that off, "To add to the evening meal of the boys with the truck train, lemonade was given to them in abundance by the Chamber of Commerce."

The same edition of the *News-Times* has a helpful ad:

Belching Caused by Acid Stomach?
Take Eatonic!!

And on page 3, a news item headlined with

Seven Women Take Aeroplane Rides!

Separately, the *South Bend Tribune* on the same day reported on the Convoy's arrival the previous afternoon: "The shrieking of sirens brought the people to the streets to watch the Convoy pass. The crowd thickened as the train neared the center of the city, and the downtown streets were lined on both sides by hundreds of interested onlookers."

In the same edition of the *Tribune*, an ad:

While in South Bend, I stopped by the Studebaker National Museum. The Studebaker company was created by two Studebaker brothers—Clement and Henry—in South Bend way back in 1852, when they made freight wagons sold primarily to settlers headed west for the California Gold Rush. The third Studebaker brother—John—trekked west to California in the 1850s, lured by the Gold Rush. He made a small fortune manufacturing wheelbarrows for miners, and then came back to South Bend to expand the company his brothers had started. Together, they did a booming business providing wagons to the Union Army during the Civil War. By the late nineteenth century their South Bend factory covered 100 acres, and they were selling carriages to the White House. Seven different presidents had Studebaker carriages, including Lincoln, Grant, and, significantly, William McKinley, who was riding in one just before he was assassinated in 1901. The museum also houses the carriage that took Lincoln to Ford's Theater.

In 1904 Studebaker produced its first gasoline-powered automobile in collaboration with Garford, and in 1911 Studebaker management decided to go it alone and incorporated, with help from financing by Goldman Sachs. During the First World War the Studebaker Corporation filled large orders for both horse-drawn wagons as well as automobiles for Britain, France, and Russia.

During the period from 1911–1917, Studebaker sold some 467,000 horse-drawn wagons, and some 277,000 automobiles. But the gap between the two was narrowing rapidly every year, and in 1919—the year of the Convoy—Studebaker discontinued its horse-drawn wagon lines entirely to focus solely on automobiles, as well as buses and fire engines.

Despite Studebaker's well-deserved reputation for engineering excellence, the Convoy did not have a single Studebaker vehicle in its 81-vehicle fleet, although there were several Garfords. But the Convoy almost certainly passed by Studebaker vehicles along the way—by 1919, Studebaker was turning out 100,000 automobiles per year. During the 1950s, when Ike was in the White House, Studebaker introduced the first reliable low-cost automatic transmission. The company flourished until the Great Depression, and a long series of setbacks thereafter led to its final demise in the early 1960s. But the Studebaker lived on in the bullet-nosed car featured in the Muppets movie. Nowadays you can visit Tippecanoe Place, the old Studebaker mansion built in 1889, right along the Convoy's route through South Bend.

While on the road in Indiana I noticed a press announcement from Uber, detailing its intention to unveil flying cars by 2020. According to the announcement, the company has negotiated partnerships with several cities and partner companies to develop the technology and infrastructure needed to introduce demonstration vehicles that would take off and land vertically, much like helicopters. An Uber spokesperson stated that Uber's original objective was to alleviate congestion and reduce pollution. "That's why we're working to make 'Push a button, get a flight' a reality."

South Bend is home to Notre Dame University, an outstanding academic institution that is nonetheless best known for its football teams. Legendary names in college football abound: George Gipp, Knute Rockne, Ara Paraseghian, and many others. There's an urban legend that Ike once had a boxing match with Rockne, but try as I might, I could never confirm that story. Everywhere I asked some people said, "Oh, yeah, that definitely happened," while others said "No way. Never happened." So it lives on as urban legend.

James Oliver of South Bend invented a Chilled Plow in the 1850s that was a great leap forward for midwestern farmers. The plow became famous world-wide, and after Oliver's death in 1908, his son JD turned their small company into the Oliver Farm Equipment Company, with global reach. By the time of his death in 1932, JD was the richest man in Indiana. I stopped off at the grandiose Oliver House, as well as the Opera House, City Hall, and Oliver Hotel, all built by the Oliver family. Ike and the Convoy passed by all of them.

Nowadays, with ever-sprawling suburbia, mega-malls, strip shopping centers, and more, it's hard to conjure up the significance of major buildings a century ago. I had to seek out the Oliver Mansion, as I did so many other old buildings along the way, but in Ike's day, such buildings were a major landmark—even THE major presence in small towns. When the Convoy passed through South Bend they would have recognized the Oliver Mansion as a key landmark and remembered the town for it.

An inviting shop sign in New Carlisle:

Sweet Revenge Barbecue Company

In the LaPorte museum, the lady at the entrance said, "Make sure you see that exhibit on the 'Black Widow.'" That would be Belle "Black Widow" Gunness. She was born in 1859, was six feet tall, weighed 200 pounds, and was not somebody to mess around with. She reportedly murdered two husbands, numerous boyfriends, two daughters, and all her stepchildren—as many as forty people in all. She collected life insurance, cash, and jewelry and made sure any witnesses didn't hang around for long. Gunness was born in Norway, emigrated to Chicago, and finally settled in LaPorte. Mayhem ensued.

Gunness put an ad in Chicago newspapers: "Comely widow who owns a large farm. . .desires to make the acquaintance of a gentleman well provided, with view of joining fortunes." She got plenty of takers on that ad, and all of them, after the requisite paperwork of signing over deeds and transferring bank accounts, quickly wound up six feet under.

Gunness was first reported to have died in a mysteriously set house fire in 1908. The charred corpse was headless, and the head was never found—fueling suspicions of foul play. But there was controversy over whether the burnt corpse was in fact Gunness, so, in search of evidence, investigators started digging on her farmstead. Lethal harvest: in the pigpen, one body after another was unearthed.

Like Elvis, there were Black Widow sightings reported for years thereafter, all across the Midwest. So no one really knows for sure when and where she died. But at the time of Ike and the Convoy, the Black Widow was already a grisly legend.

Sign in LaPorte:

Wanna Pizza
I wanna you to wanna pizza!

In Valparaiso there's a statue of Orville Redenbacher, and the town is known as the National Popcorn Capital. Every September Valparaiso holds a big popcorn festival that includes a five-mile run (the Popcorn Panic), and lots of food, entertainment, and crafts. Culminating, of course, in a Popcorn Parade. Yet another superlative, but unfortunately I had to miss it.

I stopped briefly in Crown Point to visit the John Dillinger museum. Dillinger was born in 1903 in Indianapolis and was thus just sixteen when the Convoy passed through Indiana. He wasn't robbing banks yet, but he got started soon thereafter. He pulled off bank heists all over the Midwest, and as far afield as South Dakota, but his main base of operations always remained central and northern Indiana. In 1934 he was imprisoned in Crown Point after robbing a bank in East Chicago. The local police bragged that the jail was escape-proof, but Dillinger proved them wrong, escaping with the help of—according to FBI files—a fake pistol carved from a potato. Later that same year, after several more bank robberies, Dillinger was shot and killed by police in Chicago.

By most accounts Dillinger was a polite and courteous gangster, always saying "please," and "thank you" to tellers while looting their cash drawers. He addressed all women as "ma'am," and with Dillinger every robbery was always ten minutes and out. He made a specialty of robbing banks and then immediately speeding across state lines in his Essex Terraplane V-8. The greatly increased speed of cars made fleeing across state lines (and thus crimes in multiple states) far easier. A few years later Bonnie and Clyde drove a 1934 Ford DeLuxe Sedan while they cleaned out bank after bank throughout the Midwest. With individual state police flummoxed, the FBI stepped in, and it was FBI Agent Melvin Purvis (also on the trail of Baby Face Nelson and Pretty Boy Floyd) who finally tracked down Dillinger. Dillinger's last bank robbery was the Merchant National Bank in South Bend, and then he fled to Chicago, where it all came to an end. But it was the automobile that introduced a new chapter in crime and pursuit.

From Crown Point I turned northward and crossed over the Lincoln Highway to pay a brief visit to Gary, Indiana, on the shore of Lake Michigan. US Steel opened its Gary Steel Works in 1906, and by 1910, Gary was the site of the largest steel mill in the world. Business boomed during the first World War, and was still going strong when the Convoy passed nearby in 1919. The city flourished for a while, and the population peaked at 178,000 in 1960. But Gary remained completely dependent on the steel industry, and a long, precipitous decline began in the 1970s. Today the population is only 75,000, about one-third of all houses in Gary are either unoccupied or abandoned, and Gary Steel Works has reduced its workforce by some 80 percent. It's a depressing place to drive around, and after a half hour of wandering about, I turned back southward to the Lincoln Highway in search of "The Ideal Section."

Back in the 1920s, the Lincoln Highway Association, always trying to drum up enthusiasm for automobile travel, financed several "seedling miles" all along the Lincoln Highway. The LHA consulted a full range of technical experts in designing a short stretch of road paved with thick concrete, and featuring streetlights, curbs, modern drainage, and sidewalks. The 1935 book, *The Lincoln Highway*, notes: "The Ideal Section of Lincoln Highway was one of the first, if not the first, urban sections of highway in the world to be lighted. . .Motorists were surprised and delighted to find they could drive this section at night, without headlamps on their cars, as fast and safely as in full daylight."

One of the first such "Ideal Sections" was located just east of Dyer, Indiana, near the Illinois line, and I wanted to track it down. It wasn't easy to find because nowadays all highways look like 1923's "Ideal Section," and in any event this portion had been paved over with even better material and widened to four lanes. But there is still a single bridge with a sign on the side: Lincoln Highway – Ideal Section.

This particular section was dedicated to Henry Ostermann, the LHA field secretary who guided the Convoy back in 1919 and was killed the following year in an accident on the Lincoln Highway in Iowa. Ostermann had driven his Packard Twin Six out in front of the Convoy all the way, and was accompanied by the Convoy's Public Relations Officer, Lieutenant William Doron. They often went well ahead to prepare the arrival arrangements in each town. Doron, unfortunately, appears to have created more problems than he solved, usually by providing falsely glowing advance reports to City Fathers and local press, which later led to disappointments and misunderstandings that Colonel McClure had to sort out. The first such case was when Doron evidently promised Gettysburg officials that the Convoy would overnight there. The town made extensive preparations that went for naught when McClure told them, "Nope. We're moving on to Chambersburg." Numerous other such escapades followed.

Ostermann and Doron were followed by two scouts, referred to as pilots: Captain Arthur Harrington and Lieutenant Ralph Enos. They were both mounted on Harley-Davidson motorcycles and depended heavily on Ostermann's advice, the guidance of locals, and the 1916 Lincoln Highway Association Road Guide. According to Elwell Jackson, "The simple road marking system used by the pilots proved to be a great success. The markers consisted of salmon colored. . .isosceles right-angle triangles, 11" base by 5.5" altitude, which were tacked on a conspicuous post or fence at each turn of the road. . .When the apex of the triangle pointed up it indicated the route was straight ahead; to the right, indicated right turn. Apex pointing left, left turn; two triangles tacked base to base indicated the location of the campsite. Without these markers considerable difficulty would have been experienced."

I finally found the Ideal Section and the adjacent Henry Ostermann seat; there's an original 1928 Lincoln Highway marker there as well. I had to sprint across four lanes of hurtling, honking traffic to actually sit on the seat, but it was worth it. Ostermann had guided the Convoy all the way from the White House to San Francisco back in 1919 and was a true pioneer of the Lincoln Highway. At the time of the Convoy, he and Henry Joy had probably driven the route more than anybody else, and he knew every last undulation.

I drove on westward, through the hubbub of exurban Chicago traffic, toward the nearby Illinois state line. Leaving Indiana, I was reflecting on the gorgeous old cars I had seen, the sensuous Cord-Duesenbergs, the elegant Studebakers, even the ingeniously designed RVs —all in the past now. And I could understand the pull of old auto shows like the one in Auburn for so many enthusiasts. I thought of the long downward spiral of Gary and its world-renowned steel works. On the other hand, the seedling miles, the "Ideal Sections" of 1923, were now simply ordinary. Thus thinking, I passed on through the cacophony of traffic and into Illinois.

ILLINOIS

"Any old kind of automobile can get from New York
to Chicago. . .but West of Chicago the real trip
commences. . .then we became pioneers.."

–Victor Eubank (1912)

The Convoy departed South Bend early on the morning of July 19 and made relatively rapid progress. They were escorted into La Porte by the Mayor and a reception committee, and were also greeted by the Mayor in Valparaiso. There they stopped to enjoy a lunch served by the Chamber of Commerce and the Red Cross Canteen. Big crowds all along the way.

The Convoy crossed into Illinois and arrived in Chicago Heights at midafternoon. They took the next day, Sunday, as a rest day. Elwell Jackson had a pleasant day: he spent Saturday night at the Chicago Automobile Club as guest of R. R. Newbold, Chairman of the Four Wheel Drive Auto Company. On Sunday he had breakfast with Newbold at the Congreve Hotel, followed by a drive along Lake Shore Drive and Lincoln Park. At noon, Jackson took Newbold out to the Convoy's campsite in Chicago Heights to inspect all the vehicles. Plenty of activity at the campsite. Elwell Jackson writes:

> Sergt. . .Wood did a few demonstration stunts with the Militor for the instruction and entertainment of the camp visitors. Several weekly movie camera men "shot" this exhibition and also groups of the officers. Citizens of the town took most of the enlisted men to their homes for Sunday dinner. Goodyear band is placed at the disposal of the Expedition Commander for the remainder of the trip. All necessary adjustments made.

The Goodyear Band traveled in its own five-ton Packard truck, complete with Goodyear's latest 44-inch pneumatic tires. Thus outfitted, the band team drove all the way through to San Francisco, often way out ahead of the remainder of the Convoy, playing concerts at every single stop. They appear never to have had any mechanical difficulties.

That was not the same story for the remainder of the Convoy. It left Chicago Heights early on Monday, July 21, and Elwell Jackson's log for the day is a good example of the mechanical difficulties the Convoy faced on a daily basis, as well as the constant need for adjustments:

> Class B truck. . .had to be towed by Militor a short distance to loosen up stiff motor. Stopped 45 minutes to repair fan belt on Class B 12 mi. out. Dodge. . .stopped to adjust dragging foot brake band. . .At 14 mi. from Chicago Heights G. M. C. Ambulance. . .stopped to clean dirty spark plugs. One Mack truck had trouble with magneto breaker points. Range and stack of second 2-wheel kitchen trailer drop off in street of Joliet.

At least in Joliet they could all stop for refreshments, served up by the Rotary Club and the Red Cross Canteen Service. But things didn't get much better after that. "At Plainfield, Garford. . .breaks upper fan bracket support, allowing fan bracket to fall forward so that fan tore several holes in radiator." The Convoy finally got a lunch break in Aurora, again served by the ever-faithful Red Cross Canteen Service.

This litany of mechanical woes highlights a couple of points. First, the sheer fragility of even these heavy-duty military vehicles. They were driving over what was then the best cross-country road in the country, but there were still constant problems. Second, the Convoy was well set up to deal with road breakdowns. The Militor could tow any waylaid vehicles back into camp, and the Convoy had a machine shop, a blacksmith shop, and a parts wagon, making for a rolling repair garage. This virtual garage was remarkably successful, and no vehicles had to be retired during the entire trip purely for unresolvable mechanical issues. But the fact that so many problems were already arising in the good roads of the east must have once again caused some palpitations about what lay ahead in the wild unpaved stretches of the west.

I crossed over into Illinois in the early morning, and spent some time wandering about in Chicago Heights, which has some interesting sights. First off, there's the: Frankenmufflerman!! This is a thirty-foot tall fiberglass model of Frankenstein—resplendent in blue suit coat and yellow tie—brandishing a blood-covered ax. He's been towering menacingly above a putt-putt golf course, near the entrance to an amusement park, since the 1970s. When I stopped off to see him, I saw several kiddos squealing past through the park entrance, not paying much attention to the Frankenmufflerman looming overhead.

Muffler men have a special niche in the road lore of America. The first Muffler Man was crafted in 1962 by Bob Prewitt, and thousands more followed over the next decade. They're usually about 25 feet tall, depict men, women, animals, and dinosaurs, and were used for roadside advertising all across the country. That first one was Paul Bunyan wielding a huge axe to promote a restaurant along Route 66 in Flagstaff, Arizona. After that: the Gemini Giant, Uniroyal Gal in bikini, the golfer Greg E. Normous, Injun Joe, Casino Dude, the Happy Halfwit, Harvey the Giant Rabbit, Louie the Lumberjack, and the Sinclair Oil dinosaur. None were made after the mid-1970s, and many have fallen into ruin, but there are still plenty out there to inspect for curiosity seekers wandering the back roads.

I stopped to see the intersection of the Lincoln and Dixie Highways, marked by the Arche Memorial Fountain, built in 1916, with an image of Lincoln on a penny. The Dixie Highway was originally conceived in 1914 by Carl Fisher, and, as he did with the Lincoln Highway, Fisher assembled a group of well-heeled investors to help fund the highway. Its planned route was from Chicago to Miami, conveniently opening an easy route to Fisher's Miami Beach development for northern tourists or investors. Governors along the proposed route squabbled, and a multiplicity of routes emerged, but in the end an eastern and western route were finally agreed upon. They were actually an interlocking patchwork of existing roads, but the western route did eventually connect Chicago to Miami.

Signs near Chicago Heights:

Electric Company Tattoo
And Slots Too!

and

Food! Liquor! Wine! Beauty Products!

As I drove on, through the constant, frenetic traffic of the Chicago suburbs, I was amazed by the continual railroad crossings I encountered. It seemed like every single rail line in North America funneled into Chicago. Over a century ago, Alice Ramsey noticed the same thing: "For miles and miles we crossed tracks. . .back and forth we would (go) around and over them until we almost got dizzy and wondered if there would ever be an end. Bump! Bump! Up and down, again and again."

I passed by billboards everywhere too, yet another American creation that didn't exist prior to the automobile age. Burma Shave signs were among the first, introduced in 1925 and now mostly museum relics. Wall Drug billboards were next in 1932. But nowadays there are countless thousands of billboards, as well as advertisements painted across the sides of barns all across the south. But for the Convoy, no billboards in sight.

I drove on to Joliet where I wanted to track down one of the iconic highway intersections in the US: the spot where the Lincoln Highway crosses Route 66. Even though it wasn't actually established until 1926, more than a decade after the Lincoln Highway, Route 66 is probably the most famous road in America. The route begins on Lake Shore Drive in Chicago and ends at the Santa Monica Pier in Southern California. Route 66 had the advantage of having its own hit song, "Get Your Kicks on Route 66," and a popular TV series, *Route 66*, back in the 1960s. It was the major route west for Dust Bowl migrants of the 1930s and was often called "the Mother Road." Tom Joad drove his family out West over the route in Steinbeck's classic, *The Grapes of Wrath*. But alas, the interstate highway system sounded the death knell for Route 66, and it was removed from the US highway system in 1985. Today, large stretches are abandoned and overgrown with weeds.

But America's most famous road lives on in downtown Joliet, where, at the intersection of Cass and Chicago streets, the Lincoln Highway and Route 66 meet one another. There's a seven-foot-tall monument there to mark the spot. And it's a popular spot: when I stopped by, one tourist after another posed for a photo or selfie in front of the monument of the great classic roadie spot. But back in 1919, no Route 66, and so Ike and the Convoy just motored on past.

Joliet has several more superlatives. During the 1920s and 1930s Joliet was known as the Wallpaper Capital of the World, producing one-third of all US wallpaper. This at a time when upwardly mobile households had their sights set on a pump organ, a hook rug, a radio, and wallpaper. But wait, that's not all. Joliet also had the nation's first-ever public Community College, Joliet Junior College, which opened in 1901. And on top of that: the first ever Dairy Queen opened in downtown Joliet in 1940.

I stopped off at the public library in Joliet, where, as usual, I met helpful librarians with a wealth of local knowledge. A librarian named Betty told me about the nearby Midewin National Tallgrass Prairie, where some 19,000 acres of the former Joliet Army Ammunition Arsenal have been restored as native tall grass prairie. "It's the largest piece of protected open space in northeastern Illinois," said Betty. "It's maintained by the Forest Service, but there's lots of volunteers who work out there. My husband and I are in the Nature Conservancy, and we used to go out there most weekends. They introduced a herd of bison a few years ago, and I hear they're doing well."

Betty had piqued my interest, so I took a short detour to see an authentic tallgrass prairie and grazing bison within commuting distance of downtown Chicago. There was only one other car in the parking lot when I arrived, and I didn't see anybody in the park Visitors Center building, so I just took off up a well-marked pathway. The path was clear but narrow in places, and sometimes the thick prairie grass brushed up against my thighs on both sides. There was a mixture of grasses, some flowering yellow, and I could identify golden rod and prairie dock, but didn't know the others. No trees, just wide-open views on all sides. Small birds twittering, flitting just around me, almost within arm's length, and a quail abruptly overhead. And suddenly the silence: just the soft melody of the wind through the grasses, the rustling of the swaying stalks. When I stood still, yes, I could still detect a distant faint hum of traffic. But to be so close to Chicago it was remarkable.

I walked around for much longer than I had planned, not seeing another soul. But I didn't see any bison either. Once I spotted two dark lumps way over in the distant grass, but without binoculars, no way to tell. Back in the parking lot and getting into my Chevy, I saw a woman in a uniform over by the Park Headquarters. She was walking fast in the other direction, but she saw me and waved, "Hey, thanks for coming! We don't get many visitors."

The Convoy departed Aurora after lunch, and once again there were problems. Elwell Jackson: "Militor returned 10 mi. to pick up Garford. . .Mack. . .has engine trouble all day. Class B. . .water pump becomes stuck on account seals lodging under blades.." But they still made it to their campsite in DeKalb at 5:00 p.m., having covered eighty two miles in just over ten hours.

A front-page story in the *DeKalb Daily Chronicle* on July 23, 1919, chronicled the Convoy's arrival. "The big trucks, many of them over five ton capacity and one or two of them of ten ton capacity, rumbled along as easily as a touring car, perhaps making more noise. . ..[They} sputtered along very well, and when those of the ten ton capacity rolled along the ground shook with the weight." The Convoy's powerful searchlight was always an item of intense curiosity; the *DeKalb Daily Chronicle* noted its deployment at the conclusion of the evening's events: "The big 3,000,000 candle power searchlight was started . . . people from miles and miles around stood in their front door yards watching. . .Colonel McClure. . . said that if there was anyone who did not believe it was 3,000,000 candle power he was privileged to start counting."

One of the central purposes of the Convoy, and certainly the objective uppermost in the minds of the Lincoln Highway Association, was promotion of the Good Roads movement. The *Daily Chronicle* wrote, "Dr. Johnson of Washington DC accompanied the train and during the evening . . . urged the people to boost for good roads at every opportunity. The speaker from the nation's capital made a very strong address, one appreciated by the several good roads fans in the city."

Elsewhere in that same day's issue of the *Daily Chronicle* was an advertisement:

> Mr. Man: If you were to do the family washing week in and week out, it wouldn't take long for you to decide that you should have a Thor Electric Washer. Put yourself in your wife's place and you'll decide without argument. You'll see the difference in your wife; she will and can greet you with a pleasant smile on wash day, instead of that tired weary look.

The most popular comic strips in 1919 newspapers: *Barney Google, Bringing Up Father, and Mutt & Jeff.*

I passed by mobile home/trailer parks all along the route, ranging from the luxurious to the seemingly desperate. Some 20 million Americans live in mobile homes, according to the US Census, almost a quarter of them retirees. Those folks move their RVs around a lot, particularly to the South during winter. But I saw plenty of lone mobile homes all along the route that had weeds growing up all around, a dish antenna sprouting out the side, and were clearly not going anywhere.

In DeKalb, yet another superlative: it's the Barbed Wire Capital of the World. Back in 1874, Joseph Glidden of DeKalb got a patent for what is the modern version of barbed wire, and with partners he established the Barb Fence Company in DeKalb. Demand for barbed wire soared in the west, so sales and production quickly skyrocketed. In time production was streamlined and shifted elsewhere, so by the time Ike and the Convoy passed through, business had declined. But DeKalb retains its title. Nowadays, DeKalb High School sports teams are called the Barbs. Scratch 'em, Barbs!

Early on Tuesday, July 22, the Convoy pulled out of DeKalb. There were the usual mechanical problems, but in addition a small bridge collapsed under the weight of the trucks and had to be repaired. They stopped for an early lunch in Dixon "served by the people of Dixon." But then, just an hour later, "William Ernst, of the Dixon Crucible Company, entertained all the officers at luncheon in the Elks Club, Sterling." After lunch they moved quickly on, approaching the Mississippi.

A bit to the west of DeKalb, in Rochelle, just a block south of the Lincoln Highway, is the Rochelle Railroad Park, where the Union Pacific and BNSF railways intersect. There have been many mergers and name changes over the years, but the original UP tracks reached Rochelle in 1854, and the original BNSF tracks arrived in 1857. So Ike and the Convoy passed right by one of the busiest train interchanges in America. Nowadays, 120 or so freight trains cross through every day. It's one of the only junctions in America where two double tracks cross, forming a four-diamond pattern. There's a small observation pavilion, but I just walked down to the tracks and looked around.

Several other people were milling around too, including a father with two exuberant boys. "When's it coming!? When's it coming!?" The man was on his iPhone, and I realized there must be an app to figure out when the next train was coming through. Sure enough, trusty Dad said, "It's coming. Just a minute or so." And suddenly there it was, a blip on the horizon and then quickly thundering past us. A seemingly endless line of cars, and at one point I couldn't see an end in either direction. Sound booming outrageously at such close range. But what I found most fascinating was the amazing graffiti on so many boxcars. Huge curving letters and text, swerving faces, hulking rounded monsters leaning forward. Amazing art from anonymous artists.

In downtown Rochelle there is a large wall mural commemorating Emily Post's 1916 cross-country trip, and her stay in Rochelle. Post was not too rhapsodic about this stretch of the Lincoln Highway. She wrote, "If it were called the transcontinental trail you would expect little, and be philosophical about less, but the very word 'highway' suggests macadam at the least. And with such titles as 'transcontinental' and 'Lincoln' put before it, you dream of a wide straight road. . .and you wake rather unhappily to the actuality of a meandering dirt road that becomes mud half a foot deep after a day or two of rain."

While in Rochelle I visited the Flagg Township Museum in a building originally built in 1884 as the City Hall. Ike and the Convoy passed right by it. Nowadays, it houses a wealth of esoteric exhibits ranging from prehistoric tools to Civil War artifacts to one-room school desks. But I was particularly drawn to the only known remaining Partin-Palmer automobile. Partin-Palmer started manufacturing cars in Chicago in 1913, and although they went bankrupt just a few years later, they rolled out cars with many auto innovations, like shaft drive, water-cooled engines, elliptic springs, and an I-beam front axle. A short-lived rarity, but Partin-Palmers were on the road at the same time as Ike and the Convoy.

The Lincoln Highway Association headquarters are two blocks off the highway in a historic building in the center of Franklin Grove. I stopped in and had a long conversation with headquarters manager Lynn Asp. Ike and the Convoy passed near the same building when the Lincoln Highway Association was in its infancy. Lynn had the full history: "This building was built in the 1860s by a man named Henry Isaac Lincoln. He was a cousin of Abraham Lincoln. Moved here from New York and wanted to open a store near the railroad station, so he built it here. Bottom floor was his store, and the top floor was called Lincoln Hall." Lynn showed me the old staircase heading upstairs and said it wasn't safe to go upstairs now, but that renovation was underway.

"The whole town used Lincoln Hall for social events for decades. Business meetings, dinners, plays, community dances. Back in 1914 they had a meeting of the Lincoln Highway Association here, where Henry Ostermann spoke. He was the Field Secretary at the time." The same Henry Ostermann would guide the Convoy across country five years later.

"He encouraged people to join the Lincoln Highway Association and make donations. Membership at that time was five dollars, and several people joined right on the spot. They gave all the members a certificate and a membership pin. Those were the very first Lincoln Highway Association pins given out. There's a mural down the street showing that."

Lynn told me the building had become the Franklin Grove Post Office at the turn of the twentieth century, later the local newspaper was printed on the ground floor, and later still it was a store that sold tractor parts. It gradually fell into disrepair but was renovated in the late 1990s. That's when the Lincoln Highway Association moved in.

I asked Lynn if she got many visitors, and she said "Oh yeah, several every day. People from all over the place, even foreigners. A lot of them have never heard of the Lincoln Highway, so we can educate them." She paused for a moment and then said, "Of course, there's not as much traffic through here as there used to be, since they built that interstate south of here."

Just north of the Convoy's route, on the banks of the Rock River, stands the Black Hawk Statue, the second largest concrete monolithic statue in the world. The statue is also known as The Eternal Indian, but most commonly called Black Hawk, in honor of the Indian Chief who fought the last battle against US forces east of the Mississippi in 1832. Created by sculptor Lorado

Taft, the statue measures forty-eight feet high and is situated on a seventy-five-foot bluff directly above the river, so it makes for an impressive sight from below. Black Hawk stands in a relaxed and contemplative pose, gazing serenely down the river. It was completed in 1911, so Ike and the Convoy passed just a few miles to the south.

The Black Hawk War flared up in May 1832, mostly in northwestern Illinois and southwestern Wisconsin, and ended with Black Hawk's surrender in August 1832. A young twenty-three-year-old Captain named Abraham Lincoln served in the Illinois militia during the war. He never saw any combat but came in on the immediate aftermath of a couple of battles and helped bury the dead, some of whom had been scalped. For his service Lincoln was granted forty acres of land in Iowa, and his service reflected positively on his 1860 presidential campaign.

In the delightfully named town of Grand Detour I stopped off to see the original home and shop of John Deere, now an open-air museum. Deere was born in Vermont in 1804 but moved to Grand Detour in 1836 and set up a blacksmith shop. He manufactured pitchforks and shovels, but it was his innovative design of a plow that made him famous. His business quickly flourished, and despite periodic ups and downs, the John Deere Company was a major farm implements corporation by the time of Deere's death in 1886.

Nowadays at the John Deere historic site, you can see one of Deere's original plows, walk around in his house where the Deere family raised eight kids, visit an archeological site where foundations of other original buildings have been found, and hang out in a working blacksmith shop. I wandered through it all but wound up staying for a long time in the blacksmith shop, where I struck up a conversation with master blacksmith Rick Trahan. Rick is a huge, muscular guy with an impressive flowing white beard, and he can wield a hammer and tongs as deftly as I might handle a fork and knife.

"Main thing is to keep the temperature right," he told me. He was working on a long, thin strip of black metal. "You get it too hot, and it's too soft. Too cold, and you can't work it." He was sticking the metal strip into the open oven, pulling it out and working it on the anvil for a couple of minutes, and then putting it back in. "You got to keep this thing at just the right temperature if you want to work it into something that'll last." He had a bucket of cold water close by, and every now and then he'd douse a finished product in the water, to cool it down and harden it. After a while I could see it: he was producing one beautiful unique metal stairway railing after another.

We talked for some time, about family, growing up, work, travel. Rick had been at the site for years and clearly loved his work. "Couldn't imagine I'd do anything else," he said. After a while I noticed he was working on a very small piece of metal, and I asked him what it was. "You'll see," was all he said. He got it red hot, pulled it out, and twisted and turned it down on the anvil a bit, stuck it in, and twisted some more. He used a chisel to taper it down on one side, curl around one end, arch it a bit, and then put some lines in both sides. He doused it in the cold water and then laid it out on his bench, near where I was standing. "That's one for you," he said. "Zipper pull." And then I could see it: indeed, a beautiful, elegant zipper pull, shaped like a long curling leaf. Courtesy of Rick Trahan and John Deere's ancient blacksmith shop.

The Ronald Reagan boyhood home in Dixon has been restored, and I stopped by for a visit. The Reagan family moved into the house in 1920 when Ronnie was nine years old, and he lived there for several years with his father, mother, and older brother Neil. Today it's a perfect time capsule of idyllic, small-town life in the 1920s. Reagan's Father's Model T is still parked in the garage. According to the accompanying text, his Father rarely used the car, but he religiously drove the family into downtown Dixon every single Saturday. His Father would park at one end of Main Street, and the whole family would walk the entire length of the street. Sometimes they'd stop for ice cream or root beer, or they would go to a movie. Ronnie did not even own a bicycle. Everywhere he needed to go was within walking distance: school, football field, the swimming area down on the river, church. Ike and the Convoy passed within one block of the house, just one year before the Reagans moved in.

Dixon has the distinction of having two superlatives, officially bestowed by the Illinois State Legislature: the Petunia Capital of Illinois, and the Catfish Capital of Illinois. The petunia designation resulted from twin calamities back in the 1950s: extensive road-widening combined with Dutch elm disease wiped out hundreds of stately trees. The Dixon Men's Garden Club leaped into the breach and planted thousands of petunias along the major streets. I saw plenty of petunias as I wandered around, by the iconic Dixon WWI Memorial Arch and past nineteenth-century buildings that Ike and the Convoy drove by in 1919.

West of Dixon I drove past stately old clapboard farmhouses, solitary on the hilltops of the windswept bleak hills, and ancient but still serviceable barns, some gleaming red but others with their weathered planking showing through. And then suddenly I spotted a drive-in movie theater at the edge of a corn field. Almost alone but still showing movies. "Showing Tonight: *Star Wars – The Last Jedi*."

Quilts enjoy an esteemed niche in this part of Illinois. Every museum or historic site that I visited featured numerous beautifully detailed old quilts, including the bed in which Neil and Ronnie Reagan slept. There is even a Quilters' Journey through Northwest Illinois offered by the tourism bureau, where you can view old quilts, new quilts, and a full range of quilting supplies for current-day quilters.

Billboards along the way:

Grilled Steaks
Chicken Pot Pies,
and Sloppy Joes!

and

Attorneys at Law
Specializing in:
Divorce
Malpractice
Traffic Accident Injuries

The Convoy passed through the town of Fulton, where today the windmill "De Immigrant" stands high on a dike overlooking the Mississippi River. The windmill was built in the Netherlands, taken apart, and re-assembled by Dutch engineers in Fulton in 2000. Thousands of Dutch immigrated to Fulton from the East in the late 1850s. Word got back to the Netherlands, and more Dutch arrived throughout the late nineteenth century. Still more came in the aftermath of the two World Wars, and today almost half of Fulton's population is of Dutch origin. The town holds Dutch Days on the first weekend in May every year, which coincides with the date of the liberation of the Netherlands at the conclusion of World War II.

Jane Orman Luker, Guide at the Windmill Cultural Center and Director of Friends of the Windmill, showed me around and related the town's particular Dutch history. Afterwards, I walked up the dike by the windmill, through the thick wet clover and flowering dandelions and at the crest was a wide view over the swift flowing river. To the right was the site of the bridge over which Ike and the Convoy passed in 1919. Historic floods in 1965 temporarily turned Fulton into an island and badly damaged the bridge. The ever-enterprising Dutch-origin citizens quickly constructed dikes to protect the town, the same dikes that I walked along to view the river. The damaged bridge was finally taken down in 1973.

I stood on top of the dike for a long time, enjoying the cool, damp breeze and gazing out over the massive river, rippling with eddies and swirling currents. I was thinking about Ike and the Convoy, gazing out at the same view a century earlier and contemplating the challenges that lay ahead in the American West.

IOWA

The Convoy crossed the Mississippi over the High Bridge, a rickety wooden span with protruding nails and sagging supporting structure. They only chanced two or three vehicles at a time, so it took a while to get the entire Convoy across. The High Bridge was badly damaged by a 1965 flood and eventually demolished in 1973. The Convoy was finally across at 4:00 on the afternoon of July 22 and set up camp for the evening a short time later in the riverside town of Clinton. Elwell Jackson writes, "Roads fair but very dusty." He may not have known it at the time, but dust was far preferable to the alternative: the famous Iowa gumbo that quickly developed after any rainfall.

The treacherous gumbo was well documented by early travelers. About her cross-country trip in 1916, Emily Post wrote, "As an illustration of what rain in Iowa can do, 25 minutes of drizzle turned the smooth hard surface of the road into the consistency of gruel. . .Illinois mud is slippery. . .but in Iowa it lurks in unfathomable treachery, loath to let anyone get out again that once ventures into it."

Clinton was known as the Lumber Capital of the World from 1860–1895 and had more millionaires per capita than any other US city. In the late 1800s Clinton produced over one-third of all lumber in the US, reaching peak production in 1895 with 195 million board feet. But by 1900 the northern forests were depleted, and from that point on it was all downhill for Clinton. By the time the Convoy passed through in 1919, all the mills had closed, and the population was in decline. But it's still a pleasant town today, with a minor league baseball team (Saw 'em down, Lumberkings!), riverboat gambling, rows of elegant lumber baron mansions, and a superb Sawmill Museum.

The Iowa Lincoln Highway Association and Prairie Rivers of Iowa, a state-wide nonprofit, have done a terrific job of clearly marking and documenting the original Lincoln Highway—the route the Convoy mostly followed—all the way from the Mississippi to the Missouri. Many portions of the route are still narrow gravel or dirt roads, but they're well maintained, and I enjoyed every mile of it—past remote farmhouses and lonely hillsides, wind cascading across all of it. On the back-country dirt roads of the Convoy's route, I drove through many a corn field, thigh high, swaying in the constant wind, stretching on in long arcs over the swaying hills to horizons in every direction. It was so beautiful I often stopped to get out and just enjoy the silence. The pounding solitude, the soft sound and feel of a stiff breeze. A single bird's twitter remarkable.

Now and then along the way I passed people down close to the road, and I finally stopped when I spotted a woman in bib overalls working on a barbed wire fence close by. I walked over, and she introduced herself as Becky. She had a big Chevy pickup parked in the pasture behind her. "Just checkin' this fence-line," she said. "Gettin' it tightened up." She had two huge lethal-looking pliers in her hands and was twisting some barbed wire.

"You have cattle?" I asked.

"'Bout five hundred."

"So how's everything going?"

"Lot better since Obama's gone. He had that damned WOTUS thing. Cow couldn't piss in a puddle without the damned federal government coming down on top of you. Trump sure got rid of that one. He sure did."

WOTUS is the Waters of the US Act, which placed limits on fertilizer and manure runoff from farms into streams. "So, you don't have any runoff here?" I asked.

She jerked around and stared at me, and I realized she was suddenly suspicious. "Don't get me wrong. I don't like polluted water either. You think I want a stream full of shit flowing right over here?" She waved over to the side. "But if the damned federal government wants to do something about this, they ought to at least talk to us. The farmers. We've been farming here, ranching here, for generations and we know the land. We know it a damned sight better than a damned bureaucrat sitting at a damned desk up there in Washington."

"Well, that sounds reasonable," I offered.

"Nice talking to you," she said. "I got to go. Got to finish up this line, and then go cook lunch. I got a man and three hungry boys coming down at noon. And then I got that other line over there this afternoon." And so Becky proceeded, and the pioneer spirit lived on.

Nowadays in Iowa, there are 3 million people, 4 million cows, and 20 million pigs. Land not taken up by cows and pigs is mostly used to grow food for cows and pigs: Iowa has more acres of soybeans and corn than any other state. But when Ike and the Convoy passed through there were no soybeans—they drove through cornfields and hayfields.

In the little town of Dewitt I wandered around Lincoln Park and stood by the intersection of the Lincoln Highway and the Blues Highway, which nowadays is Highway 61. The Blues Highway, constructed in 1926, runs from New Orleans to the small town of Wyoming, Minnesota, and generally follows the Mississippi River. In some northern stretches it's called the Great River Road, but from St. Louis southward through Memphis, the Mississippi Delta, and New Orleans, it's still called the Blues Highway. Robert Johnson wrote his blues classic, "Crossroads," about a Blues Highway intersection in Clarksdale, Mississippi, and Bob Dylan later recorded a classic album entitled "Highway 61 Revisited." When thousands of Southern Blacks migrated northward in the 1950s and 60s, the Blues Highway was a major exodus route.

From Wheatland I went meandering southward on a lonely county road to visit the world's largest truck stop and museum—Iowa 80—on I-80 not far from Walcott. Along my route westward I encountered other truck stops claiming to be the world's largest, but I never saw another trucking museum that could match I-80's. In the huge showroom there are dozens of trucks dating back as far as 1910, films on the history of trucking, and scads of trucking memorabilia from over the decades. I wandered around the museum but enjoyed even more walking through the acres of parked sixteen-wheelers outside. Row after row of gleaming grilles and fenders, ornate hubcaps polished to a shine. Unique ornaments bobbing from the inside rear-view mirrors.

The small town of Lowden is home to another classic Lincoln Highway establishment—the Lincoln Hotel built in 1915. Ike and the Convoy passed by it, but it slowly fell into disrepair over the years until it was restored in the 1990s. It now has a mixture of hotel rooms and apartments.

From Lowden I took another winding detour north through flowing cornfields to Dyersville to see a place I'd long wanted to visit: the site of the movie *Field of Dreams*. The 1989 baseball film starring Kevin Costner relates the story of the return to life of the disgraced 1919 Chicago White Sox Baseball team. The White Sox, led by all-star Shoeless Joe Jackson, dominated the

American League that year, and at the time of the Convoy the team was cruising comfortably in the league lead. They made it easily to the World Series, but then inexplicably flopped horrendously and lost to the Cincinnati Reds. Subsequent investigations indicated that eight players had agreed to throw games in exchange for payments from a professional gambling syndicate. The players, including likely Hall of Famer Shoeless Joe, were banned from the game for life, and the 1919 White Sox have ever since been known as the Black Sox.

In the film, Costner, who plays a small-time Iowa corn farmer, hears voices commanding him, "If you build it, they will come." He interprets this as an instruction to build a baseball diamond, so, much to the distress and ridicule of his family and neighbors, he plows up acres of thriving corn and builds a diamond. And then, in the film's key scene, Shoeless Joe and the Black Sox slowly emerge from the surrounding corn and take the field, gloves in hand.

Nowadays at the Dyersville film site, the farmhouse, red barn, and baseball diamond are still there, surrounded on all sides by windswept corn, seemingly stretching on for miles. The classic two-story white clapboard farmhouse is occupied, but the diamond is open to visitors, and it seems to get plenty. The lady in the Visitors' Center told me there had been a lengthy search for the perfect farm for the film. "They needed a long lane through corn fields, leading up to a solitary house," she said. The search culminated in the Lansing farm, which had been in the family since 1906. The Lansings gave final permission to film and plow up corn to build the diamond. They get about 65,000 visitors per year nowadays, and while I was there I saw a group of about ten little leaguers play a couple of innings, and a Dad and his peewee son do some underhanded pitch and bat. When the little boy finally hit the ball, he tore around the bases at top speed and slid into home plate like it was the seventh game of the World Series. "Attaboy!" hollered his Mom, from behind home plate. During an interlude I, too, loped around the bases, gazing out at the corn looming at the edge of the outfield, from which Shoeless Joe and the Black Sox had magically appeared.

Just west of the town of Mount Vernon, you can visit Iowa's original seedling mile, completed in 1918. So Ike and the Convoy drove right over it. It was quite the novelty back then: Hokanson writes that this mile "was among the first miles of concrete in the state. In dry weather it became popular with auto drivers who liked to feel their machines hit stride on the fast pavement. But in wet weather, people rode the trolley out to see it; you couldn't drive to it for the mud at either end."

Nearby, there's a striking sight: Grant Wood's famous American Gothic painting perfectly reproduced along two sides of a large barn close to the road. The owner of the barn commissioned Iowa artist Mark Benesh to reproduce Wood's iconic image back in 2008, and it's immediately eye-catching for anyone driving along the Lincoln Highway today. Wood, perhaps Iowa's most famous native artist, was born in 1891 in Anamosa and grew up in Cedar Rapids. He was a strong proponent of regionalism, which championed use of rural American themes. American Gothic, painted in 1930, is certainly his best-known work, but he was prolific up to his death in 1942 in many media, including lithography, ceramics, wood, and found objects. He even designed stained glass windows. I got out to take a closer look, then drove on and almost immediately passed other barns, some of them weathered, tilted-over semi-ruins.

Why is it that we find ruined barns more picturesque than new, modern barns? I stopped to take photos of many ruined, even semi-collapsed old barns along my route, with weathered planks that hadn't seen paint in years. I saw plenty of modern, gleaming, state-of-the-art barns too and hardly gave them a second look. Perhaps it's a link to the past, a semi-mythical past. Part of that particularly American restless tension between clinging to an idyllic past, and barreling ahead to develop something bigger, better, stronger, faster.

The Convoy departed Clinton at 6:30 a.m., and despite a long litany of mechanical problems, they still managed to cover eighty-seven miles in just over ten hours, stopping for the night at Cedar Rapids. Elwell Jackson writes, "Convoy escorted into Cedar Rapids by Lt. Gov. Moore, Mayor, etc. Dinner served to entire command by Chamber of Commerce and Rotary Club. . .Good hard dirt roads." Cedar Rapids citizens may also have been entertained by a mascot the Convoy had picked up along the way: Jeff the Raccoon.

Cedar Rapids was ready: the front-page headline of the Cedar Rapids Evening Gazette on July 23 was "Truck Train Due to Arrive in City at 4 P.M. Today." The article following reads in part, "Repetition of the days of the ox-drawn prairie schooners traveling across country in long caravans will be re-enacted here today, only in twentieth-century fashion." The article also notes "The cross-country tour. . .is attracting attention of the entire world."

The town went all-out to welcome the Convoy. The July 24 edition of the Evening Gazette rhapsodizes, "With the sun setting in a blaze of glory, with bands playing and with thousands of persons thronging Greene Square and the nearby streets, the. . .men and officers of the Motor Transport Corps sat down at 7:00 p.m. yesterday to what they afterward unanimously expressed as the best supper and best entertainment they had had in any city along their. . .route."

Iowans considered the passing of the Convoy to be a major event, and they turned out in droves. *The Evening Gazette* again: "All along the route from Clinton (to Cedar Rapids) the small towns through which the train passed turned out in big fashion. The highway was lined with spectators long before the hour scheduled for the arrival of the trucks. . .there was cheering when the train passed through."

And on the light side, the same article contains this item: "One of the coincidents(sic) of the membership of the train is the fact that it has one of the shortest men and one of the tallest men in its ranks that are in the army. "Pigmy," as he is called, is four feet nine inches while his boon companion the tallest man is six feet six. They created not a little amusement for the crowd. . .by their antics." One of their classic antics was having Pigmy curl himself up into a spare truck tire, which his lanky partner would then roll down the road.

The same edition had some large advertisements for some useful-sounding products:

And elsewhere:

A few days earlier, on July 21, The *Evening Gazette's* sports page had the following headline story: "Jackson's homer beats New York – It was the last half of the tenth inning. Two men were out. (Shoeless) Joe Jackson came up to bat. The score stood White Sox 1, New York 1. Almost 30,000 fans were howling for Joe to do something. And Joe delivered a heroic drive far and high, over the right fielder's head. The crowd screamed and the ball sailed and sailed and finally dropped into the right field bleacher. . .another victory for Chicago." The White Sox and Shoeless Joe seemed invincible.

Cedar Rapids is a pleasant city situated along the banks of the Cedar River. Back in the 1850s and 1860s, large number of Czechs and Slovaks immigrated to Cedar Rapids to work in the slaughterhouses and packing plants, and the wave of immigrants continued through the late nineteenth and early twentieth century. Most of them settled into one crowded area between the river and the plants, and Ike and the Convoy would have passed just a few blocks from there. Today that area is known as Newbo (New Bohemia), and it bustles with trendy shops and chic restaurants, in addition to residences.

Cedar Rapids is also home to the only Masonic Library in the US. I found beautiful nineteenth-century Masonic Temples all across the route, a reminder of the importance of Freemasonry up until quite recent times. In the nineteenth and early twentieth centuries, Freemason meetings were prominently announced in many US newspapers. At least fourteen US presidents were Freemasons, including George Washington, and the movement was still strong at the time of the Convoy. Presidents Theodore Roosevelt, William Howard Taft, Warren Harding, Franklin Roosevelt, and Harry Truman were all active Freemasons, but Ike never joined.

From Cedar Rapids I made a short detour north to see several sites that had piqued my interest. First of all, yet another superlative in tiny downtown Brandon: Iowa's largest frying pan. It was built in 2004 and stands right at the side of Main Street, almost vertical with the handle side up. It's nine feet wide, fourteen feet high, and weighs in at 1,020 pounds. If ever used, Iowa's largest frying pan could fry you up 44 dozen eggs, 352 pork chops, or 88 pounds of bacon, all at one time. As I inspected the pan, a man in blue jeans and a Chicago Cubs t-shirt walked by and said "Man, you'd need a shitload of Brillo pads to clean that baby."

Brandon has some other nice features, I learned, perhaps foremost the semi-annual cowboy breakfast. Volunteer cowboys from all over Iowa rendezvous in the Community Center and serve up a hearty breakfast of orange juice, ham, eggs, biscuits with sausage gravy, and cowboy coffee. Crowds usually surpass 2,000 happy customers, and I regretted I couldn't be one of them.

While in Brandon I stopped for gas at the town's Kwik-Stop. There were four men talking inside. As I approached the door I could just vaguely make out "goddamn Washington bureaucrats doin'," but as soon as I entered everybody abruptly stopped talking. I nodded and said hello, and they all nodded right back. "Pretty windy today," I offered up, and one of them said "Yeah," but nothing else. I paid for my gas and a bottle of water and then departed. I was hardly out the door before I faintly heard them all talking again, and there was just one snatch I could make out: "Trump'll straighten it out."

In LaPorte City I stopped in at the Auto Thrill Show Museum and struck up a conversation with its founder and proprietor, Chad Van Dyke. According to Chad, his museum houses the world's largest collection of thrill show memorabilia, and after poking around for a while I certainly believed him. There was a poster near the entrance announcing "The History of Thrills, Chills, and Spills," and then posters, programs, ads, and photos galore, depicting cars flying through the air, cars tilted sideways and running on two wheels, cars caroming off one another and speeding on. Yet another activity made possible by the automobile age.

Chad told me that auto thrill shows were popular all over the US in the 1950s and 60s, often drawing thousands of spectators, but started to fade after that. "I went to so many of those shows when I was a kid," he said. "I loved them—the speed, the wacky daredevil things they did. Even the crashes were fun to watch." He started collecting memorabilia decades ago and opened his museum ten years ago. "Don't get all that many visitors," said Chad. "Since they built the interstate, not many people come up this way anymore."

In Waterloo I visited the John Deere Museum. At the time of the Convoy, automobiles were undergoing rapid development, but so were tractors, an arguably more important phenomenon. A farmer could plow one acre per day with an ox-drawn plow, but he could plow three acres per hour with a tractor, and this brought about a sea change in American agriculture, especially in places like Iowa. The Waterloo Boy was the first motorized tractor, brought to market in 1912. John Deere wanted to get into the tractor business, and after much internal debate, they bought the Waterloo company in 1918 for $2.25 million.

John Deere had 26 employees in 1895, but as development and sales of motorized vehicles picked up steam, the company's employment had grown to well over 1,000 employees at the time of the Convoy. Deere's production was diverted to wartime needs during World War I, and the farm slowdown in the 1920s, the subsequent Depression, and a series of labor disputes caused major turmoil in the agricultural machinery sector. Many competitors went bankrupt, but John Deere persevered and prospered through it all. The Deere Model D, the first tractor designed and manufactured exclusively by Deere, was introduced in 1923, and state-of-the-art equipment followed virtually every year thereafter. In 1954, the second year of Ike's presidency, tractors outnumbered horses and mules on American farms for the first time ever.

I took a guided tour of the John Deere cab assembly factory, led by a gregarious guide named Ned. He bombarded me with details of the latest tractor technology and new innovations that were just around the corner. "JDLink Telematics," he said. "Everything's GPS-equipped with fleet management systems and wireless data transfer. Environmental field sensors—you can monitor water levels down to the millimeter. Whole fleet of vehicles can talk to one another." Ned showed me a forty-eight-row tractor that could plow an acre in one minute. "That baby's got an eighteen-speed transmission and almost a mile of internal wiring. Heated leather contour rotational seats. Everything computerized, and I mean everything."

I was the only person on the tour, so I could pepper Ned with questions. Remembering Raj Rajkumar back at Carnegie-Mellon and his talk of self-driving cars, I asked Ned how soon self-driving technology would come to tractors. "Already there," he said. "We don't advertise it really, and we don't advise folks to let the tractors self-drive, but it's definitely there in all our newest tractors. Self-driving and autonomous."

He stopped walking for a moment and said, "Let me tell you a story. Fellow came in here and told us he was out in his brand new 9520RX. Got a track system, state-of-the-art computer system, climate-controlled cab. Real plush driver's seat. He set that thing at the edge of his field, programmed it like he wanted, then leaned back, folded his arms and just watched to see what would happen. Everything perfect, nothing for him to do, so after a while he got kinda drowsy. Fell asleep. Half an hour later, he woke up real sudden. What did he see? That tractor was still perfectly on line."

Many people think of Iowa as being monotonously flat, but there are in fact huge long undulations everywhere you look: some subtle and gradual, others grand and sweeping. Together they give the impression that the land is flowing, and always in motion, and the gusting winds add to that effect. So many ninety-degree turns, marking the boundaries of a section, but on long gravel portions of the original Lincoln Highway and the Convoy's route, it was straight sailing through swaying corn, soybeans, distant solitary farmhouses. Dust spiraled up in my Chevy's rearview mirror.

The Iowa Tourism Bureau has done a great job on many fronts, but perhaps their most amusing effort is the recreation of the old Burma Shave signs on several state highways.

"Big Mistake
Some Drivers Make
Rely on Horn
Instead of Brake
IOWA!"

In little Belle Plaine I stopped for an early lunch at the Lincoln Café, a Main Street institution since 1928. I had a juicy chili burger and a slice of apple pie, and talked for a while with my waitress, Peggy. "We used to have a beautiful long oak bar all along one side of the Café," she said. "Put it in right after the end of Prohibition. All kinds of brass fittings, and a glass mirror along the wall. But new owners bought the cafe about eight years ago, and they wanted a family restaurant. So they took out the bar and changed around the whole menu. Put in more stuff that appealed to kids. And it sure worked—we're so busy, customers have to wait for a table on the weekends." And it was true. Already at noon on a weekday, Lincoln's was filling up fast.

Right across the street is a small apartment building that was originally the Lincoln Hotel. Alice Ramsey stopped there on her cross-country trip after having endured the previous night stuck in gumbo near Weasel Creek. When she and her team finally straggled into Belle Plaine for breakfast, she wrote "My! *That* was good!"

Just down Main Street from the Lincoln Café one finds George Preston's Gas Station. You can't miss it: every square inch of the station as well as an adjacent storage shed is covered with antique tin and porcelain signs advertising automobile products. Mobil Oil, Goodrich, Pennzoil, Red Crown, Star Tires, Anti-Sludge Iso-Vis D Motor Oil—George collected them all. The gas station was originally a couple of blocks closer to the center of Belle Plaine, but the original owners moved it to its current location in 1921. So Ike and the Convoy passed right by the station at its original site. Preston went to work at the station in 1925, and eventually saved up enough to buy it. George was equally famous for the endlessly entertaining yarns he could tell about decades of passersby on the Lincoln Highway. His stories were so popular he eventually set up a toll-free hot line where callers could hear his latest, and he appeared on the Johnny Carson Show in 1990. George passed away in 1993, still running Preston's right up to the end.

Since George's death the station has been abandoned and there's been little maintenance. It's no longer safe to go inside, and the roof appeared to be sagging in places. There is an antique gas pump out front, and when I approached it a startled blackbird lurched out of a hole in the middle of the pump, almost flying right into my face and startling me as well. When I looked closer I could see straw poking out of the rusty hole. As I stood there inspecting the walls of Preston's, an elderly man in overalls and a striped railroad cap came walking by, and I asked him if anyone was maintaining the station.

"Nah," he said, without even slowing down. "Everybody's just waiting for the damned thing to collapse."

As I strolled along Belle Plaine's Main Street, I noticed the usual handful of deserted, boarded-up stores, and there weren't many pedestrians. But also this: well-tended tulip and shrubbery beds, freshly painted benches. Stores apparently doing well, with their facades restored: a drug store, Tru-Value Hardware, a dentist's office, an attorney, some women's clothing stores, several bars and cafes. The historic Herring Hotel about to be restored to an operating hotel again. And on several street corners high-school kids weeding and mulching, horsing around but still working. Belle Plaine was making a serious effort to revive downtown.

The Convoy departed Cedar Rapids early on July 24 and stopped for a lunch served by the Red Cross Canteen Service in Tama. They passed over Tama's historic 1915 bridge with concrete railings that spell out "Lincoln Highway" on both sides, the only bridge of its type on the entire highway, and still used today. The Convoy reached Marshalltown already by midafternoon and camped in Riverview Park, where the Red Cross Canteen again served dinner for the entire Convoy. Elwell Jackson writes "Quiet and uneventful day. Fair and warm. Good dirt roads, but very dusty." The Red Cross Canteen contingents all across the country provided yeoman's service with timely snacks and meals. The menu in Marshalltown included meatloaf, potato salad, pickled beets, sandwiches, deviled eggs, cottage cheese, ice cream, cake, and coffee, all topped off with unlimited cigarettes.

The *Marshalltown Times Republican* of July 25 headlines "Train Attracts Immense Crowds. Leaving behind a cloud of dust that begrimed men, trucks, and equipment, the military transport train rumbled into the city late Thursday afternoon. After camping for the night in Riverview Park, the trains pulled out west over the Lincoln Highway at 6:30 this morning, although it was nearly 8 o'clock before the last of the vehicles rattled out of the city. . .Because of the dust the trucks traveled far apart in the country, the train spreading out over a distance of five to ten miles."

Just a few days later on July 29 the *Times Republican* had the headline "Night of Terror in Chicago," detailing the city's race riots that resulted in 24 deaths. The sub-headlines include: "More Whites than Negroes Killed," and "Women and Children Driven from Homes."

On a lonely stretch of highway between Tama and Marshalltown, not far from the Iowa River, is the site where Henry Ostermann, the Convoy's invaluable guide and Lincoln Highway Association Field Secretary, died in an automobile accident. It was June 1920, less than a year after the Convoy had passed through the same spot. Ostermann was driving his Packard alone. He tried to pass a slower-moving vehicle, but he slipped over into the shoulder and lost control of his car. It flipped over a couple of times, and he was killed instantly.

I was surprised and impressed by the extensive historic renovation in downtown Marshalltown, where I wandered around for a couple of hours. In addition to the famous Tremont Hotel, built in 1902 and almost certainly visited by members of the Convoy, there's also the 1910 Willard Mansion, the 1876 County Courthouse Building, and the 1898 Letts-Fletcher building, all lovingly restored to their original facades. The Letts-Fletcher building had the distinction of being one of the Midwest's first Jack Sprat food processing factories.

I stopped off to meander along the original Lincoln Highway through the small town of State Center. There were plenty of historic nineteenth-century buildings lining Main Street, buildings Ike and the Convoy passed right by, but alas many are now boarded up. Watson's grocery, which opened up in 1895 and operated successfully until the 1950s, is long since closed for business but restored for tours at select times. The old Marshall County Hospital has a beautiful ornate façade but is long closed. Just down the block was Frickeville Antiques, still very much open for business. In the window hung this sign:

"Guns are Welcome on Premises.
Please Keep Them Holstered, Unless a Need Arises,
in Which Case Judicious Marksmanship is Appreciated."

The small town of Colo lies at the intersection of the Lincoln Highway and the Jefferson Highway, originally the Pines to Palms Highway from Winnipeg to New Orleans, but nowadays bearing the unromantic label of Highway 65. Ike and the Convoy passed right by the intersection, probably unawares.

The Jefferson Highway was dedicated in 1918 and today has its own unique JH road sign, much like the Lincoln Highway. For aficionados, there is a Jefferson Highway Association—just like the Lincoln Highway Association—and they have a fine newsletter, website, and annual meetings where roadsters can swap tales.

For a small town, Colo has a lot of sights. Way back at the turn of the twentieth century, Charles Reed owned a substantial plot of land in Colo right on the Lincoln Highway, and as motor traffic picked up in the 1910s, he started allowing motorists to camp there for a small fee. Ike and the Convoy would have passed right by Reed's campsite. But Charles had bigger ambitions. He teamed up with his nephew Clare Niland, and in 1923 they set up a gas station that remained open twenty-four hours to serve passing motorists. Ever enterprising, in 1928 Reed and Niland opened the Colo Cabin Camp featuring separate cabins. They later connected them to become the Colo Motel in the 1940s. A café was opened along the way.

All has now been restored with great care as the Reed-Niland corner. Some of the motel rooms are apartments, and others are available for nightly rentals. The garage/gas station is long closed but restored to its 1930s look. Best of all, the cafe is fully restored, and features myriad Lincoln Highway souvenirs and the front grille of a 1940s Cadillac. I stopped by and dug into their daily special: cheeseburger with chili, topped off with a slice of blueberry pie. The manager told me they do a good business with both locals ("we serve good reliable food at reasonable prices") and also with periodic Lincoln Highway travelers like myself.

On the outskirts of the small town of Nevada, there is a large sign declaring "Welcome to Nevada. You Are Driving on the Original Lincoln Highway." Nevada has the distinction of organizing the first-ever annual Lincoln Highway Days Festival, held at the end of August and featuring a parade, rodeo, antique car show, and culminating in the grand finale: the crowning of the Lincoln Highway Days king, queen, prince, and princess. A bit further on I passed through Ames over the Lincoln Way, the route unchanged in over a century. It skirts along the southern edge of the Iowa State University campus, just as Ike and the Convoy had done.

Mamie Geneva Doud Eisenhower was born in Boone, Iowa, in 1896, and I visited her childhood home, which is now a museum. Her family moved to Cedar Rapids when she was only nine months old, but her maternal grandparents, Carl and Johanna Maria Carlson, continued to live in Boone, and Mamie visited frequently up to just two years before her own death in 1979.

She was the last First Lady born in the nineteenth century, and only the second (Lou Henry Hoover) to be born west of the Mississippi River. Mamie met Ike in 1915 at the home of friends in Fort Sam Houston, Texas. They married a year later when she was nineteen. She later estimated that in thirty-seven years as a military wife, she had moved and set up a new household at least twenty-seven times.

When the Convoy stopped for half an hour in Boone, Ike had a quick meeting with Eda and Joel Carson, Mamie's aunt and uncle. The Convoy got a big reception in Boone, and as usual, the Red Cross Ladies Canteen served refreshments. Upon departure, Ike was interviewed by a local newspaper and said, "I can't say too much of the condition of the Lincoln Highway." An ambiguous statement, open to multiple interpretations, and perhaps an early indicator of Ike's potential as a successful politician.

Iowa has some phenomenal early bridges still in good repair, and not far from Grand Junction you can see several of them. There's the Marsh Rainbow Arch bridge, and the simply-named L Bridge, which has large Lincoln Highway L's on the ends—both century-old landmarks on the Lincoln Highway that you can still drive over. Further along there's the West Beaver Creek bridge over a long-abandoned section of the original Lincoln Highway that Ike and Convoy would have driven over. I got out and walked along a lengthy stretch. At this point, you can see the original Lincoln Highway that I was walking over, now overgrown in pasture, the Union Pacific Railroad track, and the modern Highway 30. Interstate 80 is over there a couple of miles in the distance. All of them parallel, racing on toward the far horizon.

There's yet another famous bridge near Boone, which is the nation's highest (at 185 feet) double-track railroad bridge. Nowadays it's called the Kate Shelley High Bridge in honor of local native Kate Shelley who, in 1881 at the age of 15, crawled across the bridge in the midst of a raging storm to warn an oncoming train that a crucial bridge father down the line had been washed out. Kate saved the day, and now there's also a memorial park named for her in Boone.

In Grand Junction I stopped in at the Lincoln Highway Museum to meet with Bob and Joyce Ausberger, longtime activists for the Lincoln Highway. Bob was away, but I spent a long time chatting with Joyce, who is an inexhaustible font of enthusiasm and knowledge about anything related to the nation's first highway. For years, Bob and Joyce together have been key drivers in sparking interest in the Lincoln Highway. The museum, right on Main Street, has a trove of esoteric artifacts, and Joyce was one of the few people I met along the way who knew about the 1919 Convoy. "Yes, Main Street in Grand Junction is the Lincoln Highway, and they drove right along here," waving out front. "But it wasn't paved until 1924, so they were on a narrow dirt road."

Joyce took me out and around the museum to the backyard. "I want to show you something fascinating that we've always wondered about." There, parked in the carefully mown grass, was an abandoned Army wagon. Joyce pointed out a small label on the side, indicating the wagon had been manufactured in 1918. "This thing was found just east of Eureka bridge near an abandoned barn, and we brought it here a few years back. Nobody knows where it originally came from. I'm thinking that 1919 Convoy might have just left it there." It was the sort of wagon that would have been towed by a truck, and I thought Joyce was probably right. But perhaps we'll never know for sure.

Joyce took me back around to the front of the museum and waved her arm down Main Street. "We used to have such a beautiful Main Street here. Street the Convoy drove down. But nowadays our old Main Street is almost gone. We don't have any grocery store, variety store, clothing store, none of that. Everything moved to the new Highway 30, and then after that it all moved to Interstate 80."

I said farewell to Joyce and wandered down Main Street, past beautiful nineteenth-century buildings, ornate details everywhere, but most now vacant and starting to crumble. Windows boarded up, "For Sale" signs legion. Every now and then an Antique/Old Stuff/Junk Shop. A beauty parlor, a lonely insurance agency.

I reflected on the grand irony of the Convoy's trip and my trip: the Convoy threaded its way down Main Streets of small towns from coast to coast. The Lincoln Highway knitting the towns together into a national fabric. And then years later, well-meaning Ike, wanting to improve our nation's transportation system, helped create interstate highways that spelled doom for most of those lovely small downtowns. Nowadays dozens of small-town Main Streets across the country stand as forlorn monuments to the past, while Wal-Marts out by the interstate thrive. But here and there, fragments, even blocks, are being restored. Just in Iowa I'd already seen and admired Marshalltown and Belle Plaine, and there were still more along the route. It's a great, under-told, national story.

West of Grand Junction I got out and walked another abandoned section of the original Lincoln Highway near Buttrick Creek bridge. The original highway made a sharp L, but, as was the pattern nationwide, later routes engineered a more gradual curve. In 1919 the Convoy labored through many of these original turns: eighty-one vehicles wheezing away though a sharp right angle, clutches grinding, mired in inches deep dust.

All along the Convoy's route I noted the clever usage of antique farm implements as front lawn decoration. Wheel rims standing sentry on either side of driveway entrances, ancient hand plows parked among buckets of potted geraniums, rusted out tractors or trailers slumbering in the shade of oaks or walnut trees. They appeared as a salute to our past, and perhaps a desire to hang onto it as well—to cling to that nostalgic memory of what we were at one time in the face of self-driving tractors and the onslaught of modernity.

The Convoy was treated to ice cream by the Red Cross Canteen in Boone on July 25 before they continued on to camp in Jefferson for the night. There, everyone was feted at a dinner arranged by the community at the Jefferson Country Club. Still no rain since the Convoy entered Iowa, and the roads remained "very dusty."

Still no gumbo, and they were probably unaware of their own incredibly good luck. Henry Joy, first President of the Lincoln Highway Association, drove the route coast to coast in his trusty Packard several times. On a trip in 1916 he became bogged down to the axles in Iowa gumbo repeatedly—every time he dug himself out, he got bogged down again a few yards further. Joy, who was also CEO of Packard, was normally a temperate and level-headed man. But Iowa gumbo stretched the limits; in an uncharacteristic fit of temper he wrote, "Never in my life have I seen such roads. They are twelve to twenty inches deep in gumbo. We made 37 miles Tuesday. . .Today in the rich state of Iowa not a wheel turns outside the paved streets of her cities during or after the frequent rains. Every farm is isolated. Social intercourse ceases. School attendance is impossible. Transportation is at a standstill." You can almost see the steam rising from his head as he stood calf-deep in gumbo, next to his hopelessly sunken Packard.

About the evening's banquet, the *Jefferson Bee* on July 30 reported, "The *Bee* folks. . .cannot speak too highly of the splendid work of the ladies in preparing the banquet. It was 'swell' for all the boys said so, and Col. McClure was profuse in his thanks. . .One soldier was overheard to remark 'well boys, this lays Cedar Rapids in the shade, don't it?'."

The Jefferson Herald of July 23 has a lengthy column on "Provisions of the New Auto Law, containing this note: "The law provides that every motor vehicle shall be equipped with suitable brakes and horn. . .the horn must be sounded (motorists should note this provision) on approaching crossings, tops of hills, and intersections."

The Good Roads Movement was gathering steam across the country and Iowa was no exception. Only a week after the Convoy passed through Jefferson, the *Herald* had a front-page headline "Good Roads and Bonds Carry 3 to 1." The accompanying article details "Greene County voted for bonds and paved roads Monday by a majority of three to one. The sentiment in the county was strong for paved roads. . .very little opposition was found anywhere."

In Jefferson, I stopped by a furniture store/museum/theater called "RVP – 1875," which I had read about online. Housed in an abandoned and refurbished lumber mill, the front portion of the building features a furniture showroom and workshop in which proprietor Robby Pedersen crafts a wide range of 1875-era furniture, using only hand tools that would have been available in 1875. The rear of the building has been converted into a theater seating some 120 spectators, where several theatrical performances per year are staged to sell-out crowds.

I poked around the store, and then Robby toured me through his large workshop. Dozens of ancient wooden planes, chisels, and awls; hand saws lined up in a rack like little soldiers. A foot-powered lathe and a hand-crank ripsaw that looked lethal. Wood shavings all over the floor and work benches, the aroma wonderful. "Most important thing is to get good wood," he said. "Walnut, cherry, maple. Cedar—love that smell." He had dozens of gorgeous finished pieces—large bookcases, dining room tables, desks, beds, rocking chairs, china cabinets. No nails, just elaborate perfect dovetail joints in every one of them. "I like the past," Robby said. "Showing folks the past."

A large cast bronze statue of Abraham Lincoln, one of the first on the entire Lincoln Highway, was dedicated on the Greene County Courthouse grounds in Jefferson in September 1918 just a few months before Ike and the Convoy passed by. Jefferson also has a claim to eco-friendliness: it's one of the few places I found with publicly available charging stations for electric vehicles, in the Casino parking lot, and the Hy-vee supermarket parking lot. Downtown Jefferson is also home to the annual Hot August Night Car, Cycle, Tractor, and Truck Show, which is billed as one of the largest auto shows in the region, drawing hundreds of participants and thousands of spectators. Alas, another event I had to miss.

I saw several more Rails to Trails projects in Iowa, including the Raccoon River Valley Trail. Its seventy-two-mile inner loop is one of the longest such paved trails in the US and passes over the award-winning High Trestle Bridge Trail, above an old stretch of track high over the Des Moines River. It also passes by the Milwaukee Railroad Depot in downtown Jefferson, built in 1906 and recently restored as a museum. Ike and the Convoy passed right by when it was still a thriving passenger and freight depot.

From Jefferson I made a short detour north to Rockwell City to see a collection of old neon road signs at the Leist Oil Company. There I met Shane Leist, the third generation of proprietors. Shane's grandfather opened Leist Oil Company in 1918, then one of the few gas stations in the area. He added a garage and Pontiac dealership a few years later. When his grandfather passed away, Shane and his father discovered a large collection of vintage neon automobile signs stacked in his grandfather's attic, and Shane's father decided to display them. So nowadays they cover the walls of the garage and the gas station, both inside and outside.

Neon signs were first developed in France in the nineteen-teens, and quickly became popular in the US. The highly visible splashy signs were somehow ideally suited for the automobile age, and indeed the first-ever neon signs in the US were for a Packard car dealership in Los Angeles. They were prominent along highways for many years and reached a crescendo in Las Vegas in the 1950s. The oldest signs at Leist Oil were from 1930, and Shane told me that neon signs were starting to fade out by the late 1960s. But he had some classics: "Fireball V-8"; a large "58 Buick Limited," and the Pontiac Indian with head-feather stretched out in back.

I asked Shane if he got many tourists stopping by to see his collection, and he said, "Nah, hardly any. You're the first one in two weeks. People don't come through here anymore. You go downtown—whole lot of beautiful old buildings from the nineteenth century, most of 'em boarded up or abandoned. Some of 'em falling down. Not much left since I-80 came through down south of here."

On my way back down to the Lincoln Highway, I passed by Sac City, whose main claim to fame is one-time possession of the world's largest popcorn ball, weighing in at over 5,000 pounds. Yet another superlative.

Just west of Jefferson there's yet another elegant Iowa bridge, the multi-arched 1912 Eureka Creek bridge over Raccoon River. The bridge is right below Danger Hill looming up on the west bank, a precipitous drop around a rapid-fire succession of two right angle curves that deposited many early motorists right into the river. Those coming from the East, like Ike and the Convoy, had a straight shot over the bridge, but then faced a steep climb on the other side through dust or gumbo. Ike and the Convoy passed over Danger Hill and the lovely arching Eureka Bridge apparently without major incident.

But this is the location where the 1918 military wagon was found, that is currently in the Lincoln Highway Museum backyard. Joyce Ausberger had told me she thought it had been abandoned by the Convoy, and a potential trouble spot like Danger Hill is indeed a likely spot to abandon something.

Alice Ramsey writes, "Leaving Jefferson, we soon encountered Danger Hill. This is a climb dreaded by all, since there is a ninety degree turn at the bottom, preventing any advantage which might be gained by making a run for it. After we made the turn and started up the muddy grade we saw ahead of us. . .another automobile. The driver was having a difficult time of it. . .he (the driver) tried, but could get no traction." Ramsey and her traveling partners eventually towed the stuck car out, but Danger Hill remained a hazard until the Lincoln Highway was finally paved through this stretch. Nowadays of course it's wide and scenic, but otherwise unremarkable. The bridge was recently widened, but the classic arches were kept intact.

Scranton is home to the oldest working water tower in Iowa, which was built in 1897 and still in use today. Ike and the Convoy drove right by it. Water towers came into widespread usage in the US toward the end of the nineteenth century, but they took on an added significance and importance with the arrival of the automobile: as billboards. Before road maps or highway signs became common, motorists had little guidance on finding the next town, and often relied solely on directions from farmers along the way. Sometimes these were accurate, sometimes not.

Many communities painted their names in huge letters high on the town water tower, so approaching motorists could see a distant water tower and tell where they were. I passed by dozens of water towers on my route and saw plenty that still have town designations painted on. But nowadays there's a wide array of more whimsical designs. One of the most common I saw is the golf ball on a tee, but there are also plenty of fruit towers—peaches, apples, oranges, even bananas. There are baseball towers and football helmets of the local team. The plain ol' water tower without decoration is becoming a rarity.

Iowa Motor Vehicle Registrations:

| 1905 | 799 |
| 1920 | 437,378 |

The Convoy departed Jefferson early on the morning of July 26 and stopped at 9:00 a.m. in Glidden to pay a visit to the Mother of Merle Hay, one of the first three American soldiers to be killed in World War I.

Hay was originally buried where he was killed, on November 3, 1917, near Artois, France, but after the war his body was returned to the US and he was re-interred in the Glidden cemetery. The cemetery was later renamed the Merle Hay Cemetery, and an eight-foot monument now marks his gravesite. Ike and other officers made a point of stopping the Convoy to visit his mother in Glidden.

With the advent of prohibition right after the Convoy passed through Iowa, Carroll County developed a reputation as a major bootlegging center. Kegs of bootlegged Carroll County rye whiskey were big sellers in Chicago and became Al Capone's favorite. Capone called it "the good stuff." Numerous buildings across the county had false floors, underneath which kegs of "the good stuff" were stashed away. Nowadays you can visit the city of Carroll's Iowa Legendary Rye outlet, which features rye made from 1920s hand-me-down recipes distilled by local farmers.

"The good stuff" is not western Iowa's only link to a famous outlaw. In July 1873 Jesse James and his gang carried out the first robbery of a moving train west of the Mississippi, near the town of Adair, and made a clean get-away with over $10,000. For over 16 years Jesse and Frank James eluded law enforcement authorities throughout the Midwest, and one of their favorite hide-outs was up in the hills north of the town of Vail.

The Convoy proceeded on to Denison for the night. Elwell Jackson writes:

> Camped in Washington Park, Denison, where town erected temporary shower bath. Refreshments and dancing at Court House Square in the evening. Largest crowd in history of Denison gathered to participate in welcome to Convoy personnel. Fair and warm. Good, but dusty, dirt roads.

Lest anyone be concerned about matters getting out of hand at the dance, the *Denison Bulletin and Herald* of July 23 provides these welcome reassurances: "The dance will be in charge of chaperones provided by the Federation of Women's Clubs, and the young ladies will wear appropriate cards given them in order that the visiting officers and men will feel at liberty to invite them to dance."

Sunday, July 27, was a rest day in Denison for the Convoy. Everybody got a medical inspection, every vehicle got its oil changed, every moving part was inspected and lubricated. In the afternoon there was a baseball game in which Denison clobbered the Convoy 18-1, and that was followed by speeches from Lt. Colonel McClure, S. M. Johnson, and others. In the evening there was a band concert at the Court House and movies at the Opera House. But all was not well. On that same day Elwell Jackson writes, "Mess of officers and enlisted men very unsatisfactory, and services of an experienced Mess Officer are badly needed, to keep up morale of the command."

In Woodbine I drove over what the town touts as "the original Lincoln Highway," with eleven blocks of brick-paved streets through downtown, the longest stretch in Iowa. But the streets were not bricked until 1921. Ike and the Convoy passed over the same streets, but they were then still dirt, and one can imagine the clouds of dust generated by eighty-one vehicles passing over dry roads right through the middle of town. But the 1921 brick streets of Woodbine are illustrative of a trend that quickly developed all across the country. The explosion in the number of vehicles on America's roads, the steady drumbeat from the Good Roads Movement, and the nationwide publicity generated by the Convoy all led to a rapid surge in the number of miles of paved roads all across the Lincoln Highway's route. In 1904 there were only 150,000 miles of paved road in the entire country, and almost all of that was on the coast or major cities. By 1926 the miles of paved road more than tripled to over 520,000 and increased rapidly after that. Too late for the Convoy, but the publicity it generated certainly gave a huge boost to the road-building momentum.

I spent a couple of days wandering Council Bluffs, a pleasant city right on the Missouri. It was originally named by Lewis and Clark for the bluff where they held their first council with local Indian leaders in August 1804. In the mid-1850s the town served as the starting point for Mormons taking the Mormon trail to Utah. President Lincoln later designated Council Bluffs as the official starting point for the transcontinental railroad, and there is a mile zero golden spike that is posted downtown. Numerous railroads funneled through Council Bluffs, and there was a lively river steamboat traffic throughout the late nineteenth century. The city was still thriving when Ike and the Convoy passed through, but the decline of the railroads by mid-century led to a stagnation.

But there's plenty to see nowadays in Council Bluffs. I visited the Squirrel House Jail, built in 1885 and featuring a unique circular rotating set of jail cells. The entire structure could be swiveled so that only one prisoner could be released at a time, providing, as the designers said, "maximum security with minimum jailer attention." The jail, which is the only one of its kind in the US, was in full use when Ike and the Convoy passed by and continued in use until 1969 when it was converted into a museum.

And there was a definite need for a jail in the early days of Council Bluffs. A soldier passing through to fight in the Dakota Wars in 1863 wrote, "The streets were lined with. . .horse and mule jockeys, gamblers, thieves, assassins — and the mischief knows not what. . .Our stay at Council Bluffs was very short. . .and I think no one was sorry to leave it."

But there was also wealth and opulence in Council Bluffs. Grenville Dodge was one of the key developers of the railroads, and he earned a fortune in the process. He built an imposing mansion in 1869 in what is now known as the Third Street Historic District, which includes numerous other late nineteenth-century mansions. All there and occupied when Ike and the Convoy passed by, but many now open for visitors or sold to businesses.

The Convoy made it from Denison to Council Bluffs in about nine hours on July 28, with the usual mechanical mishaps along the way. But one is worth noting – Elwell Jackson: "Packard. . .was struck by Mack Blacksmith Shop. . .bending right steering arm, which was straightened at a nearby blacksmith shop and replaced." Part of the Convoy's mandate was to be as self-sufficient as possible, but they did find help – frequently – along the route. Once again along the day's route it was "Fair and warm. Dirt roads, heavy dust." Council Bluffs, right on the Missouri River, for the night.

NEBRASKA

"On the old highway maps of America, the main routes
were red and the back roads blue. . .in those brevities
just before dawn and a little after dusk—time neither
day nor night—the old roads return to the sky some of
its color. Then, in truth, they carry a mysterious cast
of blue, and it's that time when the pull of the blue
highway is strongest, when the open road is beckoning,
a strangeness, a place where a man can lose himself."

–William Least Heat Moon

The Convoy crossed the Missouri River via the Douglas Street bridge and
was in Omaha already by 8:00 a.m. Elwell Jackson writes:

> At 8:15 Convoy paraded through the city, escorted by the Mayor, Reception
> Comm., a band and a truck load of uniformed War Camp Community Service
> Workers. Camped by Fort Omaha. . .Privileges of the beautiful new Athletic
> Club were extended to the officers.

While the officers were enjoying the Athletic Club, what were the enlisted
men doing? Elwell Jackson again: "Work was started on removal of Dixon
Graphite Lubricants. . .a number of solid tires, which had become badly
worn due to character of roads recently traversed, were changed, necessitating
considerable work."

Staying at a military installation such as Fort Omaha gave the Convoy an
opportunity to do extensive maintenance and replacement, and they took
advantage of that. But relief arrived that evening: "refreshments and dance
for the enlisted men at Krug Park."

The Sunday, July 27 edition of the *Omaha World-Herald* devoted its entire
front page to the Convoy, with the huge headline: "War Department Testing
the Motor Convoy in Record Breaking Trip Across America." The article
provides the usual details on the Convoy, but also emphasizes its broader
significance: "Highway Building Has Only Commenced."

There were constant adjustments being made to the Convoy by McClure, and in Omaha, he decided to jettison the heavy pontoon trailer, which they had lugged all the way from Camp Meigs in Washington, and apparently never used. So McClure ceremoniously handed it off to Omaha Mayor Edward Smith. According to Davies, "Somewhat bemused, the mayor had no clue what he might do with a pontoon trailer, but said uncertainly that he would 'keep it for emergencies.'"

Two days later, the July 29 edition of the *World-Herald* headlined the arrival of the Convoy: "Truck Train Here; Came 1,500 Miles; Worst Trip Ahead." The article takes note of the work the enlisted men had to perform on the vehicles: "Elaborate plans for the reception and entertainment. . .could not be carried out because of the Army men's program. 'We don't want to be blamed by Omahans for our seeming discourtesy' said Colonel McClure. . .the men will be freed at 6 o'clock, and I understand Omaha's best-looking girls are going to dance with them at the park.'"

The same edition of the *World-Herald* carries a short article on Ruth Roach, the world's champion woman bronco-buster, in action that same week in Cheyenne. An accompanying photo shows Roach applying facial makeup "just before she won the championship."

Many people may think of Omaha as a cow town, but the city has a long history of diversity and worldliness. Owen Wister's 1902 novel, *The Virginian*, which many consider to be the first true Western novel, is set mostly in Wyoming, but has a short episode that takes place in Omaha. Speaking of a well-known restaurant in Omaha called the Palace, the narrator says, "Weather permitting, it (the Palace) opened upon the world as a stage upon the audience. . .in front of you passed rainbows of men — Chinese, Indian Chiefs, Africans, General Miles, younger sons, Austrian nobility, wide females in pink. Our continent drained prismatically through Omaha once." This diversity lives on, fueled in part by the generosity of Nebraskans. Since the beginning of the Middle Eastern refugee crisis, the state has taken in more refugees per capita than any other state in the union.

Omaha is a city of many firsts:

- Mildred Brown was named editor-in-chief of the *Omaha Star* newspaper in 1938, making her the first Black editor-in-chief of a US newspaper.
- In 1872 the Union Pacific completed the first railroad bridge across the Missouri River in Omaha.
- The Strategic Air Command's Headquarters in Omaha were the first in the world to utilize fiber optic cables for communication.

- Lewis and Clark held their first council with Native Americans on the riverside bluffs of present-day Nebraska.

I finally tracked down the Great Plains Black History Museum, which had moved several times and was now in a derelict half-empty mall. Alas, the museum was only open during a brief period every week, so I missed it. Many people are unaware of the big role Blacks played in the settling of the Plains after Reconstruction, as cowboys, soldiers, and intrepid homesteaders. In 1866 Congress authorized six Black regiments to patrol the Plains. They performed admirably and came to be known as Buffalo soldiers. Thousands of Black settlers followed after reconstruction ended in 1877. Black homesteaders established the all-Black town of DeWitty, Nebraska, in 1908 in the Sand Hills north of the Lincoln Highway. The town, which was later renamed Audacious, had its own general store, A.M.E. church, three schools, and even its own baseball team, the Sluggers. Knock 'em in, Sluggers!

There were no Blacks among the members of the Convoy, not surprising since the US military was still strictly segregated in those days. When World War I broke out, there were already four all-Black regiments, and many more Blacks volunteered for service in the war. But back home in 1919, discrimination was still rampant. Hotels all across the country routinely turned away Blacks, and in 1936 the first *Negro Motorist Green Book* was published with the express objective "to give the Negro traveler information that will keep him from running into difficulties." Davies writes that even as late as 1961 there were only nine hotels in Nebraska that would accept Black guests. In Wyoming there were three.

I visited Durham Museum, which is housed in Omaha's old Union Pacific Union Station. Built in 1931 and one of the nation's first and finest art deco train stations, it was a hub of activity in World War II, when 10,000 passengers per day passed through. Almost certainly some members of the Convoy would have passed through, perhaps even Ike himself. The station was closed in 1971 and fell into disrepair but has now been painstakingly restored to its original condition and converted into the Durham Museum of Art and History.

While Ike was traveling with the Convoy, Mamie and their infant son, Icky, were living with Mamie's parents, the Douds, in Denver. We know that Ike tried to phone Mamie at least once, in Bucyrus, Ohio, where he famously had to cadge a dime to do so. At the Eisenhower Presidential Library in Abilene, Kansas, I discovered that, although Ike presumably wrote her many times, there is only one remaining piece of correspondence: a postcard showing on one side a photo of the Convoy crew and a handwritten text on the other side. Ike began the text with a mistaken date—June 18, 1919. The Convoy didn't get underway from Washington until July 7, so he presumably meant July 18. The card reads

> "Dearest,
>
> I am not in the picture, but I thought you'd like to see it. Love you heaps and heaps.
>
> Your lover"

Despite another series of mechanical breakdowns, the Convoy made relatively good progress on July 30, covering eighty-three miles in just over ten hours, and driving into Columbus in the late afternoon. Elwell Jackson writes "Mayor and Reception Comm. with band escorted Convoy into Columbus where we camped in open field. . .Entertained at dinner in the several hotels. Street dancing in evening. Fair and very warm."

Boy's Town, now a small town and National Historic Landmark, lies on the outskirts of Omaha, and I stopped in for a visit. A young Irish priest named Edward Flanagan took several homeless boys into his own Omaha home back in 1917 and expanded his "Boy's House" into a rental house in downtown Omaha the following year. This house was fully operational when the Convoy passed right by it in 1919. In 1921 Flanagan moved to Overlook Farm on the outskirts of town, and his "Boy's House" became Boy's Town.

Flanagan possessed both high ambitions and a high energy level, and Boy's Town quickly grew and thrived. In the 1920s Father Flanagan spoke on widely aired radio broadcasts every Sunday afternoon. He organized a traveling eight-boy choir in 1928, which later became the Boy's House Band. By 1938 Flanagan had started the Boy's Town Road Show Revue, which performed all over the country and on countless radio programs.

The feature film *Boy's Town*, starring Spencer Tracy and Mickey Rooney, was shot in June 1938 on location at the real Boy's Town. When Director Norman Taurog originally approached MGM president Louis Mayer with the idea for the film, Mayer reportedly said, "It will never sell; there's no sex." Taurog persevered anyway, and Tracy later won a Best Actor Oscar for his portrayal of Father Flanagan. The film was a huge national hit, and years later Mayer claimed it was one of his favorites.

Father Flanagan died on May 15, 1948, a national hero and celebrity. Nowadays Boy's Town accepts girls and is a nationwide organization that offers Family Service Counselling, a Research Hospital, and Education Training for over 200,000 educators every year.

But wait a minute, that's not all. Inside the Boy's Town Visitors' Center, off in its own private nook, serenely stands the World's Largest Ball of Postage Stamps. I've done some research, and trust me, there's not another ball of stamps anywhere in the world that even comes close. Back in 1955 it was featured in *Ripley's Believe It or Not*, and work on the ball stopped that same year.

When I visited, it measured 32 inches in diameter, weighed 600 pounds, and contained some 4.655 million stamps. I talked to Mary, the friendly Visitor's Center guide, who told me all the stamps were wound around a golf ball, way down there in the middle. I wondered if there weren't some visitors who were tempted to slap on their own stamps.

"We try to prevent that," said Mary. "But you never know what people are going to do when you're not watching."

"So why did they create this in the first place?"

"I don't think anybody knows the answer to that question." Mary shrugged. "Maybe they were just bored. Making a ball of stamps was a lot better than some of the other things those boys could have gotten into."

I drove on up the original Lincoln Highway, right by the North Platte River through Fremont and Schuyler, and into Columbus, where I spent a couple of days. While in Columbus I stopped in at Glur's Tavern, established in 1876 and now the oldest continuously operating tavern west of the Missouri River. Founded by Swiss immigrant brothers, Joseph and William Bucher, they sold their Bucher saloon in 1914 to Louis Glur who changed the name. Today it's listed on the National Register of Historic Places, and it's still a lively spot.

Glur's was packed with a boisterous crowd eating, drinking, and playing cards, and I felt lucky to find a single empty stool at the bar. The grill was right across from me, and the chef was wearing a red t-shirt with this message on the back:

At Glur's, we drink as much of the beer as we can
Whatever's left over, we try to sell
Stop in and get your share

A man I took to be the proprietor was talking to people at every table, and after a while he came over to me. He introduced himself as Todd, and when I told him I was from Virginia, he showed me around. "Buffalo Bill used to be a regular customer here back in the day," he said. "One time he attended a big funeral here in Columbus, and afterwards he invited everyone here to Glur's for drinks on him. Tab came to over $1,000, and he covered it all."

"So how did Glur's manage to stay in business during Prohibition?" I asked.

"Hosted lots of poker games and sold near beer. Coulda been some other stuff too," he said, and gave me a sideways glance.

Waitresses were coming and going, taking orders ("Gotcha!") and delivering food and beer ("Here ya go!"). There were signs covering all the walls:

One Dollar Shot Specials!
Thursday Night Pint Night!

and

I got a shotgun for my wife. Best trade I ever made.

There was also a mounted mallard coming in for a landing, and an eight-point buck wearing a silver tiara. Todd introduced me to half the people in Glur's: "He's driving all the way across country and gonna write a book about it!" I overheard a lady at a side table half-whisper to her tablemates, "Gosh — he must be smart." Many conversations ensued, so it took a while before I got back to the bar and my fried chicken sandwich and Prairie Peace draft beer, which Todd insisted on buying for me. Immediately I was in a big discussion with folks at the bar, ranging over subjects from Donald Trump to memories of Ike as president to Cornhusker football. I lingered for a long time, mostly just listening, and when I finally departed I wondered if anyone from the Convoy had had the good fortune to stop in and spend some time at Glur's back in 1919.

Glur's was going strong, but the rest of downtown Columbus was clearly suffering through some tough times. There were empty buildings, curtained buildings, boarded up buildings, and rows of empty parking spaces on Main Street. In between there were mostly other bars and antique/junk shops. It was the same pattern I saw all across country: a once-thriving downtown thoroughfare on the Lincoln Highway in a downward spiral after the interstate came through a few miles away.

I drove on from Columbus through the Platte Valley, through land that was pristinely, geometrically flat, unlike Iowa's rolling hills. During the great western migration of the mid-nineteenth century, all wagon trains converged here in the "Great Platte River Road." One emigrant wrote, "As prity(sic) a rode as I ever saw. . .it is level and smooth as a plank floor." Another wrote, "The sight of a tree is out of the question. It is seldom we see so mutch(sic) as a bush." But the trail still held dangers. Between 1842 and 1859 some 20,000 pioneers died on the trek westward, about 5 percent of the total emigrants. They died of cholera, malaria, smallpox, measles, or dysentery. Some were crushed by wagon wheels and some drowned or were accidentally shot. Remarkably few were killed by Indians. But the Great Platte River Road remained as the prime route westward, and the Union Pacific railroad and Lincoln Highway eventually followed.

Nowadays, for miles the Lincoln Highway is right next to the Union Pacific railroad tracks, both rolling on toward the distant gleaming grain elevators towering over each small town. The only other breaks in the endless vistas are cottonwoods and willows lined up along streams, and cedars and spruces planted as windbreaks sheltering lonely farmhouses. Driving right next to the UP railroad, I passed interminable trains churning along through the vast flat space. Containers stacked two high per car, rolling on to the far horizon.

City slickers from the coasts, like me, are often largely oblivious to the vast infrastructure of flyover country, which in fact constitutes the nation's circulatory and life support system. Sprawling truck stops along the interstates and trains everywhere, miles long, with coal, oil, natural gas. Hundreds of closed containers with who knows what, stretching to the horizon, all headed toward the coasts. Keeping the lights on, the heat turned up, and the grocery stores fully stocked.

But not just trains. For days on end I passed by mysterious pipes, valves, and wires. Tangles of intersecting pipes protected behind chain-link fences, way out on the empty prairie. I had no idea what they were. Occasionally I got out to walk over and look at the signs that were on the fences: "pipeline transfer station," "Natural gas compression station," "Oil pumpjacks." I still had only the vaguest notion. Countless snaking long irrigation pipes, up on wheels, the ones that create the perfect green circular patterns we see from 35,000 feet.

The weather changed overnight while the Convoy camped in Columbus. Elwell Jackson writes, "Rain of last evening reduced dust nuisance to a minimum, and tended to produce more compact road surfaces. However. . .soft spots were encountered, which mired vehicles to hubs, requiring mechanical and manual efforts to remove them." Alas, a sign of things to come.

The Convoy made it into Grand Island at 4:15 and was once again met by the mayor, paraded through the city to their campsite, and feted in the evening. Elwell Jackson: "Dance in evening for entire personnel. Camp attendance about 3,000 persons, who were addressed by Dr. Johnson and Lt. Col. McClure. Occasional showers."

The July 31 edition of the *Grand Island Daily Independent* headlines "Motor Convoy Arrives 3 P.M.," and goes on to detail an extensive program, including arrival over the seedling mile, filming of the arrival, "whistles and bells are to announce arrival," and a parade through town to the circus grounds. In the end, a series of back and forths on the arrival route finally resulted in the Convoy's entrance by another route because the seedling mile route was judged poorly maintained and "impassable" by Henry Ostermann.

A little to the east of Grand Island I managed to track down a stretch of this seedling mile, not far from the current Lincoln Highway. This seedling mile was built in 1915, and I walked along a couple hundred yards of it, weeds sprouting up through the cracks but otherwise still solid. One side has a string of old Burma Shave signs:

This will never
Come to Pass
Backseat driver
Out of gas
Burma Shave!

Not far away I found the Seedling Mile Road, and a bit farther the Seedling Mile High School. Roll over 'em, Wildcats!

A bit farther still I passed a store for cowboy boots that had a big sign:

Convenient Drive-Thru Service

Just a block off the Lincoln Highway, right in the center of Grand Island, I ran across Fred's Flying Circus, and wound up spending two hours there. Before he passed away two years ago, Fred Schritt spent decades creating cartoon characters and exotic sculptures entirely from junked automobile parts. Most of the life-sized creations are elevated on pedestals in a large open area next to Fred's automotive repair shop, now run by his daughter and son-in-law, Doug. I met Doug and his two bird dogs, and they all showed me around.

Goofy, Tweety Bird, the Smurfettes; the Red baron in half car, half triplane, firing a machine gun at Snoopy; Shrek in the backend of a Big Mama's Cab Company Model T, driven by the wicked Old Witch. All these and many others are at Fred's Flying Circus, each in outlandish and carefully detailed vehicles, courtesy of Fred's expansive imagination. "He just loved doing this," said Doug. "He started out with just one for fun. Liked it, so he tried another. Things just sorta kept on going over the years. One time somebody offered him $850,000 for the entire collection, but he wasn't interested in selling. When he passed away he had a couple of unfinished projects underway, and he left precise instructions on how to finish them off. I'm working on them now." Automobile art at its finest.

I detoured south off the Lincoln Highway down to Red Cloud to visit the home of renowned writer Willa Cather. Red Cloud is a tiny town; Cather graduated from high school in 1890 in a class consisting of two boys and her. All three of them gave speeches at graduation, and the local newspaper the next morning reported the two boys' speeches but wrote nothing about Cather. Never mind—she went on to greatness and is greatest in her descriptions of the stark, terrifying beauty of the yawning prairie: "I wanted to walk straight on through the red grass and over the edge of the world, which could not be very far away. The light air about me told me that the world ended here: only the ground and sun and sky were left, and if one went a little farther there would be only sun and sky."

On the way back north to the Lincoln Highway I passed through Hastings, which served as the nation's largest Naval ammunition depot during World War II, producing over 40 percent of the Navy's munitions during the war. But Hastings is more famous as the birthplace of Kool-Aid. Edwin Perkins grew up in Nebraska and at age 30 invented Nix-O-Tine, a powdered drink designed to help returning World War I vets get off cigarettes. A few years later he came out with Kool-Aid, and by the 1930s it was a national hit, making him a multi-millionaire. Luminaries ranging from Elmer Fudd to Fred Flintstone have touted Kool-Aid over the years. During World War II Perkins helped the cause by inventing a lemon powdered drink that was eventually included in K rations. Every August Hastings shuts down for three days to host Kool-Aid Days, culminating in the annual crowning of Miss Kool-Aid. I was just too early, so I had to miss it.

As I was chatting with the ever-helpful librarians in the Grand Island public library, one said, "You need to come back in September for the Junk Jaunt." I had no idea what a Junk Jaunt might be, so she enlightened me. "It's every year. Last weekend in September, and it lasts for three days. It's basically a 300-mile long garage sale." The route starts in Grand Island, circles north-westerly through various Sand Hills towns, and finally returns to the starting point. All along the way vendors set up tables in front yards, community centers, even barns, selling everything from rare antiques down to unmitigated junk. Churches all along the way offer homemade meals, and many people open their houses for lodging. The Junk Jaunt began in 2003, and today it involves over 500 individual vendors and thousands of participants from all over the country. Yet another event made possible by the automobile.

The Convoy departed Grand Island early on the morning of August 1. That day's issue of the *Grand Island Daily Independent* carries the headline: "Motor Convoy Leaves at 6:30; Much Balling Up of Orders; One Arrangement Made After Another Only to be Again Canceled—Poor Brige (sic) Causes Hour's Delay." Not exactly a glowing report. The article goes on to note, "Plans had to be changed almost as soon as made, time after time, owing to conflicting orders and permissions from various persons connected with the Convoy." Alas, another example of Public Affairs Officer William Doron's woefully inept advance work. No matter, the remainder of the article makes it clear that everyone went away happy, especially the men of the Convoy—it was payday. The Grand Island National Bank dispensed cash in individual envelopes to each man.

I stopped by the Crane Trust Nature Center a little west of Grand Island to see some bison. The Center received forty-one genetically pure bison back in 2015, and the herd has since multiplied rapidly, now numbering seventy-three. I talked to a man named Tim, who told me five bison heifers were pregnant, so if they deliver as expected, the herd will number seventy-eight, almost doubling in just three years. "Bison are real self-sufficient," he said. "We vaccinate them once a year, and otherwise just leave them alone. They're thriving."

Only thirteen miles out of Grand Island on August 1, the Convoy ran into the sort of trouble that was soon to become routine. Elwell Jackson: "Class B runs off. . .road into ditch. . .and buries itself in soft dirt over axles. Rope was made fast to front end of Class B and passed around winch of the Militor, which gave a wonderful exhibition of its power, at one time lifting its front wheels clear of the ground. . .Class B was recovered in two hours."

I paused in the small town of Shelton—population 1,079—to meet Lenore Stubblefield, one of the managers of the Lincoln Highway Visitors' Center.

We met on the main street, C Street, in a nineteenth-century building that Ike and the Convoy passed right by. Lenore had a wealth of information on Nebraska Lincoln Highway lore, as well as local history in general. She had been instrumental in restoring one of the few remaining Lincoln Highway billboards, painted on the north side of a downtown building. The sign dates from about 1920 and reads:

Shelton Cash Store
The best
Bromo-Seltzer

I asked Lenore if anything came after "The best," and she said, "Oh, yes, for sure, but we just don't know what. That sign's been repainted several times over the years, but somehow that part got lost along the way." Lenore directed me to a portion of the Lincoln Highway right around the corner that still had its original bricks from the early 1900s. When I mentioned the 1919 Convoy, she said, "They would have driven over those very same bricks." The bricks were laid in a herringbone pattern, Lenore explained, to prevent them from shifting when heavy vehicles turned the corner.

I wandered around Shelton's two-block downtown and took a closer look at the billboard and the bricks, artifacts from the time of the Convoy. I noticed a number of stores that were abandoned or boarded up—victims, as in so many places, of the interstate a few miles to the south. But then I discovered that one of the buildings I thought abandoned was in fact a Hispanic Pentecostal church—Iglesia Pena de Horeb. Farther along I passed Larry's Market, Shelton's only grocery store. It has a big sign out front:

Featuring Daily
Homemade Enchiladas

A bit farther still I met a young Hispanic woman with a large bag slung over her shoulder. "Sir? You want to buy a burrito? Only three dollars. Two for five dollars. Homemade."

So I bought two chicken and cheese burritos and struck up a conversation. She told me her name was Veronica, that she was from Guatemala, and that she had been in Shelton for two years. "I like except winter. Too much cold."

She had come to Shelton with her husband, brothers and sisters, and various cousins, most of whom had found employment in a nearby Tyson's chicken packing plant. Veronica had a small child, so she stayed at home and cooked on the side. "We saving so much — soon we able to buy house. First time house for us. And my children — they go to study hard to go to college. First time college too. Cornhuskers!" She pumped her right arm into the air and smiled broadly.

I left Veronica and shortly after noticed another storefront with the sign:

"Immigration Forms; Translations; Notarials; Passport Photos"

The Convoy stopped for another Red Cross Canteen lunch in Kearney, and then made it into Lexington by late afternoon. They camped at Dawson County Fair Grounds, which Elwell Jackson praised as "the finest campsite of the entire trip thus far."

The original Oregon Trail intersects the original Lincoln Highway just east of Kearney, and the two coincide all the way to Brule, near the Colorado border. All part of the Great Platte River Road. Ezra Meeker, born in 1830, moved from Indiana to Oregon in a covered wagon with his wife and baby via the Oregon Trail in 1852. He had a prosperous life in Oregon but was concerned when the Oregon Trail's heritage was being threatened and forgotten. So in 1906 he followed the route east in a Prairie Schooner, rallying support along the way. By the time he ended his trip at the White House two years later, he camped out on the White House grounds and had received support from President Teddy Roosevelt. He later traveled the route several times, once in an automobile and once in an open-seated biplane, so it's entirely possible the Convoy passed him in 1919. Meeker died in 1928 at the age of ninety-eight.

I spent a day in Kearney, which had for years featured a sign indicating the town is the halfway point between Boston and San Francisco: it's 1,733 miles from Kearney to each. But I couldn't find the sign anywhere, just the upscale 1733 Estates housing subdivision. Kearney also has a Classic Car Collection Museum where I spent a couple of hours wandering among 200-plus vintage cars, memorabilia, and advertisements, much of it from the time of Ike and the Convoy. Model T's, Model A's, Pierce Arrows, and Packards, ranging up to Corvettes and Mustangs. Just down the street is the 1930s art deco Fort Theater, now converted into a dental clinic.

Sign in Kearney:

Gardening for God
Brings Peas of Mind

And then just down the street, the Chug-a-Lug Sports Bar.

Kearney bills itself as the Sandhill Crane Capital of the World. Every spring and fall hundreds of thousands of sandhill cranes stop off near Kearney on their migrations north or south, a pattern that fossil evidence indicates has been ongoing for millions of years. Alas, I, like the Convoy, passed through in midsummer, so no cranes to be seen.

Kearney's Museum of Nebraska Art, housed in a 1911 Neo-Classical building that Ike and the Convoy passed right by, has a superb collection of Nebraska art, much of it dating from the nineteenth and early twentieth century. There are landscape paintings by George Catlin, Thomas Hart Benton, and Wright Morris, and a nice collection of meticulous drawings of Nebraskan wildlife by John James Audubon.

Most people think of Ike as a steady, serious, rational leader, but back when he was twenty-eight, he was also a rascally practical joker. He and his pal, Sereno Brett, particularly enjoyed targeting some of the Convoy's easterners, many of whom had never before been west of the Hudson. Ike hauled off some doozies during the trip, and he describes them best himself:

> Early one morning several of us, riding in a reconnaissance car across the plains of Nebraska saw a jack rabbit loping along the road. At less than a hundred yards away, he paused. One of us had a .22 caliber rifle and, after stopping the car, shot the rabbit. Sereno had an idea. We carried the rabbit with us until we were a mile or so from our scheduled campsite. There, going off the road for a hundred yards or so, we found a bush against which we propped the now stiffened body of the jack rabbit. From a distance it looked fairly natural.

> That evening, we persuaded two of our eastern friends to drive out with us to do a little shooting. We took only .45 caliber pistols. As we drove along, Sereno suddenly said "Stop! Stop! Look over there – see that rabbit!" At that distance, and in dimming light, one could see him only in imagination. We described him so carefully, the easterners admitted they could make out his outline. Sereno said that I was one of the finest pistol shots he had ever known. "Ike, why don't you take a crack at him?"

> I carefully aimed the pistol in the general direction of the North Pole and fired. Sereno exclaimed, "You've got him! You've got him! He fell."

> Never having seen the rabbit in the first place, the easterners agreed with Brett that it was surely a fine shot, and they marveled at such skill.

I sat with them while Sereno raced out to pick up the big jack. Held by his ears, the rabbit must have been almost two feet long. Sereno brought the rabbit toward us, but when he came within thirty or forty yards and was sure that we had all seen it, he threw it aside and said, "Well, let's turn back."

The two easterners protested. The rabbit would make a nice addition to our rations. We had to explain to them, patiently, that jack rabbits were absolutely no good—they were tough, stringy, tasteless. No matter how unappetizing the ordinary jack rabbit, we didn't dare let them see one which had been shot twelve hours earlier."

Driving on through a beautiful stark landscape. Sidewinds constantly whipping my car and sand flying up. Mostly open plains, but here and there patches of trees. And there a tangled pile of uprooted trees, hacked-off branches, masses of brush, all stacked at the tree line, the product of new land cleared for plowing.

Near the tiny town of Overton I came across a small concrete bridge that was part of the original Lincoln Highway, sitting abandoned and alone in the grassy area between the current highway and the UP railroad tracks. This is the bridge that Ike and the Convoy would have passed over, years before the Lincoln Highway was realigned a few yards to the north. The bridge had been recently painted, but tramping around it, I couldn't find any trace of the old road, now overgrown by prairie grass.

The Convoy departed Lexington in a light rain early on the morning of August 2. Within three hours, Elwell Jackson writes, "It was raining steadily and road was becoming very slippery." And then a cascading series of calamities: one truck after another skidded off the road and into the ditch, until finally even the old standby, the Militor, skidded into the ditch and was buried up to the frame in gumbo. According to Elwell Jackson a total of twenty-five trucks skidded into the ditch during the day, and the Convoy made only thirty miles in ten and a half grueling hours. They finally arrived in Gothenburg late afternoon. Never a spendthrift with words, Elwell Jackson writes simply, "Rain and cool. Roads gumbo mud."

About such days, Ike wrote years later, "In some places, the heavy trucks broke through the surface of the road and we had to tow them out one by one. . .Some days when we had counted on sixty or seventy or a hundred miles, we would do three or four. Maintenance crews were constantly on the job."

I drove on over the Convoy's route through the small town of Cozad, which lies squarely on the 100th meridian. Western explorer John Wesley Powell recognized the 100th meridian as the line where "the humid east meets the arid west." Cozad celebrates its geographic significance with a small museum precisely on the line, historic markers, and even a large sign on the town's grain elevator.

In Gothenburg I stopped by the Pony Express House and Museum in Ehmen Park. The house was originally a fur trading post along the Oregon Trail, later used as a Pony Express station, and moved to its current location in 1931. Although the Pony Express looms large in western folklore, it was only in operation for about nineteen months during 1860–1861. William H. Gibson, who worked for a freighting company, created the Pony Express to carry mail from St. Joseph, Missouri, to San Francisco via a horse relay. Stations were established every ten to fifteen miles to provide fresh horses, and about every seventy-five to a hundred miles there was a station where riders could stay in between runs.

Riding this route was not for the faint of heart. Riders faced extremes of weather, bandits, hostile Indians, and food and water of dubious quality along the way. One ad for riders read:

PONY EXPRESS
WANTED
Young, Skinny, Wiry Fellows
Not over eighteen
Must be expert riders, willing to risk death daily
Orphans preferred
Wages $25 per week

There were between eighty and a hundred riders employed at one time, and each had to carry twenty pounds of mail and twenty-five pounds of equipment. The route was about two thousand miles long and required some eight days of continuous riding. The eventual completion of the transcontinental telegraph in October 1861 was the death knell for the Pony Express, and it ceased operations a short time thereafter.

The Pony Express route followed the Platte river, and subsequently the Union Pacific Railroad and the Lincoln Highway followed much the same route. Ike and the Convoy passed right by dozens of old Pony Express stations, and I also visited several that are in various states of ruin or renovation.

After the Pony Express Museum, I visited the nearby Sod House Museum, where I met proprietors Merle and Linda Block. The open-air museum features a sod house, barn, two windmills, and a life-sized bison hand-crafted by Merle out of four and a half miles of barbed wire. I was their only visitor, so I spent some time talking with both Merle and Linda. They told me that Merle's grandparents had immigrated to Nebraska from Germany, and Linda's grandparents had immigrated from Sweden. Both sets of grandparents lived in sod houses they built themselves out on the prairie. Merle and Linda remembered visiting them when they were small children.

They got the idea for the museum back in the 1990s, and started building, based on photos, written descriptions, and their own memories. But the Gothenburg city government somehow got wind of their project, and a building inspector appeared on-site one day. "He told us, 'Whatever that is you're building, you need a building permit. It's got to meet code,'" said Linda.

"People been building houses for years out of sod bricks. They called it prairie marble," said Merle. "We sure didn't want to get tangled up in building code business, so we just went ahead and built it."

I could see Merle's point. Prairie marble versus two by fours on sixteen-inch centers? Two deeply conflicting world views.

"Once we got it finished, people liked it. Nobody ever said anything about having to take it down," said Merle.

The house itself seemed snug and cozy, but a little dark: there were only a couple of small windows. Merle said it was amazingly warm in the winter, as long as you kept a good fire going. Each sod brick weighed about fifty pounds, and it took about three thousand bricks to build the typical sixteen-by-twenty-foot house.

I asked about the numerous birdcages they had near the sod house, and Linda told me those were for the women. "Men were gone for long periods, but the women stayed at the house. The silence, alone out on the prairie, was overwhelming, and it drove some women mad," she said. "Just imagine, no neighbors, no wagons passing, no church bells, no trees, no flowing water or grinding mill. No cicadas or bullfrogs or birds. So lots of women got canaries just for the sound."

Merle showed me the barbed wire buffalo he had made a few years earlier. "Took me a few weeks," he said. "Wrestling with four and a half miles of barbed wire takes a little time. I used blacksmith's gloves to work the wire, and they were real sturdy. After I was finished I wrote the company that made those gloves, just to tell them what a good product they had. Darned if they didn't send me back a lifetime supply of blacksmith gloves."

As I was leaving I noticed a large mobile home parked out to the side. Linda said, "Every winter we close up the museum for a few months and head south. We volunteer in national parks, so we get to park there for free. Come back here and open up again in the spring. So I guess you can say that mobile home is our Conestoga wagon."

But the Convoy had a misadventure in Gothenburg. According to Davies, a 19-year-old soldier from Cincinnati named Earl Thomas concluded, "Dragging trucks through this Nebraska gumbo (was) too forbidding to be borne." So he stole a Nash Six that was parked at City Hall and took off for the East. He only made it as far as Council Bluffs, where he was arrested, taken to Fort Omaha, and put on military trial. End of the road for Earl Thomas.

I drove on westward from Gothenburg over the Gothenburg stairsteps—a long series of 90-degree angle turns in the original Lincoln Highway that followed section lines and kept the road near the south bank of the Platte river. At Maxwell I stopped briefly at the Fort McPherson military cemetery, a national cemetery established in 1873 as a final resting place for Nebraska military veterans. As I wandered around, I saw dozens of 1918 and 1919 gravestones of World War I vets, and I wondered if Ike or members of the Convoy had stopped by to pay respects to fallen colleagues.

The Convoy departed Gothenburg early on August 3 and had another horrendous day, covering only thirty-four miles in about ten hours. The Militor wound up towing almost every truck in the Convoy at least once during the day. Elwell Jackson writes, "At one time, 9 trucks chained together were unable to move under their own power, and the Militor pulled them through."

The Convoy straggled into North Platte in the late afternoon, and leadership decided to take a rest day there. Elwell Jackson: "Forced to suspend movement for 24 hours and remain here, owing to many little mechanical adjustments which had become necessary through the heavy work of the trucks during the last two days."

Ike and Mamie clearly missed one another, and so it was that Mamie and the Douds drove out from Denver to North Platte (no trivial trip in those days) to meet the Convoy. They traveled in their roadster alongside the Convoy all across western Nebraska, and finally returned to Denver from Laramie, Wyoming. So instead of hunkering down in a pup tent with the Convoy members every night, Ike enjoyed several nights with Mamie in the hotels of western Nebraska.

In *On the Road*, Jack Kerouac writes, "I'd been poring over maps of the United States. . .and savoring names like Platte and Cimarron. . .Ely, Nevada." North Platte is perhaps best known nowadays as the home of William "Buffalo Bill" Cody. Cody was (he claimed) a Pony Express rider at age fourteen, served in the Union Army in the Civil War, and earned his nickname for supplying buffalo meat to workers on the Kansas Pacific Railroad. He started performing in cowboy shows when he was twenty-three, and started Buffalo Bill's Wild West Show in 1883. The show was wildly successful, touring all over the US and Europe, and it quickly made Buffalo Bill a wealthy international celebrity. With his newfound wealth he built and developed Scout's Rest Ranch just outside North Platte, where he lived from 1886 to 1913.

Scout's Rest Ranch is now a Buffalo Bill museum and I spent a couple of hours poking around there. The full name of his show was "Buffalo Bill's Wild West and Congress of Rough Riders of the World," and in its heyday there were twice-daily performances that drew crowds of 20,000 spectators. Buffalo Bill rounded up performers from all the world: Turks, Mongols, Georgians, Gauchos, and American Indians among others. Sitting Bull and a group of some twenty of his braves performed for several years.

The show's posters were informative: "South American Gauchos— Throwing the Bolo and Hunting the Llama"; "Caballeros and Vaqueros from Old Mexico"; and "Wild Rivalries" featuring a drawing of an Indian ("Savage Barbarians") and a cowboy ("Civilized Races").

There was a large poster featuring "Miss Annie Oakley, the Peerless Lady Wing Shot." Oakley performed with the Show from 1885 until 1902. Only five feet tall, Oakley was an unrivalled shot, winning her first competitions at the age of fifteen. She could shoot right through the middle of a dime tossed high into the air, snuff out candles with one shot, and shoot corks off bottles at thirty paces. On tour with Buffalo Bill in Europe, she once shot the ash off the end of a cigarette being smoked by Kaiser Wilhelm II. Oakley was severely injured in a railroad accident in 1901, and doctors told her she would never walk again. But she proved them all wrong, overcoming paralysis and enduring five spinal operations to get up and re-join Buffalo Bill's show. She was still setting shooting records well into her sixties, but she also devoted her energies to campaigning for women's rights. She passed away in 1925, a national celebrity, at age sixty-six.

Many historians contend that by the turn of the twentieth century, Buffalo Bill was the world's greatest celebrity. In addition to his shows all across America, he also performed all over Europe to enthusiastic audiences, including Queen Victoria, Kaiser Wilhelm II, and Pope Leo XIII. He passed away in 1917, just two years before the Convoy passed right by Scout's Rest Ranch.

I wandered around North Platte for a few days and eventually stopped into the Fort Cody Trading Post. It's a faux fort built of precisely-hewn logs and featuring armed mannequins standing guard along the upper ramparts. Inside, one tourist shop after another — even the Nebraska tourist guides describe it as "America's kitschiest roadside attraction." Poking around inside, it was all Buffalo Bill. Buffalo Bill moccasins, Buffalo Bill t-shirts, Buffalo Bill cowboy hats, Buffalo Bill decks of cards, Buffalo Bill baseball caps, Buffalo Bill shot glasses. Even Buffalo Bill riding whips, displayed beneath a sign with this helpful advice:

Please Do Not Crack Whips Inside the Trading Post

North Platte also has a little known and underappreciated story: World War II's North Platte Canteen. North Platte's Bailey Yard is the world's largest rail yard, with over 351 miles of track, and over 10,000 rail cars passing through every day. During World War II thousands of soldiers passed through as well on a daily basis. The Canteen operated twenty-four hours a day at the North Platte station for fifty-five consecutive months during the war, providing snacks and refreshments to soldiers pausing briefly or transferring at the station. Run entirely by women volunteers of North Platte and its environs, the canteen served over six million men during its operation. For an example of their activity, in March 1945 the Canteen served:

    7,000 cakes
    7,000 donuts
    31,000 hard-boiled eggs
    40,000 cookies

to grateful soldiers passing through. The Canteen also passed out tons of popcorn balls, each of which included the name and address of a single woman who wanted to be a pen pal. Events took their course, and after the war there were numerous popcorn ball weddings.

The August 1 edition of the *North Platte Evening Telegraph* headlines the Convoy's transit into the city. "With the roar of the 72 engines, the drivers of the Motor Transport Train threw into gear the huge motor train. . .this huge train, three miles in length. . .will be North Platte's guests." The August 4 edition of the *Evening Telegraph* notes the Convoy's delayed arrival: "They report that the last two days' trips has been the hardest of all the tour, so far. Several trucks were late in getting into North Platte and did not arrive until close to midnight."

Elsewhere in that same edition of the *Evening Telegraph*, one finds the following article: "Eight Negro Gamblers are Caught in Act Saturday Night by Chief Police." The article notes that two of the arrested men were "given a chance to leave the city."

The frequent lamentations from the Convoy's men about the food was finally addressed in North Platte, when the mess officer, Lieutenant Howard Shockey, was replaced by Captain Richard Gurvine. In Shockey's defense, he was also a supply officer, so he was performing two important jobs and may have been relieved to be released from one of them. In any event, the grub improved. According to one report, the change "resulted in excellent meals being served during the second half of the journey."

A little west of North Platte I stopped to wander around the delightful little town of Sutherland, where red, white, and blue Lincoln Highway stripes were painted on most of the utility poles. There was also a large Lincoln Highway wall mural right across the street from an immaculately tended Little League baseball park, complete with a sand warning track around the outfield.

A man in bib overalls and a straw hat crossed the street to come over and ask me if he could help me find something. When I told him I was just looking around, he said "Well, c'mon. I'll show you around." So I got a guided tour of the highlights of Sutherland. The large billboards at both ends of town: "Welcome to Sutherland!" and "Thanks, Come Again." The community horseshoe pitch in the carefully tended garden next to the UP tracks. A restored gas station from the 1920s. More wall murals. Flags flying "Go Big Red!" and "Support Our Troops." Buildings dating from Sutherland's founding back in 1891, buildings Ike and the Convoy drove right by. Sutherland joined my growing list of towns I longed to visit again someday.

Several people along the way had told me that Ole's Big Game Steakhouse and Lounge in Paxton was a must-see, so I stopped in for lunch. Rosser Herstedt, known by all in Paxton as Ole, grew up in Paxton in the early 1900s. Prohibition ended in Nebraska at midnight on August 8, 1933, and Ole opened his tavern at 12:01 a.m. on August 9. It's still going strong.

Apart from the tavern, Ole's other passion was big game hunting, and in a thirty-five-year span he bagged game all over the world. Many of them are now displayed on the walls of Ole's. Polar bear, zebra, moose, elephant, elk—some 200 mounted animals peer down at diners. In Ole's nowadays you find choice cuts of beef, Nebraska craft beers, and friendly waitresses ("You savin' room for some cheesecake, hon?"). The restrooms are marked Pointers (men) or Setters (women). The walls are covered with autographed photos of famous and satisfied patrons like Bob Kerrey, Newt Gingrich, and numerous Miss Nebraskas. If Ole's had been open fourteen years earlier when the Convoy passed through, Ole would have had a long queue of eager customers.

After the sorely needed rest day, the Convoy departed North Platte early on August 5 and immediately ran into the same quagmires. Only ten miles out they encountered a 200-yard stretch of quicksand, and all trucks had to be pulled through by the Militor, the tractor, or the combined efforts of both. The Convoy ran into two smaller sand holes later, and on top of it all, they broke five bridges during the day and had to rebuild them all. Altogether the Convoy covered fifty-three miles in sixteen and a half hours, and didn't arrive in Ogallala until 11:00 p.m.

The August 7 edition of Ogallala's *Keith County News* writes, "Enthusiastic Crowds Cheer the Men on Trucks as They Roll By," but takes note of the Convoy's delayed arrival. "On Monday when the Convoy was expected to arrive hundreds of people drove in from the country and surrounding towns but were disappointed when it was learned that the bad roads and insecure bridges of Lincoln County had delayed them."

The same issue of *The News* contained an ad: "We have reduced the Titan 10-20 price – You can now get the world's standard three-plow tractor for $1,000." The tractor included such features as a friction clutch pulley, throttle governor, drawbar, and fenders but no windshield. It was the state-of-the-art tractor at the time of the Convoy.

The *News* also dwells on the significance of the Good Roads Movement, and it printed the entire text of S. M. Johnson's speech in Ogallala in the August 14 edition. Johnson gave more or less the same speech at every stop all across the country and gave a huge boost to Good Roads advocates with lines like this: "The next step in the national advance, and indeed in the progress of civilization itself, is to be taken through the general use of the motor vehicle. . .the people of the United States demand of their legislators not less but more for roads. . .no legislation enacted by the sixty-fifth congress has met with more hearty approval than the legislation for an enlarged road program."

For many years Ogallala was known as the Gomorrah of the cattle trail because of its reputation for being the most violent and wild town on the trail. Lots of cowboys were shot and killed over the years, and many of them were buried in their boots. Thus, Boot Hill cemetery. More than twenty gravestones still remain in place today, some of them simply marked "Unknown Cowboy." Boot Hill ceased being used in 1885, and many corpses were then dug up and reinterred elsewhere. This led to a widely circulated prairie legend: When Sarah Miller, whose gravesite is still fenced off and marked today, was dug up only some twenty years after her burial, her body was found to be petrified, and could not be lifted without the help of a crane.

Wandering around Ogallala for a couple of days, I was struck by several places that featured petrified wood art. I stopped in at the Petrified Wood & Art Gallery right next to the South Platte river, where I met Harvey Kenfield, who, along with his twin brother Howard, created much of the art on display. The Kenfield twins started carving petrified wood back in the 1950s, and in 1988 they opened their gallery. Harvey told me they started working with petrified wood they found locally, but eventually started collecting wood from all over the world, as far away as Madagascar or Brazil. "You can find some interesting wood here in western Nebraska," he said, "But if you go international you get some real different types." The carvings were large, elaborate, and exquisitely precise, items like Navajo cliff dwellings, and a millhouse next to a water wheel. "Some of these woods are millions of years old," he said. "I like working with something like that."

The Convoy encountered the same morasses of sand and gumbo after departure from Ogallala on August 6, but at least the day was much shorter. They covered twenty-two miles in six hours and arrived at their campsite east of the tiny town of Big Springs at 1:30, providing a little rest time.

Just west of Brule I pulled off the Lincoln Highway by the historic marker for California Hill, a key milestone for the California and Oregon trails. The marker said that two-thirds of a mile up an adjacent dirt road, one could still view tracks and ruts from the thousands of wagon trains that labored up the hill in the mid-nineteenth century. It's the spot where the Platte River valley narrows to a point, and the settlers all had to ascend up onto the wide-open plains.

To its credit, the Nebraska Department of Roads had a sign clearly stating that the dirt road was a "Minimum Maintenance Road." But brimming with enthusiasm to see wagon ruts over 150 years old, I paid the sign no mind and went bouncing up the road. Within seconds I was hopelessly stuck in thick, soupy gumbo mud. Shades of Henry Joy! I revved forward in low gear, reversed, twisted the wheel from side to side in hopes of somehow gaining some traction. At one point my trusty little Chevy was turned almost completely sideways in the road, facing the fence line and making it seem as though I, too, was preparing to make some tracks across the open prairie. I eventually freed the car, backed onto the safe sliver of asphalt again, and set off on foot for the top of California Hill.

I stopped at the highest point on the road, then threaded through the barbed wire fence and upward farther to the highest hill, thinking about those first pioneers. On cresting the hill and gazing out ahead, they must have felt a simultaneous sense of wonderment and dread—the vast silent space and the impossibly distant horizons that took more than a day to reach and then, when finally crested, revealed only more of the same ahead. The wagon ruts were still there, down in the grass and more to be felt than seen, and I couldn't help thinking about the aspirations and fears of the people in the wagons that made those ruts, blazing a trail that so many others followed.

Big Springs is a tiny town, but it is home to the famous Phelps Hotel, founded in 1885, and in continuous operation ever since. Since it's the only hotel in town, I suspected that Ike and Mamie must have spent the night of August 6 there. So I stopped in at the hotel and spoke to the friendly owners, who were in the midst of repairing some leaky pipes. They had not heard about Ike staying there but, remarkably, told me they still had every single one of the ledger books containing records of every guest who had stayed at the hotel since the 1880s. They invited me to look through them, and the proprietress, Connie, took me into the Phelps' original kitchen from 1885, where there was a huge multi-door antique oven no longer in use. She opened all the oven doors, and there inside, in a cozy secure resting place, were all the ledger books. I found the 1918–1920 ledger and paged through it, and sure enough under August 6, 1919, there it was in a neat looping cursive: "Lt. Colonel D. D. Eisenhower and wife; Washington, D.C.; Room 2." The Douds stayed in another room down the hall.

I made a detour from the Convoy's route southward to I-80 and the Flying J Truck Stop, so I could see another work of car art I'd heard about. And out at the back of the Flying J, there it was: a fifteen-foot-tall red, white, and blue caterpillar made entirely of old tires, except for the antennae which were old exhaust pipes. The Flying J was insanely busy: dozens of trucks coming and going, dozens more parked, gift shop crammed with raucous kids and exhausted-looking parents. I retreated quickly to sleepy downtown Big Springs.

I drove on through Chappell, a small town dominated by the town's name emblazoned in huge red letters across the grain elevators right by Main Street. I passed by the Empire Hotel, now in ruins but with a "NO VACANCY" sign still standing out front on the roadside. Through the tiny town of Lodgepole, named for the spot where Native Americans cut trees to makes poles to support their lodges. Past the crumbling, famed Lodgepole Opera House, one of Nebraska's finest when Ike and the Convoy passed by.

In Sidney I stopped by the headquarters and mother store of Cabela's. Founded in 1961 by Dick Cabela as a mail-order business selling hand-tied fishing lures, the company is now one of the nation's largest outfitters of hunting, fishing, and outdoor gear. The Sidney store contains more than 250,000 square feet of outdoor supplies, including a gun library, boat shop, and "world class taxidermy, including an enormous elephant!" My economy-sized Chevy was dwarfed by the massive RVs, pickups, and SUVs that filled the parking lot.

Conservation Mountain dominates the center of the store and features a range of stuffed animals in realistic looking terrain, ranging from bighorn sheep up high on a snow-covered cliff, to gray wolves, a snarling grizzly bear about to pounce on an unsuspecting marmot, dueling male elk, a pronghorn antelope, a wily looking badger, and a diamond-back rattler among many others. While many environmentalists wince at such a display, Cabela's has a plaque mounted at the front of the display that makes a strong counterargument. Hunting is essential to sound conservation, the argument goes, because sportsmen pay self-imposed taxes on sporting goods, pay fees for hunting and fishing permits, only hunt to specified limits, support the development and preservation of conservation areas, and help maintain healthy and sustainable populations of wildlife. Ike would have been an enthusiastic patron of Cabela's.

Based on numerous recommendations, I had dinner one night at Dude's Steakhouse and Brandin' Iron Bar on the Lincoln Highway in the middle of Sidney. I stopped for a moment in the Brandin' Iron Bar, where a crowd was huddled around the bar and laughing uproariously, and then went into the adjacent steakhouse. It was a cozy, informal place that I immediately liked: Formica, vinyl, booths, and tables under western art like oxen yokes and models of galloping ponies.

I sat in a booth where I could see into the kitchen, where the two cooks were obviously enjoying their work. They, and all the waitresses and staff, were wearing t-shirts that read on the back:

FAMILY Est. 1952

There was a long row of artificial flowers separating the rows of booths, and in a glass cabinet in front of me little pitchers of syrup lined up like soldiers, waiting for the next onslaught of Dude's pancakes.

I asked my waitress about the restaurant remaining a family concern. She pointed out the young woman in the kitchen and said, "See that girl? She's our founder's granddaughter, and she's chief chef. Her brother, who is my husband, is the other chef, but he's off today. It's all family here, and I guess it always will be." I asked if they got many tourists like me and she said, "Yeah, we get some. But most of our clientele is local. We've just got us a real good reputation." And it was true: when I went outside afterward I looked at the license plates of all the cars parked around Dude's, and apart from my Virginia plate, they were all Nebraska.

From Sidney I took a brief and impossible-to-pass-up detour north to Alliance, to see one of the great works of automobile art in the US. *Carhenge* was built by Jim Reinders in the early 1980s and dedicated at the summer solstice of 1987. It perfectly replicates Stonehenge and is made up of vintage cars primarily from the 1950s and 1960s, and each buried trunk down. Cars are arranged in a circle rising up some 15 feet, with three trilithons within the circle, a heel stone, a slaughter stone, and two station stones. There is also a display of other car art nearby, like *Carronausouras Rex*, and *Carestoga Wagon*. All the cars were painted gray to simulate stones. The lady in the office told me over 10,000 people visited *Carhenge* to view the total solar eclipse, August 20–21, 2017.

I returned to Sidney and drove west past the Busted Knuckle Garage and Dude's Steakhouse and back out into open prairie once again. I noticed a sign for I-80 less than a mile to the south and "I-80 Golden Link—last segment of I-80 Completed." Even last place earns a superlative. I passed through the tiny town of Potter, which also has staked its own claim to fame: it has the only duckpin bowling alley west of the Mississippi. I took a liking to Potter because of the humor in its tourist brochure: "You know you're in a small town when you hear a dog barking and know whose it is."

A little west of Sidney I saw a white Ram pickup out on the shoulder of the road almost down in the weeds, with two men standing close by. I hadn't seen another car for miles, so I pulled over, and that's when I met two men I'll call Larry and Bill. They had both worked for the Highway Department—Larry still did, but Bill had retired. "Biggest fuckin' mistake I ever made," he said. "Just sit at home and listen to my old lady nag at me all the fuckin' day."

Larry said, "I told him so, but the goddamn bastard wouldn't listen to me."

"So, you come out here pretty often?" I asked. We were way out on the prairie, no town in sight.

"Yeah, just pokin' around. Looking for petrified wood, fossils, rocks, Indian arrowheads. You know where to look, sometimes you can find some stuff," said Larry. He pulled a cigar-sized rock out of his pocket. "Petrified wood—

found it just a coupla minutes ago, just over that rise," he said, and pointed to the north.

"Better'n sittin' at home and listenin' to 'Why don't you take out the garbage?' 'Why don't you clean out the garage?'"

"So, you cover a lot of ground?" I asked. "Every season?"

"All over west Nebraska. We got us some good spots," said Bill. "All year. Hundred and ten to twenty below."

"February?" said Larry. "Out here it can look real nice, and then next thing you know you got a fuckin' blizzard blowin' right up your ass."

"You must have to wear a lot of clothing." I asked. I was trying to loft up some softball questions just to keep them talking.

"Layers," said Bill. "Tons of 'em. You get enough layers of shit on you, you be ok."

"Biggest problem is when you out here, and the wind's howlin', and all of a sudden you got to take a piss real bad," said Larry. "You got to dig down through all them layers 'fore you hit bedrock."

"Yeah, I pissed on myself one time," said Bill. "Twenty below, double mittens, and couldn't find the goddam zipper in time."

"Probably just wiped out a six-pack," said Larry. He pointed toward Bill and grinned.

"Yeah? So, what you drinkin', shithead?" said Bill. "Lemonade?"

The Convoy departed Big Springs early on August 7, and everyone must have been relieved to encounter what Elwell Jackson described as "good gravel roads." There were no real mishaps for a change, except for a covering tarpaulin that caught fire in camp. They covered eighty-six miles in about eleven hours and camped in the fairgrounds at Kimball. Elwell Jackson writes, "Good location and irrigation ditch passing thru furnished bathing water. Commercial Club gave dinner-dance for officers at the Wheat Growers Hotel." Ike and Mamie enjoyed one of their last nights together for a while at the same hotel.

S. M. Johnson gave another Good Roads speech in Kimball, in which he said, "I have come from Washington to Kimball, and everywhere, at crossroads, villages, and cities I have been impressed with the number of autos parked and filled with cheering people who have hailed us as the harbinger of the better day, but nowhere, even at the country crossroads or the cities, have I seen old Dobbin parked. The fact that needs to be impressed today is that the entire human family is going to resort to the motor vehicle as rapidly as these can be manufactured."

On westward and into Kimball where I found plenty of interesting-sounding bars: "Beer and Loathing," "Good Times Bar & Grill," "Wind

Break Bar & Grill," and "Mad Dog Sports Bar" (for sale or lease). A motel with a big neon sign:

Sleep 4 Less Motel

But, alas, the 4 had been obliterated.

The Wheat Growers Hotel opened in 1918, and Ike and Mamie stayed there the evening of August 7 the following year. It's been out of business since 1987, but it still appears solid from the outside. The top floor windows are now boarded up, and a couple of cracks in the glass on the ground floor have been taped up. But the precise mosaic tile at the entrance still proudly proclaims "Wheat Growers Hotel" with no apparent ill effects of age.

I asked one of the town's librarians if there were other historic buildings near Kimball, and she gave me directions to two nineteenth-century buildings: a house on the old Bay State Ranch and the "Chicken Ranch." Perhaps I looked puzzled over the latter—she leaned forward in said in a semi-whisper, "A house of ill repute." I tracked down both, which are abandoned but still standing, and wondered if anybody from the Convoy happened to visit Kimball's Chicken Ranch.

The highest point in Nebraska, at 5,424 feet, is Panorama Point in the extreme southwest corner of the panhandle, very close to the point at which Colorado, Wyoming, and Nebraska meet. This is not a spectacular peak: even the Nebraska tourism brochure admits that Panorama Point "looks more like a rise in a pasture than the highest point in the State." The same brochure also cautions "NOTICE! There are buffalo roaming around these markers. . .buffalo are wild animals." Driving across the length of the state one doesn't notice the slow but steady increase in elevation. Omaha's altitude in the far east of the state is 1,089 feet, so there's an increase of over 4,300 feet in about 450 miles. Settlers on the trails, as well as their pack animals, surely noticed.

I wandered around Panorama Point for a while. No buffalo, no people, nothing but the relentless gusting wind and the swaying grass all around. And the silence. I thought again of Willa Cather. "As I looked about me I felt that the grass was the country, as the water is the sea. . .there was so much motion in it; the whole country seemed, somehow, to be running." I lingered for a long time, enjoying the moments as they stretched on. But finally I walked back down to my Chevy and drove the last mile into Wyoming.

Portion of wall mural showing Ike in uniform, Bucyrus, OH

Intersection of Lincoln Highway and Route 66, Joliet, IL

Lynn Asp, Lincoln Highway Association Headquarters, Franklin Grove, IL

Chad Van Dyke, Auto Thrill Show Museum, LaPorte City, IA

Iowa's largest Frying Pan, Brandon, IA

Lincoln Highway bridge, Tama, IA

"Field of Dreams", Dyersville, IA

Joyce Ausberger, Lincoln Highway Museum, Grand Junction, IA

Old Lincoln Highway road sign, with water tower in background, IA

World's largest ball of stamps, Boys Town, NE

Merle Block next to his barbed wire buffalo, Sod House Museum, Gothenberg, NE

Lenore Stubblefield at the Lincoln Highway Visitors' Center, Shelton, NE

Carhenge, near Alliance, NE

Lincoln Highway sign, North Platte NE

"World's Oldest Building"; Fossil House, Como Bluffs, WY

Buford, WY Town Sign: Population 1

The Virginian Hotel, Medicine Bow, WY

Boyd's Station on the Pony Express route, eastern UT

West end of the original Lincoln Highway Goodyear Cutoff,
south of Gold Hill UT

Road west of Ibapah UT, near the NV state line

Dan Braddock pouring a soda at McGill NV's Drugstore museum

Five-seat outhouse, Eureka NV

Donna Sossa ringing the dinner bell at Paradise Ranch B&B, near Austin, NV

Remains of Eastgate Station, near Austin, NV

Western Terminus of the Lincoln Highway, Golden Gate Park, San Francisco

WYOMING

The Interstate Highway System:

Total length: 47,856 miles

25 percent of all vehicle miles driven in the US are on interstate highways.

42 billion cubic yards of dirt were moved during construction, more than 100 times the amount moved for the Panama Canal

The total amount of concrete in the system could build a wall 9 feet thick and 50 feet high around the Earth's equator

Each mile of interstate contains 21,000 cubic yards of concrete

All the concrete in the system could be used to build 80 Hoover dams, with concrete left over

If every man, woman, and child in California, New York, Texas, and New Jersey took a trip to the moon, that would be the same distance traveled over the interstate system every year

Crossing in from Nebraska through seemingly boundless empty prairie, I was suddenly stopping right away to get out and gawk. First of all, a long-abandoned, dilapidated service station sat perfectly square on the Nebraska-Wyoming state line. There was a vertical black stripe painted right through the middle of the collapsing building, with NEB on one side, and WYO on the other. Wind whistling through the cracks of the building and the tall weeds, and wrecks of cars parked all around.

And then just to the north I discovered Our Lady of Peace, the largest statue of the Virgin Mary in the entire US, at over 30 feet tall. It was constructed by Ted and Marjorie Trefen of nearby Cheyenne, and it weighs some 180 tons. The Virgin is pure white, and she gazes serenely out toward the plains of the West.

Just a bit farther along I encountered Mel Gould's Buryville. I had heard about Buryville and been warned to be on the lookout for wacky metal sculptures out in Mel's front yard—unique auto art. Suddenly, there they were: a flying saucer, an insect made from an oil drum and lots of tailpipes, an elephant made from car fenders and oil drums, a skinny tubular man holding a giant pair of pliers. This was definitely Mel's place. I pulled over and got out to look around. As I was deciding whether or not to knock on the door of Mel's house, the back door opened, and a huge black dog came racing out toward me, barking like a banshee. An instant later an elderly man in a baseball cap slipped out of the same door. I assumed he was Mel, but by that time the dog was almost on top of me. As I was contemplating what sort of defense I could mount, the dog abruptly halted about two feet from me, tentatively leaned forward to smell my shoes and lower leg, and then began to lick my hand.

"Don't worry," hollered Mel. "She wouldn't hurt anybody."

It was wind-frigid with recent snow still piled up, but Mel took me around for a tour of his entire collection. Complicated creations with names like Mr. Cranky, Wild Thing, and the Purple People Eater. I especially liked Moon Beam, which is a small three-wheel vehicle with a top from a Dodge trunk lid, a tail fin from two Plymouth rear fenders, and a body of 1936 Chevy hoods sandwiched together. The engine is from a hay baler. "I just pile up old cars and then let my imagination go," said Mel.

Decades ago Mel carved out an enormous hole next to his house and proceeded to bury an old grain silo, a school bus, a camper, and a 50,000-gallon fuel tank. He covered it all back up and that complex became his workshop — thus, Buryville. He took me around to the back of his garage and showed me a pile of ruined vehicles: cars, pickups, VW Beetles, and others. "That's my supply closet," said Mel.

Mel's reputation as a creator and builder got around over the years, and eventually brought him into contact with Christo, the famous Bulgarian artist who designed huge landscape works. Perhaps Christo's best-known project is Running Fence, a huge drape running for miles across central California. When Christo first put the work into place, Whoom! The coastal wind almost immediately blew it down. In stepped Mel, who considered the problem, designed a solution, and built deep wind anchors that did the job.

Mel told me one story after another and showed me around in the cold for almost an hour. The dog was still licking my hand. Mel finally left me to go inside while we were standing over at a 15-foot metal giraffe. "Just stay and poke around long as you like," he said. "I like having visitors."

Ike and the Convoy made it into Cheyenne at 5:30 on the evening of August 8, having traveled 66 miles in 11 hours. Elwell Jackson wrote, "(Vehicles) had some difficulty in negotiating soft sand under railroad bridges. . .heavy rains during night had softened road. . .entered Cheyenne in a driving rain of an hour's duration, followed by clearing and much lower temperatures." The Convoy hunkered down in tents in Frontier Park, while Ike and Mamie enjoyed their last evening together downtown in the historic Plains Hotel, still going strong today. It was a lively evening. Elwell Jackson reports, "A rodeo was given for entertainment of personnel, including races for cowboys and cowgirls, roping, bulldogging, bronco busting, etc."

Cheyenne's *Wyoming State Tribune* of August 9 provides some detail in a front-page article headlined, "Wild Western Reception Given Motor Convoy by Old Cheyenne." Farther down the article is this note: "There was a rumor at the park that Colonel McClure, commander of the Convoy, a few days ago ran a Cadillac car into the ditch. . .when Mr. Irwin, who presided at the small end of a megaphone. . .announced during the bronco-busting that the next rider would be Colonel McClure on Cadillac, there was a roar from the men of the Convoy."

A sign of the times: elsewhere in that same edition of the *Tribune*, an article notes that since the beginning of Prohibition on July 1, arrests for public drunkenness in Cheyenne were down by 83 percent.

I dropped by Sapp's Truck Stop just east of Cheyenne, which boasts a 110-foot-tall water tower in the shape of a coffee pot, and then drove on into Cheyenne in the last light of the day. While at Sapp's, I struck up a conversation with a man named Frank, who was complaining about the traffic. "They keep widening the roads, and then more cars, and the damn trucks, they just keep on coming. Vicious circle kind of a thing. No end to it, seems like to me." This was a phenomenon I witnessed all across the country: roads and highways kept getting widened, and more vehicles quickly followed. I thought back to ten-lane I-270 in Maryland, with a politician's promise up on a billboard: "Time to widen I-270 Now!" If you build it, they will come.

As of 2016, there are some 269 million vehicles registered in the US, and some 8.66 million lane miles of paved highway. (Back in 1910, just before the Convoy, there were 180,000 registered vehicles driving on 175,000 miles of improved road, which was most often not much more than graded dirt.) So nowadays this works out to about 31.1 vehicles per lane mile of paved highway. The number of registered vehicles is growing by a little over 1.0 percent per year, and the number of miles of paved lane miles is growing at about 0.4 percent per year. Where does it all end? Let's just employ some basic math here:

Vehicles on the roads of the US range from VW Beetles to massive 18-wheelers, but let's just average them all together and assume the mean length of vehicle is eighteen feet. The standard rule of thumb is to allow one car-length of headway for every ten miles per hour of speed, so if that average eighteen-foot vehicle is driving, say, forty miles per hour, then it would take up ninety feet of road. If every single vehicle in the US was being driven simultaneously, at a steady forty miles per hour, this phalanx would take up 24.2 billion feet, or 4.583 million miles: about 53 percent of all paved lane miles in the US.

But the number of vehicles is increasing by 1.0 percent per year, and the number of paved lane miles is increasing at only 0.4 percent. Projecting these trends forward, our Nation arrives at a calamitous dénouement in the year 2186, when every single lane mile of our roads will be encumbered by a vehicle lumbering along at forty miles per hour.

Of course, this will never come to pass. Raj Rajkumar's autonomous vehicles will deliver smaller headways and far greater efficiencies. Uber, Lyft, and like-minded services will grow and prosper, and more urbanites might give up cars entirely and take to walking or public transit. But as I reflected on all of this, meandering slowly through the gorgeous wide-open spaces of Wyoming, I thought, "I sure hope the solution is not still more roads."

Okay, transitioning from highways to cowgirls. Wandering around downtown Cheyenne the next day, I came across the Cowgirls of the West Museum. The museum's introduction reads in part, "The settling of the American West has often been romanticized in the print and video media, where the lives of western women have sometimes been depicted as easy, simple, carefree, romantic, and often glamorous. Nothing is further from the truth!! These pioneering women worked very hard and right alongside the men to make the American West the one we know today. The purpose of the Cowgirls of the West is to tell their remarkable stories and to preserve their historical artifacts." The museum tells the story of dozens of characters like Prairie Rose Henderson, who dazzled crowds at the turn of the century with her bronco riding and slick horsemanship, as well as her outrageous costumes. By the time the Convoy passed through, Prairie Rose was a star in Irwin's Wild West Show.

The museum portrays just one aspect of the advanced role of women in Wyoming throughout the state's history. Wyoming women were the first in the nation to be granted the right to vote, in 1869. Women in Wyoming were also the first to serve on juries, hold public office, or serve as justices of the peace. In 1924, just five years after the Convoy passed through, Nellie Tayloe Ross became the nation's first elected woman governor to take office.

Much has been written about the paucity of high-tech facilities in fly-over country, but Cheyenne can boast a unique tech center. I visited the National Center for Atmospheric Research Wyoming Supercomputing Center (NWSC), just outside Cheyenne, right across the road from a gigantic Walmart regional distribution center. NWSC's Yellowstone supercomputer, installed in 2012, has 72,000 processors, 4,000 nodes, and over 12,000 cables stretching for tens of miles. It is capable of 1.5 PFLOPS. For the uninitiated, (like me) a PFLOP is one quadrillion calculations per second. Yellowstone was capable of 1.5 PFLOPS, but the new Cheyenne supercomputer, which came online in 2017, is capable of 5.4 PFLOPS, making it one of the most powerful supercomputers in the world. The world's first supercomputer—the Cray I, developed in 1977—had roughly the computational power of a current-day smartphone.

A supercomputer as big as Cheyenne generates lots of heat. The helpful guide named Carol told me most of the heat is recycled to warm the building and the floors, and even heats a good deal of the parking lot. "We don't have to worry about shoveling snow around here," she said. About ten percent of the facility's energy comes from a nearby wind farm, and there are large suction devices on the building's roof to suck in the cold Wyoming air, which is then used to cool down Cheyenne naturally.

F. E. Warren Air Force Base in Cheyenne today serves as command center for the Intercontinental Ballistic Missile program, and also has a museum on the ICBM program. Fort Warren was originally established as Fort Russel in 1867, and when Ike and the Convoy passed by in 1919 it was one of the largest military posts in the US. Several units had recently returned from deployments in World War I, and the dirt airstrip was used by Eddie Rickenbacker as well as the "Western Flying Circus." The first Strategic Missile Wing was activated at Warren in 1958 during Ike's second presidential term, and in the years since the base has transitioned through a series of ICBM deployments, culminating in the ICBM Peacekeeper.

These transitions have led to the retirement of some missile systems. I had earlier stopped in at the tourist information center near the Nebraska state line, where a friendly guide named Jo told me that many abandoned silos were now up for sale. She told me that one family had bought such a silo and converted it into their home. She said it was open for tours on a limited basis.

Seeing an abandoned underground missile silo converted into a Wyoming residence piqued my interest. I asked around in Cheyenne, but alas, I discovered that the couple who lived in the silo/residence had closed off the tour option just a few weeks earlier. "Crowds got to be too much," a waitress told me. "Whole busloads would just show up at their front door. Sixty tourists, all wanting to look around. So they had to shut it down."

At the nearby Arapahoe and Shoshone Wind River Reservation, the Shoshone Rose Casino appears to be the largest income earner: Open 24 hours! Over 330 slot machines. Live Table Games, a Gift & Tobacco Shop, with their own website shoshonerose.com. But there's much more to the Wind River Reservation. In November 2016, for the first time in 131 years, bison were reintroduced into the Wind River Reservation. It's a familiar story: this land once had thousands of bison, but by the time Ike and the Convoy passed through, they were all gone. The reintroduction was a combined effort of the Eastern Shoshone Tribe, Department of the Interior, and the National Wildlife Federation, and the culmination of decades of conservation efforts by Shoshone and Arapahoe tribes. The tribes jointly designated a portion of Wind River as wilderness area in 1938, introduced hunting regulations, and re-introduced pronghorn antelope and bighorn sheep as well.

Out west of Cheyenne I stopped off at Buford, which advertises itself as the smallest town in America. The town consists of a convenience store and gas station, and a few abandoned cabins out to the side. The town's big business today comes from gawking tourists like me, stopping off to snap photos of the town sign:

Buford
Population 1
Elevation 8,000

The Lincoln Highway Association's 1915 guide to the Lincoln Highway lists Buford as having a population of 80 and notes that it offers "beautiful scenery." The Convoy passed right through on August 9, but Elwell Jackson makes no mention of the town in his log.

The Ames Monument, built in 1882, stands atop a lonely windswept hilltop about twenty miles east of Laramie, and just a few miles from the original Lincoln Highway. The granite monument is a four-sided pyramid that stands sixty feet tall, and with no trees in sight, it can be seen for miles away. It was built to honor the Ames brothers, financiers of the Union Pacific Railroad, and is located at the highest point (8,247 feet) on the track of the original UP railroad tracks. The tracks have been relocated miles to the south over the years, so the monument stands starkly alone today. The day I visited, there were no other vehicles around, and the wind was howling so hard it was difficult to stand still for long. The monument is at the end of a narrow gravel road that didn't appear to get much traffic. Ike and the Convoy would have seen it up on the hill, all by itself, when they passed by.

One of the most renowned landmarks on the old Lincoln Highway is the Tree in the Rock, a short distance beyond Buford and not far from the Ames Monument. This stretch of the original highway has now been paved over by I-80, but the tree is still there in the median strip. There is even a scenic pull-out especially for the tree, with an interpretative marker. The sign on the interstate reads "Point of Interest." The tree is a somewhat stunted Limber Pine that is growing out of a small crack in a granite boulder. It was first noted by the crew building the original Union Pacific in 1867, and they diverted the tracks slightly to avoid hitting the tree. Ike and the Convoy drove within feet of it on the old Lincoln Highway, but Elwell Jackson makes no mention.

August 9 was a landmark day for the Convoy. Elwell Jackson writes, "Lunched at Sherman Hill, from which point Pike's Peak, 175 mi. southward, was plainly visible. Crossed the Continental Divide at 2 p.m. elevation 8,247' . . .Made 57 miles in 11.5 hours. Arrived Laramie Wyo 7:20 p.m.."

Exit 184 now marks the highest point on I-80 at 8,640 feet; Sherman Hill is just off to the south about a mile away. Back in 1958 a wealthy philanthropist decided that the Lincoln Highway needed a statue of Abraham Lincoln, so he commissioned Wyoming sculptor Robert Russin to produce a suitable monument that would be placed on top of Sherman Hill. Russin needed to work in a warm climate, so he completed the 14-foot-high bronze bust in Mexico City, and it was transported all the way to Wyoming by rail. When I-80 was completed in 1969, the bust was moved (during a blinding snowstorm) to its present location atop a 35-foot-high base not far from Exit 184. It is purportedly the largest bronze head in the US, and the only statue of Lincoln on the entire Lincoln Highway.

While the Lincoln statue is visible from miles around, it stands next to a far smaller and unassuming monument to Henry Joy, first president of the Lincoln Highway. In 1916, during one of his several cross-country trips, Joy camped near the Continental Divide west of Rawlins and was so enamored with the scenery he told his companions that when he died he'd like to be buried at that spot. Although he was subsequently buried elsewhere upon his death in 1936, his wife and daughter sought to fulfill his wish in part by erecting the monument on that spot in 1939. In 2001 the monument was moved and today stands immediately adjacent to the Lincoln bust—a favorite stopping point for Lincoln Highway buffs.

Two of the objectives of the Convoy were demonstration of the Army's diverse vehicles (still new to most Americans) and recruitment into the Motor Transport Corps. Recruiters made quite the impression in Laramie. The *Laramie Republic* on August 9, 1919, quotes recruiting chief Captain James Murphy: "Perhaps no branch of the service offers as great an inducement for daredevils as the motor transport and tank Convoy," he said. "One has only to watch the transcontinental Convoy pass through the streets to see that these soldiers, tearing along. . .take bigger chances than the ordinary man. . .then, too, there are the tanks. Think of the part they played in the great war. . .early promotion is sure for the man who wishes to take a chance inside one of the huge crushers or. . .whippet squashers. Get out and see 'em." The *Republic* went on to note, "It looked this afternoon as though the people of the city and vicinity will be out tonight thousands strong to see the great train and witness the demonstration."

In addition to the *Republic*, Laramie boasts another daily newspaper called the *Boomerang*. It was founded in 1881 by Bill Nye (no relation to the Science Guy), who named the paper after his mule, and is still going strong nowadays. The May 23, 2017, issue of the *Boomerang* headlined a story, "Leaks Found on Dakota Access Pipeline System."

Laramie is home to the University of Wyoming and has many of the delights of a college town. The university opened for classes in 1887 with a student body of forty-two and faculty of five. Part of the campus is near the original Lincoln Highway, so Ike and the Convoy passed right by. The university was still small back in 1919, but since that time it has grown into a major teaching and research university with a student body of 13,000. Known by locals as U-Dub, it is still the only four-year university in Wyoming.

While driving around Laramie and environs, I tuned into a local radio station, and heard the DJ refer to "tourons" and "today's touron story." I had no idea what a touron was, but when the story arrived I learned that it was a shortcut for "tourist moron." Today's touron story involved a tourist from New York who climbed over a protective fence in Yellowstone Park so he could snap a selfie with a full-grown bison. As one might expect, this did not end happily. But the touron did survive, with a few battle scars to show off to pals back home.

One longstanding highlight of Laramie is the Old Buckhorn Bar and Parlor, Laramie's oldest bar in operation since 1889. When Ike and the Convoy passed through the building housed the McCune Saloon—the Buckhorn Bar took over in the 1930s. In addition to the usual mounted antelope, elk, and deer, one can also view a mounted beehive, a two-headed calf, and check out three bullet holes left over late nineteenth-century spats.

Another delight of wandering around in downtown Laramie is the beautiful wall murals you find everywhere. The Laramie Mural Project, launched in 2011, is a collaboration of the University of Wyoming, downtown business owners, and local artists, and the results are terrific. The subject matter ranges from prairie dogs to the plight of native Americans to the role of railroads and automobiles in Wyoming's history to Wyoming's unique natural landscape and how it is changing.

Shop signs in downtown Laramie:

The Bent and the Rusty
Repurposed, Recycled, Handcrafted, Antique, Custom Designed

The Library: Handcrafted Micro Brews
"Don't Lie to your Mom – Tell Her You're at the Library"

Later I passed by the Crowbar & Grill, and Cowboy's Bar & Grill, which was located right next to a sushi shop.

Mamie and the Douds drove back to their home in Denver from Laramie, so it was a farewell for Ike. Much later he wrote, "It was a fine interlude, and I decided that it would be nice, being in the West already, to apply for a leave with my family at the end of the tour—if indeed we ever reached the end."

Laramie's Wyoming Territorial Prison Museum showcases the only jail to hold Butch Cassidy, from 1894 to 1896. After release, Cassidy became the leader of the Wild Bunch, a group of robbers that included not only the Sundance Kid, but also Kid Curry, the Tall Texan, and a couple of others. They robbed banks and trains all over the Great Plains, and evaded capture for years by hiding out in such remote spots as Robbers' Roost, Hole in the Wall, and the Red Desert. Cassidy was known as a sort of Robin Hood figure—he reportedly gave money to widows facing mortgage foreclosure and families down on their luck.

On August 29, 1900, the Wild Bunch carried out a daring train robbery near Tipton Station, Wyoming, precisely where the Convoy camped only nineteen years later. According to the Museum's account, Cassidy somehow got on board the speeding train, made his way to the locomotive, and took charge of the train. He ordered the Engineer to stop at a certain point, where more members of the gang came on board with dynamite. They then proceeded to another spot where remaining members of the gang awaited with fresh horses. The gang dynamited the safe and escaped with some $55,000. At one point, the story goes, Cassidy commented that the engineer had a nice watch. The engineer replied that Cassidy would probably want to take that as well, but Cassidy replied no, he did not rob passengers or train personnel, just the rich bankers.

Bill Carlisle was also a renowned train robber who acted alone. Carlisle, who always wore a white face mask, would sneak onto trains as they were leaving the station. Once the train was going, he would pull his revolver and rob train personnel as well as some passengers before jumping off the moving train. He was captured and sentenced to life in prison in 1916, but he escaped in 1919, and on November 18, 1919, he robbed another train near Rock River. This was just three months after Ike and the Convoy had passed through Rock River. On this particular robbery, Carlisle discovered that most of the passengers were soldiers returning from the war, and he refused to rob any of them. His takings were slim, and he wounded his hand in making his escape. He was recaptured just days later and sentenced to life once again. He was released for good behavior in 1935, married, adopted a child, and by all accounts was a model citizen thereafter.

The Convoy had a rest day in Laramie on Sunday, August 10, although they spent most of the day servicing the vehicles. "All nuts and bolts tightened up," writes Elwell Jackson. They departed Laramie early on August 11 and had lunch courtesy of the Red Cross Canteen in Rock River, site of the Bill Carlisle train robbery just three months later. The Convoy made just fifty-nine miles in eleven and a half hours that day, but as was often the case for the entire trip, the slow pace was partly caused by the extensive repair work the Convoy frequently undertook. Elwell Jackson writes, "Bridges were generally poor, and 12 wooden bridges were reinforced by Engineers with lumber furnished by Wyoming State Highway Dept."

I stopped off at Hostler's General Store, right on the Convoy's route in Rock River and spoke for a while with the proprietor, Roy Hostler. The sign at the entrance read:

Hostler's Store
Groceries
Propane
Antiques
Ice
Gas
Laundry
Tire Repair

Roy told me he was seventy-two years old and had had three heart operations. "I've only got about a third of my heart left. And probably only half my brain." He had worked and lived for years near Gettysburg, and had crossed over the Lincoln Highway nearly every day, but when he retired he wanted to move to the "wide open spaces." "So here I am out here in Rock River, and still on the Lincoln Highway. I like that." Roy said he enjoyed turkey hunting, and when I mentioned the perpetually strong wind, he said the pronghorn depend on the wind blowing the snow around so some grass would be exposed in the winter. We talked for over half an hour and not a single other customer came in. I mentioned that he wasn't too busy, and he said "Interstate 80. Everybody takes the interstate. People in too much of a hurry to take the slow road up the Lincoln Highway, but this is where the history is."

Back in the early 1920s, right after the Convoy had passed through, a man by the name of Tom "Bumpy" Boylan acquired some land between Rock River and Medicine Bow. Bumpy reportedly got his nickname from the unusual manner in which he rode horses. Bumpy knew he was not cut out for farming or ranching, so he went into commerce. His first transaction was to acquire a mail-order bride from back East named Grace. Together Bumpy and Grace built a stone house, a general store with outbuildings, and a Texaco gas station right on the Lincoln Highway. Theirs was the first and only gas station for miles around, and business was brisk, but Bumpy felt they needed some extra oomph to bring in more customers from the highway. He knew about the numerous fossils readily available at the nearby Como Bluff, so in 1929, he and Grace started building a house made entirely of dinosaur fossils. They finally completed the house in 1932, and it became an immediate sensation. *Ripley's Believe It or Not* twice featured Bumpy and Grace's house as the oldest house in the world, based on the age of its building materials. The house went through a succession of owners after Bumpy and Grace passed away, but the latest owners closed the house to tourists in 1998, and it has not re-opened. You can still see the house from the road and look around a bit, but it is fenced off with barbed wire, and the new owners have multiple signs reading, "Caution! Guard dogs will attack!," all of which dimmed my enthusiasm for closer inspection.

The Convoy motored on through high winds and a hailstorm, into Medicine Bow just after 6:00 p.m. The August 14, 1919, issue of the *Rawlins Republican* stated: "Lieut. Col. McClure reports that one of the prettiest receptions accorded the train was that given at Medicine Bow. The train was. . .late in arriving, but the barbecue was waiting. Following this an open-air dance, a novelty to many of the soldiers, was given in the middle of town."

While in Medicine Bow, I stayed at The Virginian Hotel, built in 1911 and named after the Owen Wister novel that put Medicine Bow on the map. When it was built it was the largest hotel between Denver and Salt Lake City, and it has been in continuous operation since its opening. I splurged and took the Owen Wister Suite, corner rooms on the second floor, and spent many profitable hours down in the restaurant/bar on the ground floor.

The hotel was built by Mayor August – Gus – Grimm, a larger-than-life character whose prime goal was to entice train passengers to stop off at The Virginian for high-stakes poker games, in which Grimm was a regular, profitable participant. His creditors wouldn't allow Grimm to serve alcohol in the Virginian, but undaunted, he built a special back door that led directly into his Home Ranch Saloon, already a longtime Medicine Bow fixture. Grimm was known for having the best whiskey around. On one eventful evening in 1898, some drunken cowboys rode their horses right into the saloon, and the floor caved in. Cowboys, horses, customers, furniture, and many crates of whiskey all plummeted into the storage cellar below. It took some time to get that one sorted out.

On the evening of August 11, 1919, Elwell Jackson writes, "Citizens served barbeque to entire personnel at The Virginian Hotel, made famous by Owen Wister. Street dance and refreshments in evening." Unfortunately, nobody in the Convoy actually spent the night at The Virginian and instead "camped in hillside south of Medicine Bow, soil dusty, sand, and no water facilities."

Right across the Lincoln Highway from The Virginian is Owen Wister's cabin, transported here from its original location in Jackson Hole. It was in this cabin that he wrote his most famous novel—there's a monument to him nearby, and just beyond is the Owen Wister General Store. It was here that, upon his arrival in town in 1885, Wister slept on the store's countertop because there were no other rooms available in all of Medicine Bow.

Wister wrote in the introduction to *The Virginian:* "Wyoming between 1874 and 1890 was a colony as wild as was Virginia one hundred years earlier. As wild, with a scantier population, and the same primitive joys and dangers." But by the early twentieth century: "It is a vanished world. No journeys, save those which memory can take, will bring you to it now." *The Virginian* was published in 1902, just seventeen years before the Convoy, and was an immediate runaway best-seller.

I spent many pleasant hours down in The Virginian's bar and dining room, talking with townspeople. I think everyone was somewhat bemused and puzzled with me, an Easterner driving through and writing a book, but there was always a good rapport. Once I asked everyone, "So, what do you think about this Dakota Access Pipeline?" Immediately a fanfare, and I just leaned back and listened.

"Goddamned fuckin' disaster. There's gonna be leaks in the first months."

"What? You don't want jobs?"

"It's gonna fuck up drinking water for sure."

"What jobs? Digging postholes in the prairie in fuckin' February?"

"You like collecting welfare better?"

"Gonna be goddamned oil in the groundwater. Leak in the first month, for sure."

"We gotta get jobs here, damnit. Any kinda jobs."

People disagreed about the pipeline, but they were unanimous in denouncing the route of I-80, which bypassed Medicine Bow to take a shortcut by Elk Mountain several miles to the south. Various customers told me this stretch of I-80 is impossible to keep open in winter, interferes with wildlife migration, was ridiculously expensive to build, and has been the scene of catastrophic accidents every winter since it opened in 1970. Even the wonderfully helpful and mild-mannered Medicine Bow librarian later told me, "I do rather believe that choice of route was a mistake."

On August 11, 1919, the day the Convoy arrived in Medicine Bow, Andrew Carnegie passed away at the age of eighty-three. Carnegie was one of the richest people in the world, but he eventually gave away over 90 percent of his wealth, much of it for the construction of local libraries. Many of them were already open or under construction during the Convoy's trip, and as I followed the route I saw dozens of Carnegie libraries in small towns across the country, many still in stately century-old buildings.

One morning in the hotel I struck up a conversation with a friendly breakfast customer and asked him about the nearby abandoned town of Carbon. The town had thrived as a coal mining community in the late 1800s, with a population of a couple thousand, but had been pretty much abandoned in 1903. Ike and the Convoy had passed through the almost-deserted town. "Nobody really knows why they abandoned that town," he said. "There was still plenty of coal around. Probably it had something to do with the railroad — they ruled the roost back then."

He told me he lived in a cabin out on the high plains some eight miles north of Medicine Bow. "Built that cabin myself," he said, "and I put in as much of the best goddamned quality insulation I could find. Solid stuff. Last winter it got down to fifty below at one point. Wind howling. But inside my cabin, it was seventy degrees."

I mentioned the wind farm that I had seen just west of Medicine Bow, with about forty windmills. "I don't know why they had to build that damned thing," he said. "We've still got plenty of coal, oil, gas. What I hear, gas is cheaper than wind. Before they put up them things I had a great view all around: Elk Mountain, the Medicine Bow Range, Laramie Peak. On clear days I could see way down into Colorado. Now I've got them damned windmills messing up the view."

Getting back to the abandoned town of Carbon, which seemed a particularly apt name for this location, I asked if I could get there over the five miles of dirt road with my little Chevy. "Oh, yeah," he said, "You shouldn't have a problem now, with the last few dry days. Not much to see except some foundations, but they still keep up the town cemetery. That town had some good houses — they moved two of them that I know of. One of them they moved here into Medicine Bow in 1903, and it's still here — lady's living in it, right here in town. Another one they moved up near Hanna, and somebody's still living in that one too."

With the weather sunny and breezy, I decided to drive up to Carbon, or at least as close as I could get, to see the vestiges of a town abandoned more than a century ago. I also wanted to see the rugged countryside and roads through which the Convoy had traveled not long after the town was abandoned. The town was apparently not totally abandoned right away — the 1915 *Lincoln Highway Guide* lists Carbon's population as 117. But these remaining hardy souls must have departed soon afterwards.

The road south of Medicine Bow was indeed fine — dirt and gravel winding across treeless, rolling prairie. No other cars or people in sight. After about six miles I spotted the cemetery, and after a little walking around over the prairie I finally found some foundations too. The cemetery was still well kept and neatly fenced off. People were still buried here even after the 1903 exodus — I saw a couple of gravestones marked 1919, the year of the Convoy. A sad number of markers were for small children — many of the gravestones of children had lambs carved on the top. Like Boot Hill, many stones were anonymous. Snow-covered Elk Mountain reared up to the south, and the wind swept through the wildflowers and sage, making the cemetery a somber but beautiful spot.

Over in the abandoned town there was not much left but the rubble of foundations, a combination of stacked stones and collapsed timbers, weathered and sanded smooth with age. All around in the knee-high grass I saw the detritus of departure: multicolored bits of glass, bent strips of fencing wire, rusted tin cans (their labels long gone), shards of white crockery, a busted pair of old eyeglasses, scraps of old metal tools that I could not identify. Pronghorn tracks were everywhere. And amidst it all, there were what appeared to me to be small lumps of coal.

West of Walcott I stopped by the abandoned remains of Fort Fred Steele. The fort was closed in 1886 but was rejuvenated for a time by local loggers and sheep herders. The town of Fort Steele prospered for several decades by crafting railroad ties and fence posts from felled trees floated down from upriver, and later by shearing sheep and shipping out the bales of raw wool on the adjacent UP railroad. The town was thus prospering when Ike and the Convoy passed right through on the original route of the Lincoln Highway, now long abandoned and overgrown. After several minutes of bushwhacking, I suddenly came across an old Lincoln Highway marker, and then another, deep in brush down near the banks of the North Platte. The highway was rerouted several miles to the north in 1939, and this led to the final demise of the town. The bridge across the North Platte is also long gone, and only the 1922 Union Pacific bridge stands nearby. Almost all the old buildings at Fort Steele are now reduced to rubble, and tall grass and trees obscure the old road.

Still the jokester, somewhere in western Wyoming Ike pulled off yet another great practical joke, and once again he relates it best himself:

> We had camped within a mile of a little settlement that boasted a combination restaurant and soft drink parlor. . .Sereno made friends with several of the local people in the restaurant. . .(the Easterners arrived and) the natives began to talk and argue heatedly and loudly about the possibility of Indian trouble. It appeared that an outbreak was imminent. . .As they went on, Sereno and

several of us expressed our anxiety. Before we left for camp, we proclaimed our intention of mounting a guard. We borrowed an old shotgun from one of the townspeople and loaded it with shells (from which we had removed the shot). . .Then we arranged for sentinels.

Sereno and I . . .took the early duty. We allotted the dreary small hours of the night for the officer for whom this episode was staged. Sereno, during his tour, just before midnight, let out an occasional shriek. . .in the manner of carnival Indians. This added to the tension. As Sereno came in off post, we took concealed positions to watch.

The recruit took his duties seriously, marching at attention around the camp. . .Brett. . .let out an occasional short yelp. Finally, just as we hoped, the sentry let go with both barrels – to arouse the camp he explained. . .After(wards). . .we went back to bed, pleased with ourselves.

There had been no Indian trouble since 1890. . .but another threat loomed instantly. It happened that one of the duties of our victim was writing up daily progress reports to the War Department. We learned that he had drafted a telegram in which. . .he described the local Indian trouble.

Faster than any vehicle in the Convoy, we shot off in all directions to find the man who was carrying the message to the telegraph office.

Ike and Brett did manage to intercept the telegram just in the nick of time before it was sent and got the portion involving Indian trouble deleted. But it was a close call. As Ike wrote later, if the portion describing Indian trouble had in fact made its way to the War Department's adjutant general, "he was unlikely to understand our brand of humor." The butt of this joke was the person responsible for writing daily progress reports, and thus was none other than Elwell Jackson himself.

The Convoy arrived in Rawlins at 7:30 p.m. on August 12 after a tough day. Elwell Jackson reports that fourteen bridges had to be reinforced or rebuilt entirely, and that "Road is an abandoned Union Pacific R.R. right-of-way, and very winding. Some dangerous trails at natural grades; in general very tedious going. . .territory of a most desolate character. 40 mi. gale, extremely dry atmosphere and intense sandy dust entailed considerable hardship." Matters didn't seem to improve much once they reached Rawlins. Elwell Jackson: "Camped in Fair Grounds northeast of Rawlins, on barren, dusty field."

The *Rawlins Republican* August 14, 1919, issue had a somewhat sunnier view of the Convoy's arrival. The newspaper features four front-page headline photos of the Convoy, and the accompanying article notes, "camp was made at the Fair Grounds where supper had been prepared. . .and was awaiting the arrival of the Convoy. The supper was a feast to the boys, as trout was part of the bill of fare. . .The Red Cross also sent down a bunch of pies. During the evening a dance was given at the Elks Hall for the visiting soldiers. . .Lieut. Col. McClure stated to the *Republican*, 'You may assure (the citizens) that we will always remember Rawlins, Wyoming, with only the kindliest retrospections.'"

Rawlins nowadays is a lively town of some 20,000 people spread into a valley at almost 7,000 feet, with the bare high plains looming up all around. I visited the interesting museum at the state penitentiary, in operation since 1903. Hangings took place there on a regular basis until 1936 when modernity arrived and a gas chamber was introduced. It too was used on a regular basis.

Thomas Edison visited Rawlins in the summer of 1878 in order to view a total solar eclipse. He stayed around for several days afterward to do some fishing and hunting just south of Rawlins. Local lore has it that Edison got the idea for the incandescent light bulb while camping out on this trip and gazing up at the "beautiful stars and clear sky light" of Wyoming, although the evidence on this is sketchy.

At the same time of Edison's visit to Rawlins a bandit named George Parrot was wreaking havoc all over Wyoming and Montana with a string of daring highway robberies. Parrot was called "Big Nose," and in 1878, the year of Edison's visit, Big Nose murdered a deputy sheriff and a Union Pacific detective after a bungled train robbery a short distance east of Rawlins. It took two years, but Big Nose was finally tracked down and brought back to Rawlins, where he was sentenced to hang. But before the hanging could take place, a lynch mob of 200 men hauled Big Nose out of the Rawlins jail and strung him up from a telegraph pole. Lynchings weren't that uncommon in those days—there were nine in Wyoming in the period from 1879 until the final lynching in 1912, just seven years before the Convoy.

And now for the lurid details. After Big Nose's lynching, local doctor John Osborne took possession of the body, ostensibly to do research on brain structure. Osborne sawed off the top half of Big Nose's skull and presented it to fifteen-year-old Lillian Heath, who went on to become the first female doctor in Wyoming. She reportedly utilized the skull alternately as an ash tray or a door stop. The skin from Big Nose's thighs and chest was sent off to a tannery in Denver and returned to Osborne, who had the leather made into a pair of shoes and a medical bag. Osborne was later elected governor of Wyoming, and he is said to have worn his Big Nose shoes to his inaugural ball. You can see those very same shoes nowadays in the Carbon County Museum.

The 1915 *Lincoln Highway Guide* notes that the speed limit in Rawlins was twelve miles per hour, but that this limit was not enforced. Apparently, some took notice of this absence of enforcement. In the August 14, 1919, *Rawlins Republican* there is a small item on page two:

Notice to Owners and Drivers
of Autos or Trucks

As the ordinances of the city concerning the driving and parking of cars, and concerning lights and speed seem to be ignored by many;

You are hereby notified that these ordinances are going to be strictly enforced without any further warning and without any favors whatever

WILL HAYES, *Marshall*

In that same issue of the *Republican* was the following notice:

"Big Blow-Out at Saratoga!"
Saratoga people always show their visitors a dandy time and it is a safe bet that this "blow-out" will be no exception and that every person who attends will be shown the time of his life"

August 13 was a tough day for the Convoy. Elwell Jackson:

22 mi. west detour. . .around dangerous bridge. . .truck slipped off road. . .spare parts truck ran off road on abandoned Union Pacific R.R. grade. . .water tanker ran off road. . .and rolled over 270 degrees. . .trail mobile kitchen broke spring and bent axle. . .machine shop ran off road into soft sand hole. . .right wheels of blacksmith shop sheared through bridge floor planks and narrowly averted dropping into 12' ravine.

Just another day in the office: All vehicles were rescued and brought back into service, and meanwhile the Engineers reinforced seven bridges along the way. But things didn't get better at the Convoy's campsite. "Camped on Red Desert on barren sandy plain, no inhabitants or buildings. . .Nearest natural water supply 16 miles." They dragged into Tipton Station, site of a Wild Bunch train robbery only 19 years earlier, at 5:00 p.m.

I eventually found the site of Tipton Station, next to the old U.P. railroad tracks. All is abandoned now, just a couple of collapsing buildings and the wind whipping through the prairie grass.

Things didn't get much better after the Convoy's departure from Tipton Station. Elwell Jackson, writing on August 14, catalogued another long litany of mechanical problems and added, "The intensely dry air, absence of trees and green vegetation, and parched appearance of the landscape exerted depressing influence on personnel." The Convoy covered seventy-six miles in almost fourteen hours of slogging, and didn't arrive in Green River until 8:15 p.m.

About this stretch, Davies writes: "They had trouble sleeping; the temperature in the open desert had dropped to forty-five degrees. Now the weather gave them dust storms, with winds touching fifty miles an hour; one of these near Rock Springs was so thick, said McClure, that it 'totally obscured vision.'"

The August 15, 1919, edition of the *Green River Star* reports that the Convoy tumbled into town and proceeded immediately to its campsite at the baseball park. "When the Army trucks arrived, almost every man, woman, or child of Green River, with several auto loads from Rock Springs, were gathered . . .to view the train as it passed through town."

The *Star* went on to editorialize about the trip:

> We wonder if the public fully appreciates the tremendous significance of the great motor Convoy. . .The Convoy is the largest ever sent over any distance anywhere. The distance traversed by the Convoy is the longest ever undertaken by any motor transport unit. . .To quote General Drake: "This trip over the Lincoln Highway is. . .the War Department's contribution toward the good roads cause." The Lincoln Highway Association has never stopped in its effort to demonstrate to the Nation the need for interstate highway improvement. . .The War Department. . .throws its tremendous prestige. . .in favor of a properly improved connecting America Highway system.

Elsewhere in the same edition of the *Green River Star* was a baseball article that quoted Connie Mack, the legendary manager of the (then) Kansas City Athletics: "The White Sox will win the pennant in the American League. . .the Chicago players are, collectively, a smart crew."

When Ike and the Convoy passed through southern Wyoming, the number of sheep had already overtaken the number of cattle, but ongoing tensions between the two camps was still strong. By 1900 there were 5 million sheep in Wyoming, and violence peaked around this time. In one 1896 incident

12,000 sheep were killed by being driven off a cliff by angry cattlemen. Similar violence continued until 1920 when cattlemen finally started being prosecuted for the attacks.

Thousands of Chinese men migrated to Wyoming in the late 1860s to serve as laborers on the construction of the transcontinental railroad. Many had first come to California after they heard about the Gold Rush, and then moved on to Wyoming when they were recruited by labor contractors. After completion of the railroad, the Union Pacific hired Chinese laborers to work in the coal mines it operated in Wyoming—there were some 700 Chinese workers in Rock Springs. Anti-Chinese sentiment began to develop among white miners, and this culminated in the September 1885 Rock Springs massacre. White miners attacked Chinatown, killing twenty-eight men, wounding many others, setting all the houses on fire, and driving everyone else out of town and into the prairie. The governor eventually intervened and sent protective troops to Rock Springs and Evanston, which also had a sizeable Chinese population.

Many Chinese departed Wyoming after the massacre, but enough remained in Evanston to maintain an active Chinatown for many years. Located next to the Bear River, Chinatown featured a substantial community center building and a temple, known as a Joss House. The Chinese community in Evanston—a couple hundred at the turn of the century—also celebrated Chinese New Year every year from 1879 to 1922, when the Joss House burned down. The *Evanston Age* writes that the 1879 celebration involved "feasting, drinking, smoking opium. . .burning queer little tapers and bits of colored papers. . .beating a rude drum, sounding a gong, ringing a triangle, firing off firecrackers by the bushel, shooting sky rockets, in short, making all the noise they can."

Evanston's Chinatown was still active in 1919 when Ike and the Convoy passed through, but it had started to dwindle in size. Chinese people had been banned from working in the mines, so they found other occupations. Some served as clerks, messengers, cooks, or dishwashers, but some operated their own businesses, such as laundries or restaurants. One memorable character in Evanston was a Chinese man named Long Choong who went by the name of Mormon Charlie. He had his own vegetable garden and made home deliveries on foot. He was a well-known fixture around town when Ike and the Convoy passed through.

The city of Evanston oversaw a reconstruction of the Joss House in 1990. Many of the elaborate gold panels that had been rescued from the 1922 fire were used in the reconstructed Joss House, which now serves as a museum of the history of Chinese people in Wyoming.

When Ike and the Convoy passed through, coal mining in western Wyoming was still going strong. A few years after the Convoy, trona (sodium sesquicarbonate) was discovered, and trona mining now rivals coal. Sweetwater County alone contains an estimated 100 billion tons of trona, the most massive deposit known in the world. That's enough to last hundreds of years at present rates of consumption.

Omnipresent billboards advertise Little America for miles around in all directions. Established in 1934 to shelter travelers, it is now purportedly the world's largest gas station, with 55 pumps. The billboards promise such luxuries as "17 marble showers," and "75-cent ice cream cones." I couldn't resist stopping in for a look at Little America, located on I-80 just west of Green River. There are indeed gas pumps all over the place, but I never quite got an accurate count because they were so spread out and in my quest I kept inadvertently wandering into the path of accelerating eighteen-wheelers. Dozens of trucks were parked in rows off on several sides, and as I strolled around I marveled at the beauty of the chrome, the elaborate paint jobs, the extra frills. Almost all trucks were immaculate, the object of obvious studied attention from their drivers.

There was a diner and shop for professional drivers that I poked into, and I quickly got that particular sense: what you might also sense when wandering into a professional baseball dugout, or a high court judges' chambers. This was a professional club, with its own talk and gear and codes, and I—a lanky guy in khaki pants and shabby sneakers, wearing reading glasses and scribbling furiously in a little black notebook—was clearly not a member. Everyone was friendly, and I struck up a few light conversations, but after a few minutes I retreated.

The shop for ordinary motorists like me features rows of Little America memorabilia: t-shirts, mugs, caps, shot glasses, along with such specialties as cherry-limeade flavored popcorn and roadkill jerky. There's a swimming pool and playground out back for the kids. The shop was crammed with families and little kids were everywhere, all no doubt happy for a break from the interstate.

James Cash Penney was born and grew up in Missouri, where he was diagnosed with tuberculosis and advised to move to the West. He eventually wound up in Evanston, Wyoming, managing a general goods store called Golden Rule. He and his wife scrimped up enough money to open another

Golden Rule store in nearby Kemmerer. The store opened in 1902, and Penney and his wife and infant child lived in the attic above the one-room store. Penney's business acumen was clear: he called all his employees "associates," and they all shared in the profits. He progressively took over more of the Golden Rule company until, in 1912, he incorporated as the J. C. Penney company. Ike and the Convoy passed right by the first Golden Rule Store in which J. C. Penney worked in Evanston, on Front Street. I stopped by it as well — it's now Dino's Bar & Grill. Right next door is a busy thrift shop called Second Hand Rose:

No Checks
No Credit Cards
All Sales Final
Donations Accepted

The Convoy had a cascade of problems on departing Green River, early on August 15, perhaps best summarized by Elwell Jackson: "A great many weak wooden bridges over culverts of dry creek beds were broken through during the day, causing much delay. . .made 63 miles in 17 hours." But then, "Bivouacked on site of old Army post, in beautiful oasis." That was in Fort Bridger.

I stopped by Fort Bridger, and it still is a beautiful oasis: the picture-perfect Groshon Creek meandering over small stones, with cottonwoods and aspens lining both sides. A wide expanse of flat green meadow, with high mountains rearing up in the near distance. A perfect campsite where one would ideally linger for a couple of days. But not the Convoy.

The fort was established by legendary mountain man Jim Bridger in 1843, who wrote, "I have established a small fort, with a blacksmith shop and a supply of iron, in the road of the emigrants." Bridger envisioned the fort as a key supply stop on the Oregon Trail, and for a while it saw heavy usage from not only emigrants, but also Indians, the US Army, the Pony Express, and the Overland Stage. It was purchased by the Mormons in the 1850s to support the Mormon pioneers who were passing through and became an army outpost in 1858. It remained so until the army abandoned it in 1890, and the buildings were thus in serious decline when Ike and the Convoy camped in the "beautiful oasis." But historic preservation began in the 1930s, and the site remains a historic crossroads where the Oregon trail, California trail, Mormon trail, Pony Express route, Overland Stage route, and Lincoln Highway all passed through.

A portion of the old fort, including the Commanding Officer's house, was purchased by Margaret Rochford. She lived in the house with her family and rented out extra rooms to travelers. But when traffic on the Lincoln Highway began to increase dramatically, she built the Black and Orange cabins in 1926 to house travelers. This is something I saw all along the route: in the years immediately after the Convoy's trip, tourist cabins and motor courts began to spring up all along the Lincoln Highway.

William A. Carter was a shopkeeper who traveled with the US army. When he wound up at Fort Bridger he decided to stay put, became a judge, and through clever trading with the army and local suppliers, eventually became Wyoming's first millionaire. He had high aspirations for his family, and in 1860 established the first schoolhouse in Wyoming at Fort Bridger for the use of his six children and other children in the fort. He imported experienced teachers from back East, and the school was so successful that graduates were accepted into several colleges in the East without further requirements. The school is still standing today, after some renovations, and Ike and the Convoy would have bivouacked within walking distance of it.

On their final full day in Wyoming, the Convoy drove the thirty-five miles from Fort Bridger to Evanston in 7.5 hours. Just an average day for this part of the trip. Elwell Jackson: "proceeded through canyons. . .negotiated about 8 miles of grades up to 12 percent. . .Excessive dust. . .Engineers repaired or reinforced five bridges and three culverts."

I was grateful to once again escape I-80 and follow the Convoy's route over a steep and winding gravel road. I passed by the site of an old gas station, built shortly after the Convoy but now abandoned, by the boilers, a series of hot springs right by the road, and by Eagle Rock, so named because it is a favorite roosting spot for Bald Eagles. Eagle Rock also served as a convenient landmark for early travelers on the Lincoln Highway, and shortly beyond the road leads into Evanston.

Historic preservation is clearly a big priority in Evanston. In addition to the Chinese Joss House, the city has done a great job of restoring the historic railroad roundhouse and depot square, as well as a long row of nineteenth-century buildings along Front Street, which is the original Lincoln Highway that Ike and the Convoy passed along. I mentioned this to one of the librarians, and she said it all started with just a few people who were determined to preserve and renovate, and it all grew from there. Nowadays,

Evanston has a Preservation Ball every year that raises money for ongoing and new projects. As I wandered around, I saw kids working in flower beds at downtown street corners. I visited the Chinese garden with its gazebo and the excellent museum in the old Carnegie Library built in 1906. And finally, I stumbled across archeological excavations underway in old Chinatown. I went away impressed with Evanston and its determination to maintain an attractive city and its links with its past.

Elwell Jackson on August 17, "Departed Evanston 12:30 p.m. Militor towing Class B Machine Shop." Headed toward Utah.

UTAH

"They left camp to wander along the terraces, into the aspen ravines, under the gleaming walls. . .to the grand archway over the entrance to the valley. . .Wild flowers sprungupeverywhere,swayingwiththelengtheninggrass."

—Zane Grey

U tah is renowned for striking landscapes, and I saw it right away. Just over the state line I fled the interstate and got onto Echo Canyon Road, part of the original Lincoln Highway and the exact route that the Convoy followed. Except for a worn and scraggly layer of asphalt, the road hasn't changed much since 1919. There were towering steep cliffs to my right, and a sharp slope downward to Echo Canyon Creek to my left. The Utah Lincoln Highway Association has done a great job of placing markers at noteworthy sites, mostly natural features with names like Steamboat Rock, Death's Rock, Jack in the Pulpit, and Castle Rock, which was listed as a town of twenty persons with meals, lodgings, gas, oil, telephone and post office in the 1915 *Lincoln Highway Association Guide.*

My favorite was Billboard Bluff, a smooth rock face protected by a long overhanging shelf of solid sandstone, on which was painted in huge letters still visible today "Plantation Bitters." It was one of the first billboards in the West, originally painted in 1869, touting a new miracle painkilling medicine that turned out to be 33 percent rum. Ike and the Convoy would have seen it as they drove past fifty years after it was first painted, and when I stopped off to take a look, the sign was still visible and sharp after so many re-paintings over almost 150 years.

The 1915 Lincoln Highway Association guide reported, "Between the Wyoming line and Salt Lake City via Echo Canyon. . .the roads will be found to range from fair to excellent." Sounds good, but alas, the Convoy had a different experience. On August 17, 1919, Elwell Jackson wrote, "Departed Evanston 12:30 p.m. Traversed worst road in Utah entire distance through

Echo Canyon on rough trail at natural grade, with many d angerous (sic) turns, deep cuts and cliffs on left of road, total decent(sic) of 1000'." The challenging road apparently flummoxed Elwell Jackson into making uncharacteristic typographical errors. The Convoy eventually scraped into the tiny town of Echo, having made forty-one miles in seven hours.

I drove on down Echo Canyon Road, loving the scenery and stopping every five minutes just to get out of my car and wander around aimlessly. I drove two hours just to cover ten miles, no other cars in sight. Out of the car and walking, I scrambled upwards over loose sandstone chunks, slipping sometimes and the rocks dribbling down behind me. I peered up at the towering red bluffs, glowing impossibly in the harsh sunlight—flat, smooth rock faces and then suddenly crags jutting crazily outward. Every now and then a lonesome little pine grove appeared, each one looking somehow cool even before I reached it.

This trail was blazed by Native Americans in hot pursuit of herds of bison— they rode through the canyon bottom for centuries. In 1847 Brigham Young led Mormon settlers through Echo Canyon, and thousands of Mormons followed his trail over the next couple of decades, many of them hauling handcarts on foot. The Pony Express stampeded through in 1860-1861. In the mid-nineteenth century the first explorers, trappers, and gold-seekers came along, and eventually the Union Pacific Railroad rolled through in 1869. The "Plantation Bitters" sign was painted expressly for UP passengers. The town of Echo was settled in 1854, and I found the tourist brochure story of its growth with the railroad very telling: "Echo remained a quiet little town until the Union Pacific Railroad was being built, when. . .saloons and brothels sprung up everywhere."

I drove onward into the now barely-there town of Echo where I parked again and walked around. There are several landmarks in Echo that have a long history as iconic stops on the Lincoln Highway. Brian Butko writes, "The Kozy Café & Motel has served travelers for decades." A vintage gas station was right next door. Alas, it was closed and abandoned, weeds growing up all around, no sign of people or vehicles. I walked around and took photos, and down into the town I didn't see any signs of people either, just forlorn old buildings, seeming to waver in the harsh sunlight, ready to collapse. No cars came by until, after forty minutes, a camper with Pennsylvania plates pulled up and stopped. An older couple got out, and the lady, who I later learned was Betty, said "Jeez, Louise. This looks like a ghost town about to happen."

I said, "This used to be a big stopping point on the Lincoln Highway. All falling apart now."

It turned out that neither Betty nor Hank (her husband) had heard of the Lincoln Highway. So I filled them in on some of the history and the story of the Transcontinental Convoy. "That's neat," said Betty. "Never heard of any of that. But sure is falling apart in a heap. Right here, right now. Great photos."

Betty had two Nikons strapped around her neck, and she hurried around to the side of the Kozy Café to get the sun at her back and started shooting. Hank volunteered, "Just retired last December. State Farm Insurance. Forty years. This is our big cross-country trip, something we've been dreamin' about for years."

I traipsed around a bit, reflecting on the thousands of Lincoln Highway travelers who had stopped for gas or refreshments at the Kozy Café. Lemon ice box pie. Fresh coffee. Or spent the night, a safe rest at the Kozy Motel. All finished now, just flaking paint and sprouting weeds. Way down at the north edge of Echo, I suddenly saw a pickup truck moving out of a driveway and onto the highway, heading north — the only other movement in Echo.

From Echo I backtracked slightly to the Visitor Information Center on I-80 to look for maps and get some information about roads west of Salt Lake City. Back in 1919 the Convoy had taken a newly marked shortcut south of the lake and across the desert that was called the Seiberling Cutoff, named after Frank Seiberling, Chief Executive of the Goodyear Company and President of the Lincoln Highway Association at the time of the Convoy. The same route later was called the Goodyear Cutoff. I would have preferred to follow that route, which is still unpaved, but it now lies within the US Military's Dugway Proving Ground and is strictly off-limits. So, I decided to take the older route that ran farther south, now just outside the Dugway Proving Ground perimeter. This is the route Henry Joy had taken on his cross-country Lincoln Highway trip in 1915. But it's a very isolated route nowadays, meriting just a dotted line on the official Utah state map, running some 180 miles across wide-open empty, blowing desert. I was curious about the condition of the road.

The friendly ladies at the Information Center didn't have much information on this route. "Not many people go way out there anymore," said one. "You might see a few folks in off-road vehicles. Maybe."

"Some of them go out there to see the wild horses," said another. "Or pronghorns. But it's pretty much real empty."

They did not have any maps or any specific information on the road conditions but cautioned that if it rained the road would probably turn into "a real big mess."

An older man in a Colorado Rockies t-shirt had been flipping through tourist brochures nearby, and he chimed in. "I drove through that stretch once in a four-wheel drive Jeep," he said. "Few years ago. Ran across a fellow in a sedan that had two flat tires. He'd changed one, but then the damned spare went flat too. Lotta sharp rocks out there. He'd been waiting six hours, said I was the first person to come along. No cell phone reception way out there. But I couldn't help him none cause my spare wouldn't fit, and I didn't have a repair kit. So I just gave him a coupla Snickers bars and some water and promised to call Triple A in another five or six hours, once I reached Ibapah."

I stood there at the counter for a moment, digesting this glum offering without saying anything. Perhaps he saw that, after his friendly contribution, I was having a few qualms, so he quickly added, "But don't worry about a thing. No way! You'll do fine."

Thus fortified, I returned to Echo and headed northwest toward Morgan. Nowadays the route leads right up through Morgan's Main Street, the same route that the Convoy took a century ago. Past the nineteenth-century City Hall and old church, buildings Ike and the Convoy passed right by. The town is nowadays known as the location where the movie *Troll* 2 was filmed, but back in 1919, it was best known as the site of the Morgan Pea Cannery, the largest in the West.

The Convoy continued onward into Morgan, where a grand welcome awaited them. Elwell Jackson: "Female Relief Society of the Mormon Church served refreshments. Bishop Anderson of Mormon Church made address of welcome and presented Expeditionary Commander with two 4' keys – gold, to Utah; and silver to Morgan. Massed school children with flags and band furnished music. 6 boxes famous Morgan canned peas presented to Convoy for mess."

The Convoy edged onward toward Ogden, negotiating a string of steep grades and sharp curves. Elwell Jackson, always economical with words, reports "considerable dust and no wind caused much inconvenience."

A short distance beyond Echo the road curves sharply to the West and passes Devil's Slide. Alice Ramsey passed by here in 1909 and wrote,

> We had heard Devil's Slide mentioned and were curious to see it. . .Beside our road was a mountain. Descending its steep side were two vertical parallel ridges of solid stone ten or twelve feet high and not too many feet apart. The declivity was terrific. It would have made more of a drop than a slide for the

aforementioned Devil. . .I believe I should have felt a bit sorry for (the devil) if he had had to slide down it. . .So all-by-itself and so stupendous.

Ramsey was off a bit in her estimation of the height of the sides, which are actually closer to 30 feet high. Although the Convoy passed right by the Devil's Slide on the same road that Alice Ramsey negotiated, and which I took a century later, Elwell Jackson makes no mention of it. Today, there is a small scenic outlook stop on the north side of the highway right after the curve, with a last-minute sign. I slammed on the brakes abruptly and steered over to take a look at the Slide on the other side of the highway. It's a startlingly high slide, with a crazy steep angle and almost perfectly parallel sides all the way down to the road. While I stood there on the empty stop, cars and trucks both accelerated past around the curve and up the hill, and all the fumes wafted back down in my face. The Devil's Slide deserves better.

The Convoy reached Ogden at 4:30 p.m. on August 18 and enjoyed a gala reception and parade through the town on the way to their campsite in Loren Farr Park in north Ogden. The headline of the August 19 edition of the *Ogden Examiner* reads, "Ogden Greets Transcontinental Motor Transport with Open Arms: Personnel and Officers Shake Dust of Wyoming Desert and Accept Hospitality of City." The accompanying article notes, "Ladies of the Ogden Red Cross Canteen, in their natty uniforms of blue, supplied the personnel of the Convoy with watermelons, ice cream, cantaloupes, and fruits."

This same edition of the *Ogden Examiner* also headlines an evening banquet hosted by Ogden officials and business leaders at the Weber Club for Colonel McClure and the Convoy's officers. The *Examiner* reports that, as happened so often across the country, "though primarily intended as a banquet of honor to the visiting Army men, the banquet developed into an enthusiastic Good Roads meeting." After an increasingly exuberant round of speeches, the assembled crowd went on record in favor of "a system, north and south, east and west, of hard-surfaced national highways." They also went on record urging that one billion dollars (a huge sum in those days) be allocated for construction of the highway system. The crowd endorsed the text of telegrams supporting these views that were quickly sent to Secretary of War Newton Baker, and Utah's congressional representatives and senators.

Next day, wandering around aimlessly in downtown Ogden, I passed a few storefronts:

Jack and Jill's – Intimate Apparel
Blood and Ink Tattoo Parlor
Pawn and Loan – Payroll Checks Cashed

At the latter, the parking lot was packed.

There were plenty of historic buildings in Ogden, buildings that Ike and the Convoy passed by and that I inspected up close—the library, the Smyth mansion, Peery's Egyptian Theater, Union Station with beautiful huge murals at both ends of the grand hall. I read about the placing of a historic marker for the Convoy at the east side of City Hall Park, and so I went searching for that. But it was nowhere to be found, and everyone I asked had no information. This would have been the only historic marker for the Convoy between the White House and the trip's end point in San Francisco. But at some point the road was widened from two lanes to six, and alas, the monument was lost to history.

Just south of Ogden an unforeseen calamity: the Militor, the single all-purpose, go-to vehicle that could always be counted on to winch out and free any vehicle that was stuck, was itself stuck. Elwell Jackson reports "Class B broke through the surface crust, and the Militor, in trying to pull it out, also broke through and was buried in soft mud to a depth of about 4.5'. About 3 hrs. were required to extricate the Militor. A steel cable was broken several times."

But once again, there was a grand welcome awaiting them ahead. "Convoy escorted into Salt Lake City by Reception Comm. and followed by parade of several hundred commercial trucks, with two bands and blowing whistles. . .Large purple and white floral motor truck presented Expeditionary Commander. Dinner–dance at Hotel Utah Roof Garden." I walked by the former Hotel Utah, a still grandiose structure that nowadays is the Joseph Smith Memorial Office Building.

Anticipating the Convoy's imminent arrival, the Sunday August 17 issue of the *Salt Lake Tribune* featured an entire special "Automobile Section." In addition to the usual details about the Convoy—"Giant Caravan Due to Arrive Here Tuesday!"—there was a long article headlined "Ship by Truck Time Now Here." The article links the arrival of the Convoy with the Ship by Truck movement and exults that the Convoy "established beyond doubt the utility of the truck. . .and the vital importance of improved highways." On the same subject, Salt Lake City's *Desert Evening News* reports, "With the arrival here today of army motor transport Convoy, 'ship by truck' will be the legend of. . .trucks participating in the big parade to welcome the Convoy here. . ..'Ship by Truck' is the great taproot of America's transportation system."

Separately, the August 17 issue of the *Salt Lake Tribune* carried the following quarter-page ad:

Liberty Theater
Are You Fit to Marry?
Women Only – Wednesday, Thursday, and Friday
Men Only – Saturday and Sunday
Positively No Mixed Attendance
Revealing for the First Time Life's Darkest Secrets to All Humanity
Scenes of Realism That Stagger the Imagination
Never Before Seen By The Human Eye

This piqued my curiosity, but alas, the film is nowhere available on the internet. Lost in the dustbin of history.

I spent a couple of hours in the Salt Lake City library, and as always, the librarians went overboard to be helpful. When I was finished and ready to depart, one librarian asked where I was going next. When I told her Pioneer Park, she leaned in close and whispered "Just be careful. There are [*emphasis here*] HOMELESS PEOPLE down there."

Pioneer Park indeed had dozens of HOMELESS PEOPLE, some leaning back against trees, others lounging on sleeping bags, and others bending in to figure out how much cash they had left. I walked up to a man sprawled out on a straw mat.

"Hey, how you doing?" I asked.

"Okay. You?"

"You from Salt Lake?"

"Naw. I'm from Tulsa. Came out here 'bout eight years ago."

"You like it here?"

"Like it?" He sat up straight and peered in at me very directly. "Like it? I'm sittin' here on my ass in wet, muddy grass, ain't had nothin' to eat or drink for a day, and you askin' me if I like it? What the fuck?"

"Sorry. I've got a bottle of water here. You want some water?"

"Water!? You think it's fuckin' water I want to drink!? What the motherfuckin' fuck!?"

I walked onward. After Pioneer Park I meandered around the Temple District for an hour, fascinated by the groups congregating there. Koreans, Tanzanians, Paraguayans—all there to worship in the highest temple of the Mormon faith. I stopped off at the statue of Brigham Young, which is inexplicably situated so that his back is to the Temple, and his right hand is pointing across the street at the Zion Bank. Nearby is the Beehive House, designed by Truman Angell, who also designed the Temple, and right next to that is Lion House, Brigham Young's home. It features twenty gables with windows on the second floor—all small, solitary rooms for children and childless wives.

I finally walked into the Temple, aiming to just poke around anonymously in the corners, but soon discovered a group of young tour guides that promptly latched on to every single person who entered. I wasn't inside more than twenty seconds before a young woman with a heavy Slavic accent, named Tanja, came up to me. "Please, you like to see Temple? I like to show you around. So much to see!"

On an enthusiasm scale from one to ten, Tanja came in at about fifty-three. With every recited fact she smiled ecstatically, clapped her hands together, and exerted a mighty effort to avoid jumping straight up into the air.

"The pipe organ!" she exhorted. "Can you guess how many pipes are being in this organ!? Please try to guess!!" Hands clapping together all the while, and up and down on her toes.

I had no earthly idea, so I just launched "Maybe around two hundred?"

"Two hundred?! Two hundred?!" she exulted. "No, no, no. In this pipe organ there are being 11,623 pipes!!! Can you believe it? 11,623!!!" She bounced up and down, preparing for take-off.

I somehow managed to slip a couple of words into the midst of her avalanche. "So, are you a student?"

"I am being missionary. One year. I already graduate Brigham Young. Listen – I tell you about the acoustics here. So good!!! Because this room shaped like human mouth!! Unbelievable!! You see? Curving on the top just like human mouth, so sound is going out so perfectly. Beautiful, yes?!!!"

Although I felt mean-spirited about it almost immediately afterwards, I couldn't resist asking Tanja, "So that statue of Brigham Young outside? Why is he pointing at the bank, instead of the Temple?"

Tanja paused for about two nanoseconds, and then said, "I am thinking this thing does not matter so much." And then hurtled onward: "Do you know about lighting? It is so amazing!!! I will tell you!!!"

Later, wandering around downtown near the Temple complex and beyond, I passed multiple pawnshops and tattoo parlors. Scallywags Bar. A sign in a shop window:

We Fix Baggy Eyelids!
Proof the Bible is True!

I marveled at the contrasts from one block to another. Sometimes even within one block. A boarded up weed-covered house next to a spotless white clapboard house with manicured lawn and flowering azaleas. Three homeless people all in one block, asking for loose change. But then an old parking meter, with the sign:

Don't Give to Panhandlers!
Donate to a Better Cause

The meter's slot was open for contributions that would, the sign assured, go to support homeless shelters for all.

I eventually made it over to the State Capitol and wandered around the lush manicured grounds. There were numerous statues of famous Utah natives, including Daniel Cowing Jackling, a copper mining magnate; Marriner Stoddard Eccles, Chairman of the Federal Reserve Board; and Martha Hughes Cannon, a doctor, women's rights advocate, and state senator. Inside, I found a statue of Philo Farnsworth, who is named as the inventor of television, although he held over 300 patents in a wide variety of fields, including nuclear fusion. Back outside and over to the west I encountered some dozen members of Falun Gong, playing recorded music, holding signs, and handing out literature to anyone who happened to wander within reach. I went back to my Chevy and headed south.

Billboard ad near Salt Lake City:

Five Wives Vodka!
Made in Utah!

And another:

Utah! Don't Be Blind to our Opioid Crisis!
Stop the Opidemic!

And another:

First Class Cars
Bad Credit? No Credit?
We Finance Everyone!

And finally:

We Fix Bulges
And Love Handles too!

In the suburb of Murray, I tracked down the first-ever Kentucky Fried Chicken franchise, opened back in 1952. There's a bronze life-size statue out to the side: Colonel Sanders next to the original franchisee, Tom Harman. Inside, amidst the current-day customers chowing down on crispy chicken legs and coleslaw, are a range of displays including an original Colonel Sanders white suit, several KFC signs from the mid-1950s, and a glass chicken bucket. There's another huge red and white striped bucket outside. Nowadays there are some 20,000 KFC restaurants in 123 countries serving 12 million customers per day, but it all started right down there in little Murray, Utah.

Driving down toward Tooele, a billboard that appeared several times:

Showgirls:
Southern X-posure

The Convoy departed Salt Lake City on August 20 and was in for a long and tiresome day. In addition to a lengthy litany of mechanical breakdowns, Elwell Jackson also writes that the road "was natural desert trail of alkali dust and fine sand up to 2' deep, with numerous chuck holes. No rain for 18 weeks and traction exceedingly difficult. In places chasses of trucks grounded on road surface leaving wheels free, making jacking up and digging out necessary. Sage brush was cut from desert to fill in wheel ruts." The Convoy finally straggled into Orr's Ranch at 10:30 p.m., having covered fifty-two miles in seventeen hours.

I departed Salt Lake City in the early pre-dawn hours, with a long day's drive ahead. I passed quickly through Tooele, site of an early twentieth-century smelter, and a World War II ordnance depot, with historic nineteenth-century buildings lining Main Street. I passed the Ritz Theatre, still showing films. I was still feeling a bit uneasy about the hours-long lonely crossing through the desert, especially after the woeful story from the man at the Visitor's Center. By the time I reached Tooele it was 8:00 a.m., and I phoned Jay Banta.

Jay had been recommended to me by Brian Butko as an extremely reliable source of information on the history of the Lincoln Highway and the current condition of the road in Utah. Jay worked for years as manager of the Fish Springs National Wildlife Refuge down at the southern end of the route and is a decades-long member of the Lincoln Highway Association. Once I got through to him, he was friendly and reassuring. "Don't worry, I've driven that road several times, and it's really not too bad. If you just take your time and are careful, you won't have any problems." But then he added, "Of course, if it rains, you need to just find a high spot and stop. Don't try to drive. Once that soil turns to mud—forget it."

I felt better after talking to Jay. At the last chance gas station in Tooele I filled up and was pleased to see there were no clouds in the sky. I drove on southwest, through hills with scattered pine trees and dust blowing from all sides in a relentless wind. I passed a cowboy in a ten-gallon hat, mounted on an appaloosa horse, way out on the wide-open plain, talking on a cell phone and gesticulating with his free hand. Over Fisher Pass, named for Carl Fisher in part because he had donated money for the road's construction and argued in favor of this route being included as part of the Lincoln Highway. No other cars anywhere. Empty, blowing space.

Zane Grey's classic Western *Riders of the Purple Sage* is the most renowned Utah novel, set in the barren canyonlands of southern Utah in the 1870s. It was written in 1912 and was one of America's most popular novels at the time of the Convoy. Many classic Westerns suffer from weak or cliché female characters (the prim and proper Eastern schoolmarm, the kind-hearted prostitute), but *Riders of the Purple Sage* features a fully-rounded female main character in Jane Withersteen, who can ride as well as any man, manage her own ranch, and does not back down to anyone. But she comes under relentless pressure to marry by the Mormon Church, and eventually the mounting harassment causes her to flee with her trusty cowhand, Lassiter, who famously says, "Where I was raised a woman's word was law. I ain't quite outgrowed that yet." At least some members of the Convoy would have certainly read Grey's novel before they passed through Utah.

I arrived at Dugway and the entrance to a top-secret US military base. There were signs posted along the chain link fence:

"Absolutely No Trespassing Use of Deadly Force Authorized!"

I had hoped to track down Orr's Ranch, where the Convoy and hundreds of other Lincoln Highway travelers over the years had stopped. But I had some-how missed the ranch driving down through the rocky hills and gray sand, and the guards at the Dugway entrance said only, "This base is off-limits, sir. You cannot enter." They claimed they had never heard of Orr's Ranch.

After this I backtracked for several miles and eventually came across a classically well-built farmhouse about 500 yards off the road. I drove up and knocked on the front door, somewhat fearful that I would be offending some-one inside with a disturbance so early on a Saturday morning. But a friendly fortyish-looking woman came to the door and immediately set me at ease. "Hey! Hi! What you lookin' for?" When I said Orr's Ranch, she was ready. "Yeah, close by. Down that road over there." Waved her left arm way out to the side. "Then left, then right, then another left. Gravel, then dirt. Look for the two birch trees. Little ways past there and you're at Orr's."

I followed her directions and found myself at Orr's Ranch. Orr's Ranch was established in 1890, and the 1916 Lincoln Highway Guide describes it as, "Excellent ranch meals and lodging. Gas 45 cents. Drinking water." But when I was there, Orr's Ranch was abandoned. Weeds growing up everywhere, and the roof of a building seen in photos from the Convoy's trip? Caving in. There was a Lincoln Highway column out to the side, but it was leaning at a 30-degree angle with weeds nearing the top. The only sign of habitation: way over to the side there were two ferocious-looking German Shepherds, both on neck leashes, howling and lurching and longing to rip into my legs. At the entrance there was a rickety gate crumpled way over to the side, with "Orr's Ranch" letters on the top. And a brand-new archway sign over the entrance: "Ensign Ranches." I later learned that Ensign Ranches is a company that specializes in free-range hunting of antelope and other species.

The MVP Militor had suffered some damage in the previous days, but those had by and large been repaired by August 20. Nonetheless, Colonel McClure ordered the Militor to return to Salt Lake City for further repairs, with the hope that it could rejoin the Convoy later in central Nevada. Elwell Jackson, in a rare display of strong feelings, disagreed vehemently with this decision and wrote on August 21: "Expeditionary Commander ordered Militor to return to Salt Lake City. . .this action entirely unwarranted."

From Orr's Ranch westward the Convoy encountered some of the toughest going of the entire trip. About this stretch of the trip, Ike later wrote, "From Orr's Ranch, Utah, to Carson City, Nevada, the road is one succession of dust, ruts, pits, and holes. This stretch was not improved in any way and consisted only of a track across the desert."

Elwell Jackson reports on August 21: "First portion of Seiberling Cutoff under construction and impassable. Detour necessary on salt marsh with thin, hard crust of sand and crystallized alkali. Practically every vehicle was mired, and rescue work required almost superhuman efforts of entire personnel from 2:00 p.m. until after midnight. Made 15 miles in 7.5 hours."

Captain William Greany, in his final report, chronicles "the most arduous and heroic effort in rescuing the entire Convoy from impending disaster on the quicksands of the Salt Lake Desert."

The Convoy camped for the night at Granite Rock, which sounds nice but in fact is merely a name for a solitary natural feature in the middle of the empty desert. This may have been the low point of the entire trip. Elwell Jackson: "Unexpected delay on desert caused serious situation regarding water and gasoline. Tanks were placed under guard and water ration limited to one cup for supper and overnight. Stalling of fuel truck prevented a cooked dinner. Supper consisted of cold baked beans and hard bread, mere existence being chief concern. Impossible to distribute baggage and personnel obliged to sleep wherever they could. . ..personnel utterly exhausted by tremendous efforts."

The fuel and water shortages were eventually resolved by sending a gasoline tanker ahead and by utilizing a horse team provided by Utah State Highway Commission to haul water from a source twelve miles distant. But the difficulties surely weighed on the Convoy's personnel as they contemplated what else might lie ahead. Never a spendthrift with words, Elwell Jackson merely writes, "Reduced morale."

I pushed off from Dugway, onto a gravel and dirt road, starting off right along the southern perimeter of the military base. But within minutes I was on a minimal dusty road, out of sight of the Dugway fence, bouncing on through empty desert. Thick, gray dust billowing up behind me. There was a huge boulder out to the north, with "Dave + Carla" painted on the side. Later, a single pronghorn to the left, and then, half an hour later, wild horses to the left, moving away. Black smoke rising up to the right where there looked to be a grass fire. Suddenly an off-road vehicle approaching me. I stopped and waved, but he just rumbled by. But then another, and this time the driver stopped.

"Hey, how you doing?" he asked. "You going far?" I later learned his name was Patrick.

"All the way through," I said. "Nevada."

"Whoa! Get out!"

"Road OK?"

"Yeah. OK, I guess. We're just out here looking for wild horses and prong-horns." There was a young woman with a Canon and a long lens next to him. "Saw some, but that grass fire scared 'em off. Gone down south," he said, pointing out to my left.

"Big fire?" I asked. I had seen the smoke and black charred grasslands in the distance.

"Enough to scare all them horses up into them hills over there. That's for damn sure."

Patrick drove on, back toward Tooele, and I continued down the hills toward the plumes of black smoke and the empty desert, yawning all the way across to the Nevada state line. Another "Dave + Carla" on a boulder. The grass fire smoldered, a black expanse of grass and dark smoke wafting up, but no flames. I crossed over a rock-strewn hill and lost sight of the fire. A lone wild horse, standing way over to the south. Didn't see another vehicle for the next seven hours, when I finally made it through to Ibapah.

On the way to Ibapah I stopped off at the Fish Springs National Wildlife Refuge headquarters, where Jay Banta had worked for years. But there was nobody there on a Saturday. So I took some time to meander around, down toward the springs where there is still water, and then on to the site of Thomas Ranch, which had been a station both on the Pony Express and the Wells Fargo stagecoach run.

John Thomas is a legendary figure in Lincoln Highway lore. The 1915 Lincoln Highway Association Guide says, "If trouble is experienced, build a sage brush fire. Mr. Thomas will come with a team. He can see you for 20 miles off." Although I never found any documentary evidence, it is widely believed that Thomas flooded the road on purpose to support what was a money-making enterprise. When he met stuck motorists with his two-horse team, he would immediately announce his price for pulling the car out to high, dry ground. According to Hokanson, "Usually a dollar a foot. He'd silently listen to the driver argue for a few minutes, then raise the price to two dollars. Smart travelers shut up and paid the fee – the longer one argued, the higher the price."

Thomas also sold gasoline, which he hauled in with his horse team all the way from Ibapah, and offered meals on a sporadic basis. When Alice Ramsey passed by in 1909, she and her companions were offered a meal of dry cereal, canned tomatoes, and coffee. "I'm sure I shuddered," she writes. "Maybe the others shuddered too!"

There's not much left of Thomas Ranch nowadays, just the hint of a foundation lurking down in the spongy grass. But the setting is still beautiful with the flowing spring, standing water filled with waving green reeds, sagebrush, and a handful of poplar and pinyon trees. And a solitary Lincoln Highway pillar, planted proudly right there in the middle.

I drove on through the empty desert. Not much of a road, but I could just follow the tire tracks. Huge, long views, and the thin, gray dust spiraling up. At a certain point, after Fish Springs but before Callao, along the Pony Express trail, I pulled over and got out to walk.

This was like what I had experienced before, in Wyoming, Nebraska, Iowa. That moment of emptiness, and total, complete, almost overwhelming silence. Did Ike ever experience this on his trip? For me, that utter silence, that astounding long view, that overwhelming cloudless sky, were all transfixing. A moment of reflection and a moment of amazement.

It was late afternoon, so I drove on through Callao and Gold Hill, way up at nearly 6,000 feet. Both now ghost towns, but with beautiful aging buildings still standing. In Callao the one-room schoolhouse and the Kearney Hotel, sitting forlornly out in the dust. Gold Hill was close to the spot where the Goodyear Cutoff rejoined the highway, and it had an ancient but still sturdy Mercantile Store proudly established at the east entrance.

I finally made it through to Ibapah, where I saw some other people. The Ibapah Trading Post, with a big Royal Crown Cola thermometer and sign, right out front. It was almost disorienting, after all those hours, to drive into town on the slate-gray, dusty road and then suddenly see a pickup truck headed right toward me. As we approached, I waved madly, but the driver of the pickup just looked straight ahead and motored on. I did manage to catch that he was wearing a Los Angeles Dodgers cap. I filled up with gas, credit card auto-fill-up, with no actual human beings in sight. Only station for miles. I drove around an empty town, crumbling few houses. Weeds and wind. And then pushed onward toward Nevada.

The Convoy ground on throughout August 22, covering thirty-six miles in seven and a half hours, and they finally made it to Black Point. Another solitary landmark in the open desert, but at least it was near the end of the Goodyear Cutoff. On August 23 the Convoy soldiered on westward toward the Nevada state line, passing through the tiny towns of Gold Hill and Ibapah. But it was a terrible day for mechanical breakdowns: "hole punched in crank case," "connecting rod cap loose," "connecting road crack(ed) through eye for wrist pin," "piston forced upward through top of cylinder block," "broke valve spring," "wheel work(ed) loose," "carburetor trouble on account dust," "spare parts truck turn(ed) over." Because of these difficulties the Convoy gradually spread out over tens of miles, as some vehicles pushed ahead and others languished awaiting repairs. But, at some point, the entire Convoy crossed the probably unmarked Utah/Nevada state line. The main part of the Convoy made it to Anderson's Ranch, Nevada, at 8:00 p.m., having covered fifty-one miles in thirteen and a half hours. And everyone else camped for the night under the stars, somewhere out there in the wide-open empty spaces of eastern Nevada.

NEVADA

A trip, a safari, an exploration, is an entity, different from all other journeys. We find after years of struggle that we do not take a trip, a trip takes us. . .schedules, reservations. . .dash themselves to wreckage on the personality of the trip.

–John Steinbeck

Once into Nevada, the Convoy passed by Tippet's Ranch and eventually straggled into Anderson's Ranch at 8:00 p.m., having made fifty-one miles in thirteen and a half hours. The following day, the Convoy had to negotiate the precipitous Schellbourne Pass. Of this crossing, Elwell Jackson writes on August 24: "Roads very narrow and continuous sequence of U and S turns at very steep grades, with nearly vertical, unprotected fills dropping hundreds of feet. That this pass was successfully negotiated without accident considered remarkable." But once safely past, there was no slowing down: "Sunday rest period abandoned on account being behind schedule."

I came rumbling over the corrugated dirt and gravel, ashen-colored dust spiraling out behind me, down from the Utah state line and through the Gosiute Indian Reservation. All emptiness. Out in the distance to the south a dust devil spouted up, hundreds of feet high, and then quickly another. Sage brush stretching off to the far horizon. I drove by a lone house trailer next to a raggedy low mesquite tree with weeds all around, the only sign of habitation a DirecTV satellite dish sprouting from the side. Miles later, another lone trailer. No cars, no people. And then, inexplicably, a row of four brand-new GM SUVs, parked neatly out in the desert. No people, no buildings, just the forlorn vehicles standing sentry. Long expansive views to the south, rocky bare mountains far ahead to the west.

I passed by the remains of Tippet's Ranch, where the Convoy had stopped briefly a century earlier. Tippet's was a major stop on the Lincoln Highway for decades, but it was finally shut down in the 1970s. Today it's a lonely dust-covered ruin, the wind whipping through and the sand piling up on the sides. I got out and walked around for a few moments, trying to imagine the busy glory days of Tippet's Ranch all those years earlier. The 1916 Lincoln Highway Guide writes about Tippet: "Pop. 10. Meals, lodging. Campsite. Route marked through County. Extensive road improvement. General Store." I walked all the way around the ruins. The wind whipping through the various cracks and openings of the structures made a high-pitched whistling sound. The tired buildings almost seemed to slump in hopelessness, as though waiting for the first valid excuse to collapse entirely. I drove on, past abandoned Anderson's Ranch and over the same route through Schellbourne Pass. Not much had changed since Ike and the Convoy passed through a century earlier.

Coming down from the pass within minutes I could see a clump of buildings in the distance and then a solitary house off to the right. A pickup pulled out on the road behind, the first vehicle I had seen in hours. Soon I was back on asphalt, headed south toward Ely.

The Convoy eventually limped into Ely and set up "on municipal campgrounds for tourists, adjacent to camp of itinerant Shoshone Indians, who visited camp all afternoon showing keen interest in equipment," according to Elwell Jackson.

The *White Pine News* of August 31, 1919, reports: "A hearty welcome was given the Transport Corps upon its arrival in the city, and the ladies of the local Red Cross soon made the weary soldiers forget the "chow" of the regular service by serving a variety of creations of the culinary art not on the army menu, topped off with cigars and cigarettes galore. . .while the boys were cleaning up and scraping their faces for the evening inspection, many of the young ladies of the city circulated among them and presented the astonished boys with flowers. . . .which will let the people of the far east know that Nevada is not all sage brush."

I reached Ely in the late afternoon and found it somewhat jarring that, after plodding on for hours since Tooele, Utah, through a boundless mostly-empty desert, I was suddenly in a hotel with a packed all-day casino right in the middle of the lobby. There was a little balcony up above the lobby where I ate breakfast and dinner every day, sitting by the edge so I could watch all the gambling and other activity below. (When I write "other activity," I will merely remind you, dear readers, that prostitution is legal in the state of Nevada.)

Already at 8:00 in the morning there were dozens of people on the floor below, milling around, flirting, playing machines with names like "Shadow of the Panther," "Tales of Hercules," or "Moo-Lah," which featured an oversized smiling cow leaning in above players. There was also "Penny Megabucks," which had "1 cent" broadcast all along the top, but only had a slot for dollar bills. A multicolored flashing display showed the ever-growing potential payout, and it grew from $11,514,613.21 to $11,735,297.83 just in the few moments while I watched. Back to the rear, tucked out of view, was a small, shallow swimming pool where kiddos could be safely parked away while Mom and Dad devoted their full and undivided attention to "Early Retirement!," or "Lucky Larry's Lobster Mania!"

From my hotel room in Ely I wandered around the central part of town every morning, past sites like the Old-Fashioned Soda Fountain, and the Loneliest Thrift Store in America. Most mornings I usually wound up sooner or later in the historic Nevada Hotel and casino, where a long row of Harleys was unfailingly parked out front. There were stars in the sidewalk outside just like the Hollywood Walk of Fame. Names like Charlie Pride, Mickey Rooney, Evel Knievel, Harry Reid, Ronald Reagan. Walking around and gawking inside the casino one mid-morning, I met a tall thirtyish blonde woman in a bright red miniskirt. She had been playing a slot machine called "Outback Cashback" but had suddenly, after a particularly depressing kawhump sound, waved her right arm up high and hollered "Fuck!" very loudly. She yanked out a cigarette from her purse, lit it, and took a long draw. She swiveled around and saw me and asked, "You ain't playing today, hon?"

"No, just watching. How about you?"

"I was on that fuckin' heap 'a junk. Fuckin' rust bucket." She took another deep draw. "Lucky smoke now. I'm a thinkin' 'Witches' Riches' next."

"You ever play blackjack?" I asked. It was mid-morning, and the blackjack tables were just opening up.

"Nah, I don't like any of them damned card games. Everybody starin' at you all the time. Starin' at you like, 'What the fuck you gonna do? C'mon.' No time to think." Another long draw. "Just them machines for me. I just come up here for something else to do, cause there sure as hell ain't nothin' to do down where I live."

"You're not from Ely?"

"Ely? Fuck no. People say I'm from the middle of nowhere, but that ain't right. To find my place, you first got to go down there and find you the middle of nowhere. And then you got to ask directions." She slanted her left hip outwards and looked at me in a way that made me think her desire for diversion might extend beyond slot machines.

I yanked out my trusty black notebook and said, "Well, gotta run. Got an interview to do." She didn't say anything but blew out a narrow jet of smoke, spiraling right toward my face.

One morning I backtracked from Ely to the town of McGill, formerly a big copper mining town but now much diminished. But it was home to the McGill Drugstore Museum, with the century-old Rexall sign still hanging out front. The museum was closed, but there was a sign in the window with a phone number to call to get someone to open up. So I called, and that's how I met Dan Braddock.

Dan, an older man with white hair and an infectious grin, arrived full of enthusiasm. "I'm so happy you phoned! I love showing people around here! It's like a time capsule! You won't believe it!" He opened up and ushered me in.

McGill Drugstore was constructed in 1908 during the development of McGill as a company town designed to house the employees of Nevada Consolidated Copper Company. The building was constructed of corrugated steel to make it fireproof, and the drug store had one of the only soda fountains in the area. It was in its heyday when Ike and the Convoy passed right in front in 1919.

"Fellow by the name of Jerry Culbert bought this store way back in the 1930s," Dan explained to me. "McGill Drugstore and Soda Fountain was a focal point of the town until Jerry died in 1979. His widow shut it down then. Hey, come over here and take a look at this." Dan led me over to a low array of wooden cabinets. He opened one and pulled out a tube of Ipana toothpaste from the 1950s. "Jerry never threw away anything," he said. "He had stuff in here from the 1930s when he bought the store. Some stuff even earlier. And once they closed it, nobody else touched anything. Time capsule."

Dan led me around the store, displaying early to mid-twentieth-century items one after another. Geritol, Bryl-Crème, Dippity-Do styling gel, Wild Root Cream Oil. Film cartridges for Kodak Brownie cameras. Ancient greeting cards. Dipping snuff and chewing tobacco. In a card catalog case near the back of the store, Dan showed me medical/prescription drug records from patients dating back to the store's opening, all perfectly arranged in alphabetical order. Dan gave me a detailed look at the soda fountain. "Isn't this thing beautiful?" he said. "Don't see them like this anymore. We've got to get one more part and then it'll be completely restored and working just like it did a century ago."

I departed reflecting on the fact that I had actually just seen and experienced a small slice of something like what Ike and the Convoy would have seen a century ago. And I was thankful for people like Dan Braddock for preserving and caring for this slice. It was something I had seen all across the country. A few people who wanted to hang on to these slices, to nurture them. This insistent urge to protect even a small sliver that could somehow demonstrate to us all: this is what it was like back then.

Early one morning I drove out to the south of Ely to visit the Ward Charcoal Ovens. These elegant thirty-feet high beehive-shaped stone structures were built in the 1870s to produce charcoal for silver smelters at the nearby Ward silver mines. By the 1880s they had already been abandoned, and by the time Ike and the Convoy passed by, the abandoned ovens had earned the reputation of serving as hideouts for bandits. Today the six structures—still perfectly intact—stand alone in a quiet, remote setting below a ridge lined with piñon trees. I wandered about for close to an hour and did not see or hear another human, just the wind whistling through the piñons.

The ovens had been built and operated by Italian stone masons, and this made me think of the numerous wall murals I had seen in Ely, reflecting the historic diversity of the town. Italian stone masons, Basque sheepherders, Greek merchants. There was one mural depicting a Shoshone woman gathering pine nuts. And one grand mural honoring Slovenian, Basque, Italian, Greek, Chinese, and Native American, all together. It was a good reminder of the astonishing diversity that already existed when Ike and the Convoy passed through.

On the way back to Ely I passed the turnoff for Cave Lake State Park. I had read earlier that Cave Lake is the site of the annual Great Bathtub Races, held every August since 2009. The races feature both motorized and non-motorized bathtubs, and from photos I had seen, competing bathtubs are ingeniously modified with devices ranging from oil drum flotation attachments to pedal-powered paddle wheels. Yet another event I regretted having to miss.

The Lincoln Highway heading west from Ely all the way to Carson City Nevada also goes by the name of "The Loneliest Road in America." A *Life* magazine article back in 1986 described this portion of the highway as "The loneliest road in America," claimed this 287-mile stretch had no points of interest, and recommended prospective travelers along this route have "survival skills." But in a stroke of genius, the Nevada State Tourism Department decided to adopt this name as a marketing tool. Today Nevada tourism brochures and other materials loudly proclaim the excitement awaiting travelers on the Loneliest Road, and the state dispenses Loneliest Road paraphernalia ranging from caps to water bottles to t-shirts bragging, "I survived The

Loneliest Road in America." There is even a Loneliest Road pocket-sized survival guide with a list of highlights along the route – if you get each of the highlights checked off, you win a prize from the tourism department.

The Convoy departed Ely on August 25, and Elwell Jackson wrote, "Heavy grades and deep alkali dust. Poor gravel roads. Made 46 miles in 15 ½ hours. Arrived Pinto House Nevada 10 p.m." The 1916 Lincoln Highway Guide's full description of Pinto House is "drinking water, radiator water, campsite." I asked librarians, gas station attendants, waitresses, and others in Ely, Austin, and every spot in between about the precise location of Pinto House, but alas, not a single person had ever heard of Pinto House. So I retraced my route back to the Convoy's campsite in Ely, and then drove precisely 46 miles to see if I could locate the mysterious Pinto House. Voilà! This effort landed me right at an abandoned ruin of a stone house, with two ponies grazing to the rear. There was a beautiful stream flowing nearby and a broad, flat, grassy space that practically screamed, "Camp here!"

Thus convinced that I must have found the ruins of Pinto House, I returned to the Austin library and spoke once again to the friendly librarians. I told them with some enthusiasm that I thought I had discovered Pinto House. But after hearing me out, one librarian, ever circumspect and precise, stroked her chin a couple of times and said, "It is quite possible you are correct. But I am not aware of any other documentary evidence to support this claim."

Okay, that's close enough. I'm convinced that I found Pinto House, where the Convoy camped the night of August 25. Onward!

The Convoy departed Pinto House on August 26, passed briefly through the town of Eureka, and then encountered some heavy going. Elwell Jackson: "About five miles across Alkali flats with dust-filled ruts and chuck holes 1.5 feet deep, necessitating slow and tedious going. Remarkable that all equipment remains serviceable with abuse given." The Convoy made it only forty-four miles in a little over eight hours that day and camped in an isolated spot called Willow Springs, which Elwell Jackson described as "mountainous country of most desolate character." Today, of course, on the perfect asphalt of the Loneliest Road, I could cruise along this stretch at sixty miles per hour with the air-conditioner humming. But I preferred driving with the windows down, and I pulled over and stopped frequently, just to walk around and gaze at the "country of most desolate character"—the wide towering skies, the impossibly long vistas, the subtle hues of the desert rocks and sand, and most of all the absolute stunning silence.

The Convoy had planned to overnight in Eureka but stopped short to remain at Pinto House because of the waning light and concern over driving up the narrow canyon roads leading into Eureka in the darkness. But the trusty Goodyear Band, traveling slightly ahead of the Convoy, made it into Eureka by nightfall. The *Eureka Sentinel* of August 30, 1919, reports: "The band arrived in Eureka Monday afternoon. . .and the people of Eureka had a real musical treat that evening in hearing it render a varied programme of selections in front of the Europa Hotel. . .the social dance that had been arranged by the local Red Cross Chapter in honor of the visiting Convoy was held at the Eureka Theater." The townspeople and the band had a grand old time while the Convoy hunkered down in tents out in the field by Pinto House.

Today, a large billboard at the entrance to Eureka announces: "Welcome to Eureka—the Friendliest Town on the Loneliest Road in America," and the town lived up to this claim during the days I stayed there. Even though Eureka's population is only 610, every single time I walked down Main Street (also the Lincoln Highway and the Loneliest Road) I met somebody with whom I struck up an interesting conversation.

Most of the brick buildings on Main Street were built in the 1880s after fires had destroyed earlier wooden structures. During the mining heyday years of the late nineteenth century, Eureka's population had reached 10,000. According to one person I met, in those days Main Street boasted more than twenty saloons, always a trusty barometer of economic prosperity. But by the time Ike and the Convoy rumbled down Main Street, the town had already gone into a slow but steady decline.

One day, as I was ambling slowly along Main Street, I struck up a conversation with an older man who asked where I was going. I mentioned my interest in history, and the next thing I knew I was getting a personalized guided tour of the courthouse (one of the largest and most ornate in Nevada), the Sentinel Museum (originally site of the *Nevada Sentinel*, one of the state's first newspapers), and the Eureka Opera House. The Opera House was beautifully restored in the 1990s and is now used for a wide variety of events that draw audiences from Eureka and the entire county. When I visited, the lady in charge told me that that evening there would be a piano recital for all elementary and middle school students in the county who were taking piano lessons, and she expected "a pretty good crowd."

My meanderings eventually brought me by the Bartine Outhouse, billed as the only five-hole outhouse in Nevada. The outhouse was built by Frederic

Bartine, who immigrated to Nevada from Finland in the early 1900s and was a successful businessman, running the Ruby Hill Water Works, the Bartine Ranch, and the Bartine service station. The outhouse was built for his family's use but moved to its prime location on Main Street after his death.

I couldn't help but wonder about the underlying motivation for constructing a family five-hole outhouse. No family member could accuse another of hogging the bathroom. Each family member could have his/her individualized toilet seat. Perhaps Bartine's familiarity with the intimate coziness of Finnish saunas led him into a quixotic effort to extend that concept to the Nevada outhouse. Who knows?

On the way out of Eureka I passed a store with the sign:

Antiques!
Old Stuff!
Eurekatiques!

The Convoy drove on from Willow Springs and made it into Austin on August 27 with the usual panoply of mechanical mishaps. Perhaps most noteworthy was this entry: "Trailmobile kitchen overturned on very steep grade, was wrecked and retired from service." But otherwise Elwell Jackson notes that "roads generally fair," and the Convoy moved at an above-average clip of sixty miles in eight hours.

I happened upon an off-the-beaten-track bed & breakfast out in the desert southwest of Austin. The proprietor and host, Donna Sossa, told me that she and her late husband, Bob, had lived in Cleveland but always planned to move to "the wide-open spaces" after his retirement from a long career at the *Cleveland Plain Dealer*. Donna said they bought 160 acres of land sight unseen, designed their dream house (a true-to-life replica of a medieval castle), and started acquiring building materials all while still in Cleveland. "So you knew a lot about construction?" I asked. "Didn't know anything," she said. "We just decided we'd figure it out as we went along."

So Donna and Bob loaded four containers full of their possessions, building materials for the castle, and farm animals, and moved with the entire caboodle from Cleveland out to their new 160-acre spread in central Nevada. They had the foundation and I-beam frame of the castle done by local contractors, but built the remainder of the building themselves, all the way down to kitchen cabinets, tile floors, plaster, plumbing, and electricity.

Bob passed away in 2015, and shortly thereafter Donna officially opened the Paradise Ranch Castle Bed & Breakfast.

The Paradise Ranch Castle is indeed an unmistakable replica of a medieval castle: two stories of painted stucco the color of granite with square towers at each corner, simulated gun turrets, a full functional basement that Donna called the dungeon, and a flat roof that provides great stargazing at night. With virtually no light pollution, the Milky Way was spectacular for the two nights that I stayed there. I went out for a walk at sunrise one morning and saw that her nearest neighbor is at least two miles distant, the house just barely visible across the flatland. There were jackrabbits everywhere, and several pronghorns grazed peacefully, not paying much attention to me until I came within fifty yards and they trotted away.

Out back Donna had parked two sedans, a four-wheel drive SUV, a pickup truck, and a bulldozer/backhoe. To my query as to whether she drove all these vehicles, she said, "Of course I do. What else would I do with them? Used to have a snowplow too, but I gave that to a neighbor in exchange for him promising to plow my road whenever it snowed." Donna also had thriving flower beds and a vegetable garden, but she said prairie dogs were wreaking havoc on all the gardens by tunneling underneath. "I had a guest who said he was a good shot, so I gave him my twenty-gauge and told him to go to town on those prairie dogs. He shot twelve one morning before breakfast. Didn't even make a dent." She spread her arms out wide, and said, "the Great Basin of Nevada."

The Convoy arrived in Austin midafternoon, so they had time to enjoy the extensive welcome prepared by the townspeople. Austin's *Reese River Reveille* of August 30, 1919 ran this front-page headline:

"Transcontinental Convoy Stayed Over Night in Austin
Local Red Cross Served Ice Cream and Cake"

The article notes that "the (welcoming) committee placed shower baths in the four cells of the jail. . .one of the young men remarked that he had never seen so many men trying to break into a jail." And there was still more entertainment: "Captain Joe Gilbert delivered an address in Shoshone. . .after which about sixty braves and dusky maidens gave an Indian dance in front of the Court House."

I wandered around Austin for a couple of days, noting that most of the current brick buildings along Main Street, buildings like Gridley's General Store, the Masonic-Odd Fellows Hall, and the International Hotel, were all there when Ike and the Convoy rolled past in 1919. The street one sees today is almost exactly the same one they saw a century ago.

Of the Convoy's trip from Austin down to Eastgate on August 28, Elwell Jackson wrote: "Wrecked Trailmobile kitchen shipped back to Washington. Second Trailmobile kitchen broke a wheel and was loaded on truck. Dust caused trouble with magneto of one (truck) and gasoline line of another. Two Class B trucks skidded off road into canyon. Class B Spare Parts truck was stuck in the sand. Usual mountain and desert trails. Made 80 miles in 12.5 hours."

But they found some respite in Eastgate. The 1915 Lincoln Highway Association Guidebook lists Eastgate as being at an altitude of 5,291 feet and having: "Meals, lodging, gas, oil, drinking water, radiator water, campsite. A fine place to stop."

Just west of Austin on my way toward Eastgate, I passed through Cold Springs, a tiny roadside settlement today. But a two-mile walk to the south, uphill through the sagebrush and jackrabbits, brings you to the Cold Springs Pony Express station, one of the main stations on this stretch of the route. The British explorer Richard Burton, famed for discovering the source of the Nile, passed through here in October 1860 and wrote about it:

> A wretched place, half built and wholly unroofed; the four boys, an exceedingly rough set, ate standing and neither paper nor pencil was known amongst them. Our animals found good water in a rivulet from the neighboring hills and the promise of a plentiful feed. . .whilst the humans, observing that a beef had been freshly killed, supped upon an excellent steak. We slept under the haystack and heard the loud howling of the wolves, which are said to be larger in these hills than elsewhere.

I stopped to walk around at Eastgate, a handful of low buildings crouched beneath an enormous looming rock formation just to the north. James Simpson first passed through here back in 1859 and named the location Gibraltar Gate for the towering rock. Eastgate was for many years an active ranch, trading post, and stopping point for overland travelers like Ike and the Convoy, but today it appears abandoned, its buildings slowly but resolutely falling into ruin.

I noticed a large black boulder right out in the middle between the houses and the barns and stables and later learned that this was a medicine rock for the Paiutes and Shoshone. It was sacred for them, and Paiutes and Shoshone would come from miles away to rub their heads on a particular spot on the Rock. That spot was completely smooth and still gleamed brightly in the sunlight.

I also later learned of a big cavern called the Water Baby cave in the rock face right up above Eastgate. There were allegedly mystical spirits, powerful spirits, in that cave, and local residents would not enter. But one year, researchers from Berkeley came out, entered the cave, and removed several items. Never was the same after that. An earthquake in 1954 changed the course of the streams, and then a heavy cloudburst in 1961 silted everything up. All because of what one person called "those professors in pith helmets."

The Convoy departed Eastgate on August 29 and Elwell Jackson reports they stopped for "noon chow at Frenchman's station near enormous sand dune 380 feet high." Sand dunes that big tend to move slowly, so this one is still there but is now, according to the Bureau of Land Management, 600 feet high. The BLM today manages the dune and surrounding 4,800 acres as the Sand Mountain Recreation Area, visited by some 30,000 tourists per year. A young man in a dune buggy was parked at the base of the dune, so I went over to talk with him. He told me his name was Rob and that he came out from Fallon on a regular basis to ride over the dune.

"What's it like up there near the top?" I asked.

"Can be pretty scary," he said. "But it's fun—I love it."

"Sand pretty deep?"

"Deep in places. You also got razorbacks. And it's always shifting around. Different every time I come out here."

"What's a razorback?"

"You go racin' up to the peak of the dune. Everything looks cool. Then that thing just drops off vertical on the other side. That's a razorback. Flipped over and gone flyin' on razorbacks couple of times—that ain't no picnic."

Well, at least you're not landing on rock," I said.

He peered at me for a moment through his goggles. "You go slidin' down the side of a hot sand dune flat out on your butt—believe me, it ain't no picnic."

I tried to envision the 300 men of the Convoy, resting during noon chow on this very same spot shuffling through what they'd just passed through, what might lay ahead, and where they'd be at nightfall. I wondered if Ike or any others climbed at least part of the way up the dune. But there was no record of that, just Elwell Jackson's terse "three wheels changed on Class B trucks," and then onward.

Before returning to the Convoy's trail I walked over to the nearby Sand Springs Pony Express station, just half a mile or so from the base of the dune. Richard Burton had also visited Sand Springs in 1860, and about this station he wrote: "The water near this vile hole was thick and stale with sulphury salts: it blistered even the hands. The station house was no unfit object in such a scene, roofless and chairless, filthy and squalid, with a smoky fire in one corner, and a table in the center of an impure floor, the walls open to every wind and the interior full of dust."

The Sand Springs station was covered in sand and forgotten for over 100 years until it was rediscovered and excavated in 1976. So when Ike and the Convoy passed by, it lay hidden beneath the drifting sands. Despite the fact that every Pony Express rider had to swear, "I will drink no intoxicating liquors," the most common items found during excavation were fragments of liquor bottles.

Next from Elwell Jackson: "Conditions crossing Carson Sink similar to those on Great Salt Lake Desert, although Fallon Fill was passable but very rough and dusty." I drove on along the Loneliest Road, past the ruins of the old Frenchman's Station, which had been destroyed by the US Navy in 1984 in the process of turning the entire area into a Naval bombing range. Carson Sink and Fallon Fill were indeed very much like the Great Salt Lake desert. I got out to walk for about half an hour, and while I meandered around only two cars passed. The impossibly white sands shimmered. The sun was intermittently behind clouds, but when it thrust out in full force the reflection was blinding. I could imagine members of the Convoy experienced some anxiety about getting through this stretch after what they had endured crossing the Great Salt Lake desert, and they must have been mightily relieved when they were safely past it.

I had the easy passage of the Loneliest Road of course, but I also had another souvenir of modernity: graffiti. All along the road were larger rocks with painted graffiti, or smaller rocks arranged to spell out someone's name. "Eddie'; "Marie," "Tyler"; "Bobby." "Susan + Rodger." I assumed this was all recent, but given the climate, the graffiti, like the dune, was unlikely to move anytime soon. I drove on toward Fallon.

Just short of Fallon I stopped off to see the millennia-old petroglyphs at Grimes Point, an isolated expanse with views miles-wide under a high glowing sky. To the south you could see the ancient sea-level markings in a sandstone rock face. It was a lonely spot that required some serious hiking uphill over rocks, boulders, and ankle-deep sand through the afternoon sun. But it was worth it, to stand in the swallowing wide-open spaces amid art created over 8,000 years ago, the wind whipping through the rocks and over the sand, and no other sound anywhere.

Suddenly, there was a zooming noise, growing louder and deeper. It was unmistakably the sound of an aircraft, either taking off or landing—I couldn't tell. I couldn't tell which direction it was coming from either, and the prolonged roar was disconcerting out in the middle of what I had thought were wide-open empty spaces. I looked all around but saw nothing—no planes, no vapor trails, no sign of anything.

I drove on toward Fallon, past signboards warning "Caution! Low Flying Aircraft." And then the sign for the turnoff to the Fallon Naval Air Base, which I later learned was the Navy's Top Gun naval air training base. The source of the zooming out in the wide desert. I remembered Donna at the Paradise Ranch Castle B&B telling me she had complained about sonic booms, and then they had stopped, even though she had never actually seen any planes. And in my several days of poking around in Fallon, hearing the zooming on a regular basis, I still never actually saw a plane.

As in so many towns along the route, the arrival of the Convoy in Fallon was an opportunity for some civic boosterism. The *Churchill County Eagle* of August 30, 1919, proudly reports: "Let it be recorded that the military Convoy passed through Churchill County over the Lincoln Highway on schedule time and without mishap, which is very gratifying." The civic pride that the safe and uneventful passage of the Convoy generated was also accompanied by an increased attention to the condition of roads and a renewed enthusiasm for the Good Roads Movement. An earlier article in the *Churchill County Eagle* reports on a town meeting prior to the Convoy's arrival: "It is hard to realize the vast importance of this Convoy. . .the roads should be put in the best possible condition. . .the Good Roads boosters will plan for the improving of the roads."

In Fallon I dropped by the Coverston Garage and spent some time at the Overland Hotel and Saloon, both of which were open and right on the Convoy's route back in 1919. Although there's no record, it seems a certainty that at least some of the 300 men would have paid the saloon a visit, and the garage—one of only a few along the route in Nevada—must have been worth a visit by the Convoy's mechanics. The Overland has been in business continuously since 1907 and is still a lively spot, with delicious Basque cuisine and a bustling saloon. Coverston's garage was opened in 1911, making it one of the oldest garages in Nevada, but it closed in 1974.

Signs in Fallon store windows for upcoming events:

"Octanefest! Fairgrounds!"
"Heart O' Gold Cantaloupe Festival!"
"World Cowboy Fast Draw Championships!"
"Bucking Horse and Bull Bash!"

The Convoy departed Fallon early on the morning of August 30. The *Churchill County Eagle* of that date reports: "Reveille was sounded while most of the Fallon people were still deeply wrapped in the arms of Morpheus, and the big Convoy swung into line and left over the Lincoln Highway on the way to Carson City at 6:30 this Saturday morning."

The Convoy encountered some of the heaviest going of the trip just west of Fallon. Elwell Jackson: "Required 11 hours to move Convoy from Fallon to a point 12 miles west, on account several stretches of unstable, dry sand up to 1.5 feet deep and wet quicksand. All heavy vehicles. . .had to be pulled and pushed through by combined efforts of Tractor and men. . .Two tankers sank to a depth of 5 feet in sand, requiring extensive excavation." The Convoy didn't reach Carson City until 11:00 that evening, having made just sixty-six miles in over twenty hours of effort. One can almost feel the exhaustion in Elwell Jackson's laconic description of their arrival in the capital: "Convoy met by Gov. Boyle, etc. Chicken dinner."

After a few days in Fallon, I, too, headed west on the Convoy's route, over the Loneliest Road, toward Carson City. Along the way a large sign:

The Treasure Hut!
We Buy, Sell, or Trade Anything!!

A series of small signs, set up in a column like Burma Shave signs:

Jesus is the Truth! Trust Jesus!
Phone 888-FOR-TRUTH!

A large billboard:

Crystal Meth + Ice + Speed = Death

And another:

Meth is a Nevada Epidemic
Don't Give In To It

Abandoned farm equipment, pick-up trucks, RVs—all parked and rusting in the weeds and relentless sun. A Conestoga wagon parked out in the blowing sand with "Jesus Saves!" painted in red on the side. I passed along a stretch of the Central Pacific Railway and later read that in 1869 Chinese laborers completed a ten-mile stretch of the railroad here in a single day, a record that still stands today.

On my way toward Carson City I stopped off in the small town of Dayton, right off the Loneliest Road, to look around and visit the History Museum. There I met Patrick Neylan, a volunteer curator and fount of information on local history. "Most people have never heard of the Sutro Tunnel. It's one of the greatest engineering marvels of the nineteenth century," he told me. The tunnel, built in the 1870s, was the brainchild of mining magnate Adolph Sutro and was intended to transport ore from the high mines near Virginia City down to the envisioned town of Sutro, near Dayton. But by the time the tunnel was completed, ore was being carried by railroads, so the four-mile-long tunnel dug through solid rock lay unused, and the town of Sutro withered. But during a late nineteenth-century blizzard, Virginia City was completely snowed in, and tons of potatoes were hauled up through the empty tunnel to save the day.

When gold was discovered at the mouth of Gold Canyon in 1849, Dayton was founded on the site, making it one of Nevada's oldest towns, and a few years later the historic Comstock Lode was discovered nearby. In the 1870s, hundreds of Chinese laborers were brought in; Patrick told me that at first they weren't trusted in the mines, so they labored on the town's waterworks and on other construction. But as gold and silver fever escalated, the Chinese went to work in the mines as well. At one time there were so many Chinese in Dayton that the entire town was known as China Town. Today visitors can take a look at China Mary's House, the only structure remaining from the Chinese community and a reputed former gambling house, opium den, and who knows what else.

Patrick filled me in on plenty of other local lore, such as Dayton Cemetery, Nevada's oldest; the special spot where ice was harvested on the Carson River; and of course, the bar where Clark Gable and Marilyn Monroe hung out while filming *The Misfits*, the last movie either of them made. By 1919, when Ike and the Convoy passed through, Dayton's population had dwindled to some 500, and the county seat had been moved elsewhere. But when I walked around there for an hour, virtually alone in streets largely devoid of either car or human, I could marvel at the many threads of history all now intertwined in such a small town—from fortune-seeking desperados to grasping would-be magnates to struggling Chinese laborers and all the other supporting cast all the way down through the Convoy that passed by, perhaps oblivious to much of that history as they struggled over a barely passable road, and finally culminating in Clark Gable and Marilyn Monroe down to today as the town tries to reinvent itself as a tourist destination.

I departed Dayton and made another short detour, twisting northward up through the mountains to Virginia City. I was primarily motivated to see the spot where Mark Twain got his start as a writer with a two-year stint as city editor of the *Daily Territorial Enterprise*. But I was also curious to see the frontier town that featured prominently in the wildly popular 1960s western TV series *Bonanza*. Most people my age can no doubt remember tuning in on Sunday evenings to follow the exploits of Pa Cartwright and his three sons, Adam, Hoss, and Little Joe. They ruled over a huge cattle ranch known as the Ponderosa, but whenever they had business in town, they duly rode into Virginia City. This usually led to trouble, but all inevitably ended well, and one of the sons got to be hero for the week.

Bonanza memorabilia and signs are everywhere in current-day Virginia City, including saloons like the Ponderosa, the Red Dog, and the Bucket of Blood, where actors in period costume frequently enact staged shootouts. Right across the street from the Bucket of Blood is the Delta saloon, which features Little Joe Burgers and Hoss Burgers with fries.

Sign in a Virginia City store window:

"Handguns are better than women; You can put a silencer on a handgun"

Mark Twain ventured west in 1862, a stagecoach trek from St. Louis memorably recounted in his first book, *Roughing It*. He stayed on as city editor at the *Territorial Enterprise* until 1864, and the desk where he worked, along with many of his books, are all on display at the former newspaper office, now the Mark Twain museum, just down the street from the Bucket of Blood. The entire newspaper office was located in one long room in the basement. The press was steam-powered, and next to Twain's desk stood a long composing table where he often took short naps if publication was running late. I flipped through some old copies of the *Daily Enterprise* and noted that "Rumorsville: Factville" was a daily front-page feature to which he contributed. Twain wrote "The Celebrated Jumping Frog of Calevaras County" at this desk, and began work on *Roughing It*, which he ultimately completed after moving to California.

Staged gunfights are re-enacted regularly in Virginia City nowadays, but in Twain's day real gunfights were a common occurrence. As Twain notes in *Roughing It*: "The first twenty-six graves in the Virginia City cemetery were all occupied by murdered men. . ..in a new mining district the rough element predominates and a person is not respected until he has killed his man." In writing about his efforts to fill his column inches as a new reporter, he notes his growing desperation as publication hour approached and he had nothing to write about. "When things began to look dismal again, a desperado killed a man in a saloon and joy returned."

Twain writes that he felt he had "found his calling" as a newspaper reporter, and it's a good thing he did because he failed miserably, even catastrophically, at everything else he tried. He once, through sheer carelessness, started a massive fire in virgin forest on the shores of Lake Tahoe, and on another occasion lost a valuable silver claim through incomprehensible neglect. Virginia City's *Daily Territorial Enterprise* rescued him from not just obscurity but also likely ruin. Twain died in 1910, and at the time of the Convoy he was one of the country's most revered and widely read writers.

From Virginia City I proceeded steeply downhill back to the Loneliest Road, past a huge spider made entirely of parts from Volkswagen beetles, and into the center of state capital Carson City, where the Convoy spent a couple of days resting up. *The Carson City Daily Appeal* for September 2, 1919, headlines: "Welcome to the Army Transport Corps!" and details the grandiose welcome accorded the exhausted Convoy, which straggled in from midafternoon August 30 until late morning August 31. No matter. As the *Appeal* writes: "But if the boys of the train had a hard time in overcoming the obstacles and difficulties which confronted them on the road between Fallon and Carson, it was dispelled and turned into joy by the reception they received when they arrived in this city." The entire Convoy was taken — in stages as they arrived — to the capital grounds where an enormous banquet had been arranged. The *Appeal*: "The tables were beautifully arranged, spread with linen and ornamented with flowers and real silver. . .and flocking above them, like ministering angels, were the ladies and girls of the local chapter of the Red Cross, anticipating and attending to their every want."

Carson City, named after Kit Carson, has been territorial or state capital since the city was founded in 1858. Nevada's transition to statehood was somewhat tenuous, but the state abruptly gained strong support in Washington when silver from Nevada played a key role in financing the Union during the Civil War. During the war, passage of the Thirteenth Amendment looked questionable, so Nevada was admitted to statehood in 1864 in exchange for the crucial two votes needed for adoption.

The silver deposits of the Comstock Lode were the deciding factor in siting a US mint in Carson City. The mint issued its first coins — both gold and silver — in 1870 and continued operations until 1893. Ike and the Convoy passed right by the mint building in 1919, and at that time it was the US Assay Office for gold and silver. Today the building serves as the Nevada State Museum. Morgan silver dollars minted in Carson City are now prime collectors' items.

Just on the outskirts of Carson City, the Stewart Indian School opened in 1890 with thirty-seven students from the Washoe, Paiute, and Western Shoshone tribes, and three teachers. The school was established as a boarding school and managed by the Bureau of Indian Affairs. As enrollment increased over the years, new dormitories and classrooms were added, and the school earned its own train stop in 1906. By 1919, when Ike and the Convoy passed through, the school had over 400 students and was considered the premier school for Indians in the entire US. Classes included the basics of reading, writing, and arithmetic but had a sharp focus on vocational training such as stone masonry, agriculture, and the service industry. Boys could take classes in ranching, mechanics, carpentry, and painting, and girls were offered cooking, sewing, nursing, and laundry.

But there were many allegations over the years that students were beaten and severely mistreated, and that the school was a thinly veiled attempt to westernize Native Americans. Native dress and languages were strictly forbidden, and transgressors were severely punished. The school closed in 1980 due to budget cuts and over concerns about building safety in an earthquake zone, but the attractive masonry buildings, built by students with the guidance of Hopi stone masons, are still standing although now mostly boarded up. The

Bureau of Indian Affairs has an office on the campus, and limited training programs are still offered. When I walked around I saw six squad cars with "Peace Officer Standards Training" emblazoned on the sides.

Ad in Carson City's *Nevada Appeal*:

2 Tie the Knot!

"We will come to the location of your choice and set up one of our themed, complete wedding packages. Or maybe you just need an officiant. Either way,. . .you'll be amazed at our flexibility. From Wild West – to Romantic – to Elegant, we offer you a range of themes,,, and are happy to be a part of making that dream come true."

The Convoy enjoyed a well-deserved rest day in Carson City. The men got a chance to wash off the desert dust at hot springs near the town, which are still open and bustling with activity today—the parking lot was full when I visited. Convoy members attended religious services on the capital grounds and were officially greeted by Governor Boyle. They spent the remainder of the day preparing for the next day's challenge: a long and treacherous crossing of the Sierra Nevada via the 7,800-foot King's Grade, and then down into California at Lake Tahoe.

Everyone was aware that the King's Grade crossing would be one of the most arduous stretches of the entire trip, so preparations were extensive. Elwell Jackson writes:

> Convoy arranged with heaviest vehicles in lead. Temporary control established at base of King's Grade for inspection of steering gears, brakes, tow chains and wheel blocks, also for spacing vehicles 100 yds. apart. . ..Experienced drivers only allowed to drive and one man on each vehicle stood ready to block the wheels at each halt. . .Nevada State Highway Dept. suspended all eastbound traffic from 6:30 a.m. until after Convoy had crossed the Sierras.

I had seen photos of the Convoy on this portion of the trip and longed to see the King's Grade Crossing today, and to relive that same experience of the crossing of the Sierras. I went into the Carson City tourist office and met a pleasant man with piercing blue eyes and thinning blond hair. I told him about my quest and said I would love to follow the Convoy's trail over the King's Canyon Road. "I know it's a tough road nowadays, but I'd love to follow their trail," I said.

He looked at me for what seemed like an extraordinarily long amount of time, and then he said, "Yeah. You just might be able to make it. Maybe. Lotta snow and ice up there. Deep gullies from the run-off. No place to turn around. You got you a tough, high four-wheel drive?"

"Well, no," I said. "I've got a small Chevy sedan. Will that be okay?"

He did not say anything right away. This was not your normal pause, but a fingers stroking the chin, looking up at the ceiling, shuffling your feet pause. He gazed around, to the right at the tourist brochures, left at the restrooms, and then up at the fluorescent lights. For a short time, he looked out the front window like he hoped to see some kind of helpful advice parked out there. But finally he looked back at me and said, "I really would not advise you to do that road. That particular road? In a sedan? No. Don't do it."

So I didn't do it. But instead, the following morning, I drove up as far as I could go to a trailhead on King's Canyon Road, parked my Chevy, and started walking uphill on the narrow curving road. Within moments I was thankful for his advice. There were gullies two feet deep and a vertical drop-off on one side hundreds of feet into a rock canyon. No possible way to turn around. In the first fifteen minutes I saw three bicyclists, but after that nobody. After about ninety minutes of sweaty uphill climbing, I rounded a corner and encountered a sign: "Warning: You are Entering Bear and Mountain Lion Habitat." This gave me pause, but I rationalized that any sensible mountain lion or bear would, unlike me, never venture out in the 100-degree midday sun.

I kept on going. At every curve I thought that at the next curve there must be a spectacular view, but that always turned out to be just one more curve right ahead. Sweat pouring, dusty uphill climb, no other people, and ravenous bears and mountain lions lurking and ready to pounce on the hills right up above me. I wondered if Ike ever had days like this.

I finally rounded a corner, crested a hill, and abruptly had a spectacular view. I stopped for a moment to reflect on how Ike and the Convoy must have felt when they had exactly the same view a hundred years ago. On the way up I had thought that at the top I'd have a great view down into California, but such was not the case. Instead, there was a gorgeous valley and then a still higher, snow-covered mountain range looming right ahead. This might have caused Ike and the Convoy some consternation, but they were no doubt prepared for this stretch of road. Imagine the thousands of wagon-train settlers that preceded them. Many of these earliest settlers, like the doomed Donner

Party, were racing against the clock to get down out of the mountains and into California's central valley before the onset of winter snows, so the sight of an even higher peak to surmount must have been disheartening.

The Convoy labored onward throughout the day. Elwell Jackson writes:

> Reached altitude of 7,630 at summit over narrow winding road of sand and broken stone, cut out of, and in places, built up on mountain side. Total climb 14 miles made in 6 hours, slow progress being necessary to prevent accident. Grades of 8% to 14%. Crossing Sierras without accident may be considered noteworthy achievement for heavy vehicles.

Reno and Carson City had vied with one another in trying to attract the Convoy through their towns, and once the Convoy had decided on Carson, Reno newspapers had wasted no time in slamming the route west from Carson. So the *Carson City Daily Appeal* took particular pleasure in reporting the successful passage over King's Canyon Road in the September 2, 1919, issue.

> None of the calamities which were predicted by Reno or Reno papers developed on the trip yesterday from Carson to State Line. The roads stood up well under the test and the Cave Rock Bridge proved a Gibraltar, despite the suspicion put out by the Reno Gazette that. . .the bridge. . .would crumble under the weight of the trucks. . .It was a nasty knock that Reno gave the road, and it was absolutely uncalled for.

I backtracked from King's Canyon Road and returned to the safe and sure Lincoln Highway, heading south out of Carson City, and then west over the Sierras. Curves, switchbacks, steep grades, all over the perfect wide asphalt. I passed Spooner Summit at 7,100 feet and saw snow still piled up in shady areas, even in midsummer. Suddenly, I came upon towering trees and a thick conifer forest.

Friends had told me that I wouldn't believe the deep blue of Lake Tahoe in the sunlight, and indeed, at the first clear sight of the lake I pulled over just to take a longer look. Even the consistently businesslike Elwell Jackson had been struck by the beauty of the scene. On September 1 he wrote: "Scenery throughout day of greatest beauty, especially at Lake Tahoe." The lush forest, the snow-capped peaks in the background, the impossible blue of the lake — they were all somewhat overwhelming after the days of windswept desert I had just traversed. I made slow progress along the lake because I stopped every few minutes just to gape and gawk. But I drove on, past snow-streaked Mount Genoa looming off to my left at 9,200 feet, past Zephyr Cove, past Cave Rock, past a slew of last-chance Nevada casinos, and finally crossed into California.

CALIFORNIA

"Those were all good times. . .when the tourist business was poor and the time passed extremely slowly, as time should pass, with the days lingering and long, spacious and free as the summers of childhood."

–Edward Abbey

Crossing in through the tacky last-minute casinos and then along the forested road with resorts and scattered hotels. Rooms! B & B! The highway was now miles removed from Lake Tahoe. I wandered down a couple of roads off northward toward the lake and ran into luxury homes, clubs, and gated communities. I retreated and kept on going westward through thick stands of spruces and firs, up and over more of the Sierras.

On September 1 Elwell Jackson wrote:

> At California-Nevada line the War Camp Community Service and Mayor's Commission of San Francisco gave fine barbecue and enthusiastic welcome. Mr. Celic, owner of Meyer's Ranch, served refreshments in evening around huge campfire, while the Firestone representative furnished movies and smokes. The Convoy overnighted and rested at Meyer's Ranch, and took off early the next morning at 6:30 a.m.

I continued downhill through steep forested slopes with occasional houses clinging to the hillsides. The tiny town of Kyburz featured a single Main Street sign: "Welcome to Kyburz! Now leaving Kyburz!"

The Convoy departed Meyer's Ranch early, up at 6,000 feet on a cold morning. Elwell Jackson: "Temperature 30 degrees F early in morning. . .12% to 15% grades 3.2 miles to Sierra Nevada Summit, from which point the remainder of the route is down grade through the beautiful American River Canyon. Fair and warm. Made 50 miles in 11.75 hours."

Placerville is a delightful little town where I stayed several days, just wandering around Main Street and environs and checking out the shops and signs: "The Original Mel's—Offering Breakfast All Day Since 1947." Home of the Movie *American Graffiti*. "Liar's Bench Bar." And of course:

Buttercup Pantry Breakfast!
Lunch! Dinner! Pies!

The Buttercup had it all.

I poked into one fascinating shop after another. "The Good Earth Tea and Elixir Bar," "Canines on Main," "Placerville Hardware" (oldest hardware store west of the Mississippi), "The Shabby Rabbit Boutique," "Artisanally Crafted Olive Oil," "Metaphysical Tools." Tortilla Flat Restaurant," which was built around an original 1928 Lincoln Highway marker. A doleful mannequin of a hanging man at the site of the original Hanging Tree, which gave Placerville its original name, "Hanging Town," and the name of a renowned local dish called the Hangtown Fry, a grilled combination of eggs, oysters, and bacon. All of this later gave rise to the Hangtown Street Stomp.

Placerville has seen its share of outsized antic characters over the years. One of the first settlers arrived with a grizzly bear and a donkey with the intention of staging public fights. Emigrant Jane Johnson drove a herd of horses across the Great Plains and over the Sierras to Placerville in 1859 and used the proceeds of their sale to construct a prominent building on Main Street that still stands today. One of the most memorable characters is John A. "Snowshoe" Thompson, who immigrated to the US from Norway back in 1837 when he was ten years old. Thompson eventually settled near Placerville in 1859 and quickly discovered the challenges posed by the massive annual snowfalls in the Sierras. He carved some Norwegian-style skis out of solid oak (later skis were pine) and used them for years to cross the Sierras even during the wildest blizzards, all the way from Placerville to Virginia City. Once he skied from Placerville to Genoa Nevada—90 miles of steep slopes and meters-deep snowbanks—in only three days, then promptly turned around and made the return trip in two days. "Snowshoe" carried mail, supplies, the latest news and weather reports, and frequently rescued wayward travelers floundering about in the High Sierras. Thompson's snowshoes are now on display in the El Dorado County Historical Museum.

The museum also has a small exhibit on Charley Parkhurst, one of California's most famed stagecoach drivers in the mid-nineteenth century, operating along the bandit-infested stretch from Placerville to San Francisco.

Charley in fact helped pioneer the trail that later became the Lincoln Highway and eventually the route for Ike and the Convoy. A horse's well-aimed kick to Charley's left eye led to his nickname, "One-eyed Charley," but this never slowed him down. Upon Charley's 1879 death, neighbors preparing his body for burial discovered that Charley was in fact a woman. Later investigation revealed that Charley had been born Charlotte Parkhurst in Vermont, was orphaned as an infant, and at some point had given birth to a child. The story quickly became a national sensation.

I spent hours at the Historical Museum, reading over the *Placerville Mountain Democrat* and the *El Dorado Republican* from 1919, and also chatting with the ever-friendly librarians. The *Republican's* headline from September 5, 1919, was:

Army Men Are Touched By California Welcome Barbecue and Sports Go Through Without a Hitch Menu Perfect

The article notes that sports included "bronco busting, roping, foot races, including races for ladies."

The *Mountain Democrat*, on September 6, reports on a bit of confusion in the welcoming festivities:

> After a considerable wait at the Court House, during which time the Sacramento Boys Band regaled the crowd. . .it was announced that owing to the fact the crowd was split between the court house and the tower, where the Goodyear Band was giving a concert, all would go to the tower, where the speaking would be held if opportunity knocked.

Opportunity failed to knock, and the dance became the chief attraction. No speeches, just music and dancing! Ike must have been delighted.

One day, a librarian named Nancy told me there was a county fair underway nearby, so I headed there right from the museum. Big crowds of people lined up to get in, and once inside it was nonstop entertainment: kids screeching around on Ferris wheels and roller coasters, caramel popcorn balls and cotton candy. And then there was the Studebaker Wheelbarrow Race, a Placerville annual event for decades. John Studebaker—"Wheelbarrow Johnny"—got his start crafting wheelbarrows in Placerville long before he moved back to Ohio and joined his brothers in crafting carriages and eventually automobiles.

Rules for the Studebaker Wheelbarrow Race include: "All contestants must wear long pants, shirts, and shoes. Absolutely no throwing of equipment." The race requires shoving an unwieldy wheelbarrow up a steep hill, filling it with hefty packs of ore, then piloting the whole thing back down again, swerving past insane obstacles until the finish line. I joined everyone else lining the final stretch and cheering like maniacs for every contestant, even the laughable bumblers. The bumblers mostly crossed the finish line, sat down and wheezed, and then laughed at themselves.

The Convoy set off from at Placerville at 6:30 a.m. and must have almost immediately been cheering—the first paved road since Chicago!! Elwell Jackson: "Departed Placerville. . .Entire route down grade over bitumen surfaced concrete roads lined with palm trees, through peach, almond, orange, and olive ranches and vineyards. Populace showered Convoy with fruits."

The end was in sight. In the years after the Convoy's arrival in San Francisco, Ike had only limited contact with his colleagues from the trip. The Convoy's commanding officer, Lieutenant Colonel McClure, retired from the military immediately after the trip. Ike's buddy Sereno Brett had a tough time. According to General Jacob Devers, who spoke about World War II for the Eisenhower Oral History Project in 1974, "And then we had Sereno Brett of the infantry, who was a top tanker, but inclined to drink too much. . .General Marshall told me he was drinking too much and to do something about it. So I gave him a chance; I got him promoted, and he was my chief of staff. Then I sent him out to a division as a general officer. But later on, he slipped by the wayside."

Captain William Greany, who served as expeditionary adjutant and statistical officer for the Convoy, later became a senior executive with Packard and was also a renowned scoutmaster of Scout Troop 194, Church of Saint Cecilia, Detroit, Michigan. Greany wrote to Ike on July 18, 1950, to say he had seen Ike give a speech and was very proud of him. Ike wrote back with thanks. Greany and Ike exchanged Christmas cards for several years, and Ike wrote him a nice note on the occasion of Greany's retirement from Packard in 1953. Greany wrote back: "Dear President Eisenhower: Thanks a million for your gracious and much-appreciated letter relative to my recent retirement. With every best wish. Sincerely, William Greany."

Captain Art Herrington, who was one of the two advance guides who took off early every morning on Harley-Davidsons and marked the way with those "salmon-colored isosceles triangles," later became a highly successful businessman and eventually the CEO of the Marmon Herrington Company.

He wrote Ike several times in the years just before Ike's presidency, and they had a low-key correspondence for a few years.

There are still lonely portions of the original Lincoln Highway that you can track down, winding up and down through the beautiful curving grasslands just west of Cameron Park. They are rare stretches that were paved with concrete even before 1919, so the Convoy rolled over exactly the same pavement that now has weeds sprouting up through the cracks. I parked and wandered around alone with no person in sight, the heat and the rolling hills and golden dry grass all around. Relentless sunlight. Thinking this could be the last solitary moment of my trip. I was about to encounter the gathering jams of Sacramento down to San Francisco. I savored this moment and thought about those other solitary moments of the trip, and about the solitary moments of Ike and the Convoy members, reflecting on what they had done, what lay ahead.

About entering the state capital of Sacramento, Elwell Jackson writes:

> Entered Sacramento leading parade of motor trucks. Camped in State Fair Grounds with Fair in progress. Dinner and cabaret to entire personnel by courtesy of Mr. John Willys. Dances for both officers and enlisted men. Fair and warm. Perfect roads.

Ike wrote:

> Governor William D. Stephens. . .compared us to the immortal Forty-Niners. He reminded everyone of the hardship, privation, discouragement, and even death incurred to reach this new land. "Their blood is the blood of the western country," he said. "Strong – virile – self-reliant. . .So, in this journey of yours across the plains. . .etc." the speeches ran on and on in a similar vein.

Sacramento in 1919 was a city of superlatives, and it still is: State's oldest city, highest trees, greatest diversity, most almonds. But there were some negative superlatives back in the mid-nineteenth century. The Squatters' Riot Plaque in downtown Sacramento commemorates an 1850 bout of citywide mayhem involving hundreds of settlers with dubious land claims, unscrupulous fortune-hunters, clamoring squatters, and an overmatched city government. The Sisters of Mercy statue on the state capital grounds commemorates the 1857 arrival of the first contingent of Sisters of Mercy with the mission "help the sick, the homeless, the poor." With the maelstrom of chaotic forces unleashed by the Gold Rush, all three categories existed in abundance in Sacramento in those days. To top it all off, shortly after the Sisters' arrival a raging cholera epidemic broke out.

I wandered around Sacramento for two days, visiting libraries and just meandering. I resisted the urge to take a detour to the northern suburbs just so I could stand and snap a selfie at the intersection of Klingon and Romulon streets. The Convoy pushed off from Sacramento early on September 4. Elwell Jackson writes, "Departed Sacramento. Route through most productive fruit ranches and vineyards in the world." A century later it's still plums, apricots, almonds, pears, strawberries and cherries everywhere you look.

Passing through Stockton nowadays, one might see: "K Mart: Everything Must GO!" Little Vietnam Plaza, a Mexican Restaurant that had been converted into a fire station, and a movie theater that had been converted into a Thai Restaurant. Noodle shops everywhere. And later the Sunny Valley Baconfest: "Bacon! Beer! Bands!" A Sikh Temple and Sal's Foreign Cars. The Lincoln Way right through downtown Galt, Lincoln Highway signs and historical monuments on all sides.

Arriving at Stockton, Elwell Jackson noted:

> Escorted into and through Stockton by Mayor, Red Cross. . .and commercial truck parade. Populace called out by fire whistle. . .Personnel tired out by continuous, strenuous efforts of past several weeks, but morale is high at immediate prospect of attaining final objective. Dinner and dance at Hotel Stockton. Fair and warm. Fine concrete roads. Made 48 miles in 7.5 hours.

Nowadays you have the Wat Dharmararam Buddhist Temple in Stockton. I asked several pedestrians about the location of the temple and got answers ranging from, "What are you talking about?" to "Go away!"

The Convoy spent the night in Stockton, everyone no doubt glowing at the knowledge that this was the next-to-last stop on the journey. Of the next morning's early departure, Elwell Jackson writes:

> Departed Stockton 6:15 A.M. . .Drove over best section of entire Lincoln Highway. 2 Rikers & Packard broke fan belts. Class B trucks had broken spark plug porcelain, broken fan belts & brakes required adjustment. Indian motorcycle broke control wire.

About this entry in Elwell Jackson's log, Ike later wrote "But that was the last of our troubles, except for the final speeches."

I stopped off to visit the historic Summit Garage at Altamont Pass. Altamont is, alas, best known for a calamitous 1969 rock concert featuring Jefferson Airplane; Crosby, Stills, Nash, and Young; and the Rolling Stones. It was a free concert attended by some 300,000 people, originally billed as "the

Woodstock of the West." Accounts differ, but several say the Stones hired Hell's Angels to provide security in exchange for $500 worth of beer. The results were ugly: one person was stabbed to death, two were killed in a hit-and-run accident, and another drowned while looped on LSD. But the nearby Summit Garage, servicing vehicles for over a century, serenely perseveres to this day, now serving not only as a garage but also a post office and an antique store. Ike and the Convoy passed right by it.

The Duarte Garage is a longstanding landmark in the town of Livermore: Francisco Duarte bravely built his own lonely garage out on a hillside in wandering open spaces on the only highway that existed in those parts in 1915. He sold gas and oil products and performed repairs in a sizeable garage that he later tacked on out behind the petrol pumps. His was the only garage on what soon became the Lincoln Highway down in the San Joaquin Valley, so he got lots of business. In 1923 he expanded further and began selling Durant, Flint, and Star automobiles. Francisco's son, Frank, continued the garage until he passed away in 1973. The city of Livermore purchased the garage and land and had plans to demolish it and use the land as a park, but the Livermore Heritage Guild signed a lease to restore and maintain the garage for use as a museum, so it still stands today. Ike and the Convoy passed right by it.

Just down the road from Duarte's Garage lies Livermore Labs, founded in 1952 by Ernest Lawrence and Edward Teller, one of the creators of the atomic bomb. Livermore set its course during Ike's Presidency: enhancing US security by advancing nuclear weapons technology—the cornerstone of American defense policy during Ike's years in the White House. But nowadays Livermore does plenty of other things, like decoding DNA, perfecting airborne surveillance, and bringing fusion power to fruition.

I spent two days in windy Hayward, of which Elwell Jackson makes no mention. There was a large Japanese population in Hayward that was forcibly moved in 1942 to the Topaz Relocation Camp in Utah due to fears about Japanese infiltration. They endured three years in Topaz and other locations, and after World War II almost all returned to Hayward as model US citizens.

Hayward suffered a 7.0 earthquake back in 1868, and the forecast is for a similarly large quake every 140 years or so. They are way overdue. I strolled through the Castro Valley Car Show on half a mile of Hayward's Castro Valley Boulevard on a Saturday afternoon. I saw thousands of visitors and over 300 vehicles on display, including the first-ever Batmobile from the original *Batman* TV series. This was the eleventh annual event, sponsored by the

Castro Valley Moose Lodge. Various vendors lined both sides of the street, including Castro Valley craft breweries doing a brisk business.

I heard a lot of spectators commenting on the colors of the cars: bright colors versus original look. Which one is appropriate for a MAJOR CAR SHOW? Black or Chartreuse? At precisely 4:45 all 300 cars attempted to start up and drive away. It was not smooth. Some cars sputtered and wheezed, smoke spiraling up from behind. Some rumbled and lurched lamentably. Others made discouraging deep bass moans and then checked out permanently. But most started up and cruised off, a fine show of Black Model Ts, Yellow Model Ts, Tangerine Packards, Fuschia Impalas, Purple GTOs, Baby Blue Mustangs. Big round of applause from all of us.

The September 3, 1919, edition of *the Oakland Tribune* headlined, "Uncle Sam's Motor Fleet Arrives Today! Oakland to Welcome Motorists with Caravan, Banquet, Dance, and Other Forms of Entertainment" and further elaborated, "Vehicles that have come 3,000 miles from Washington DC, over mountains, through valleys, across great plains and parching heat-scorched deserts. . .arrived in Oakland this afternoon."

The Oakland Tribune holds the distinction of being the first newspaper in the US to publish the work of an African American woman on a regular basis. Delilah Beasley wrote for the *Tribune* from 1925 to 1934, but perhaps more importantly, she single-handedly chronicled the myriad achievements of African Americans in settling California, in her book *The Negro Trail-Blazers of California*. That book was published in 1919, just about the time Ike and the Convoy were passing through Oakland.

A couple of months earlier I had started phoning Alice Waters' famed Chez Panisse restaurant in Berkley for reservations. "Breakfast, lunch, dinner, anytime, any day," I said. But all was hopeless. The courteous but firm lady on the phone said, "Sir, we book up months in advance. We may have something to offer you in November." So instead of savoring Chez Panisse, I ate a midafternoon lunch in downtown Oakland at Mountain Mike's Pizzeria located on a lively street corner that offered great opportunities for gazing at pedestrians.

While sitting there at my Formica table in Mountain Mike's, I started ruminating about the Slow Food movement—of which Alice Waters has been a central driving force—and a possible comparison with something I thought of as Slow Travel. I had travelled slowly all across the country, following the track of the Convoy over dirt and gravel, stopping to poke around here and there and yak with complete strangers, and often covering only fifty miles per day. I was almost never on an interstate, or even a four-lane highway, and I had loved every moment of it.

I recognize that not everyone has the luxury of travelling at such a leisurely pace. You may have the boss hollering, "Conference at 9 a.m. and you're presenting!" Or you have Grandma warning, "The turkey's coming out of the oven at 2 p.m. and you better be here!" But for those who do have an option, why not consider a Slow Travel movement? Avoid interstates. Seeking out backroads, like William Least Heat Moon did in *Blue Highways*. Eat at mom-and-pop cafes. If you have a destination that you could reach over the Interstate in two days, take four days and do it in Slow Travel mode. Discover and savor America. Whether they knew it or not, that's precisely what Ike and the Convoy did, way back then in 1919.

On approaching Oakland, Elwell Jackson wrote:

> Convoy met 10 miles east of Oakland by city officials, reception committee. . .Escorted through Court of Honor and flag-festooned streets, while all whistles around Bay were blowing. Elaborate electrical and fireworks display. Dinner, Hotel Oakland. Dance, municipal auditorium. Fair and warm. Unexcelled roads.

I wandered around Oakland for a few days, checking out sites like the historic art deco Paramount Theater, an art school that was previously a YWCA, a vegan soul food restaurant that, alas, was closed for the day, as well as Biryani Kebab and a Taqueria nearby. Sauntering through Merritt Park I passed by Whites, Blacks, Latinos, Asians, men in Sikh turbans and women in hijab. I saw the Oakland Embarcadero, where the entire Convoy boarded ships to cross over the Bay and into San Francisco, and Heinold's First and Last Chance Saloon, a harbor institution since 1883, and no doubt visited by members of the Convoy. The "Whoops! Don't Worry, We Can Fix That" cell phone repair shop. A bar with a sign "Why Can't Every Hour be Happy Hour?" Jack London history everywhere.

Eventually I passed by the Hotel Oakland, site of the last banquet for the Convoy before arrival in San Francisco. The Hotel Oakland is now the Hong Kong Home for the Elderly, and all signs are in Chinese with English subtitles. When I approached the front door, residents milling around or sitting in rocking chairs all stared up at me and started chattering among themselves in Chinese, no doubt wondering what a WASPy-looking stranger like me was doing wandering around there. I said hello and then retreated, but I couldn't help noticing the neatness of the grounds: perfectly trimmed hedges, carefully groomed mulch, flowering trees in Euclidean symmetry.

There were mesmerizing wall murals everywhere in downtown Oakland. Vibrant colors, amazing designs. Outsized graffiti on brick, concrete, plaster, and every other surface. On walls by parking lots, empty spaces, derelict old buildings. I found them all amazing and took many photos as I wandered around.

And then I ran into a graying lanky man in a red sweatshirt and a 49ers cap. "It's a goddamned mess. Goddamned shit on every wall, everywhere you look. If you're out walking, you can't even look up without seeing some kinda shit stuff somewhere." I made some small talk with him, and he told me his name was Norman. "I grew up right around the corner here. Nice, respectable neighborhood. Always. Seventy-eight years I've been in this neighborhood. Clean. Hard-working. But now it's all changed, and you got this shit all over the walls."

I let him go on for quite a while, but when he was silent I ventured, "But some of the murals are quite artistic, don't you think?."

"Artistic? Fuckin' artistic?! This shit is nothing but fuckin' garbage," Norman said, and he swept his arm around 360 degrees. "This country has gone down to nothin'. Nothin'. Whole fuckin'country. We're at the very bottom. The very fuckin' bottom."

"Well, we fought a civil war against one another back in the 1860s," I said. "That was surely worse than nowadays."

"Never been so bad as now. People puttin' shit all over the walls. Everywhere. And nobody doing a goddamned thing about it! Shit everywhere! Never been so bad!"

I halted at this point and watched as Norman continued up Jefferson Street, still waving his arms and ranting to himself.

On the final day of his journey, September 6, 1919, Elwell Jackson wrote:

> Convoy crossed San Francisco Bay on two ferry boats, and immediately paraded through the city to Lincoln Park. "The end of the Trail," where medals were presented to the entire personnel by the Lincoln Highway Association, and the Convoy was formally received by. . .(officials). Milestone marking western terminus of Lincoln Highway dedicated. Red Cross Canteen Service served lunch. Convoy parked at the Presidio. Fair and warm. Paved city streets.

Paved city streets after the bothersome swirling dust of Iowa or the deep sinking sands of Utah no doubt seemed like a particular godsend. Everyone in the Convoy must have been reflecting not only on the perfectly paved roads of San

Francisco, but also on what they had just accomplished. What they had just experienced over the past two months, now that the road's end was at hand. Sometimes we take part in momentous events that don't fully register at the time. So perhaps some of the 300 men in the Convoy looked back years, even decades later, and thought, "That trip was one of the greatest experiences of my life."

The milestone in San Francisco's Lincoln Park marking the Convoy's end and the western terminus of the Lincoln Highway is somewhat of a letdown, forlornly situated amidst litter and weeds next to a noisy bus stop. The parking lot for the Palace of the Legion Honor is on one side, and the Lincoln Park golf course is over the other way. Through the low trees there's a terrific view of the Bay. The Palace of the Legion of Honor design was based on the French Pavilion at the 1915 Panama/Pacific Fair, and builders sought the permission of the French government to copy the design. This was duly granted, but World War I delayed groundbreaking until 1921, so Ike and the Convoy ended their long journey on a high bare spot surrounded by underbrush and scrubby trees, but it was flat and ideally suited for a ceremony that involved several hundred people and dozens of heavy vehicles.

All of the members of the Convoy were honored at a lavish banquet on the evening of September 7, hosted once again by the reliably supportive Willys-Overland Company. The menu included:

California Ripe Olives

Salted Almonds

Razor Clam Chowder

Sacramento River Salmon, cold en mayonnaise

Country Fried Chicken Hot Rolls

Evergreen Corn on Cob

Roast Sweet Potatoes

Hearts of Lettuce with Dressing

Turkish Melon

Overland Ice Cream

Coffee

Cigars and Cigarettes

California Fruits

Nuts and Raisins

Quite a step up from K rations.

There were many speakers, including Henry Ostermann and S. M. Johnson, as well as Colonel McClure and California Governor William Stephens. All used the occasion to advocate for better roads, including a federal highway program. Colonel McClure: "A national highway system is too important to be left to local whims and prejudices." But the speakers knew there were limits. According to Davies, "The dinner's organizers knew not to let the rhetoric drag too long on weary men. Over the list of honored guests they put this reassurance: 'Don't be alarmed, boys, all speakers have agreed not to exceed the speed limit – which is five minutes.'" Entertainment for the banquet was provided by the likes of the San Francisco Jazz Trio, the Royal Hawaiians, the Whistling Doughboy, and Charles Leonard, advertised as a "Singer of Songs."

In an unplanned coincidence, the entire US naval fleet, with some 15,000 sailors aboard, anchored in San Francisco harbor at precisely the same time as the Convoy's arrival. With thousands of thirsty sailors and soldiers all over the city, barkeepers must have been deliriously happy for a few days at least, as they contemplated Prohibition looming just weeks ahead. Newspapers were full of headlines such as, "Fleet Arrives!" "Truck Convoy Arrives!" It was a massive accretion of national pride coming on top of the recent glories of World War I.

I wandered aimlessly around San Francisco. My hotel room was right on the ocean, and two separate days I walked in various outings toward the bay and back. Van Ness/Post Avenue and Automobile Row. The cable car museum, still an operating cable car garage, after more than 100 years. The Presidio, with the Major W. A. Jones tree, planted to "beautify the post, sharpen the contrast with the surrounding city, and thereby accentuate the power of the government." Some 100,000 trees of 200 distinct types were planted there at the end of the nineteenth century, making it the most ambitious landscaping project ever undertaken by the US Army.

After arriving in San Francisco, the Convoy broke up and everyone went their separate ways. The trucks were all carefully inspected and then sent to various military bases around the western US. Some valuable lessons had been learned. Hokanson writes, "It was apparent to the military that if war should ever come again, a carefully planned and built system of highways would be needed."

In Elwell Jackson's final report (30 single-spaced pages, plus appendices) he writes: "The most uncertain factor in the operation of these motor

vehicles. . .was the inexperience of the drivers. . .some drivers had considerable difficulty in keeping their trucks on the road, while others fell asleep at
the wheel and ran their trucks into the ditch."

But he reports a steady improvement. "As the Convoy proceeded across
the country, the men gained experience with their trucks and confidence in
themselves so that by the time the mountains and desert were reached. . .many
of the men were really competent drivers."

Not exactly glowing praise, but at least there was improvement. About the
vehicles, Jackson's report enumerates a lengthy litany of mechanical and
structural problems but is generally positive overall. He notes, "The fact
that only three trucks were retired from service en route bears tribute to the
effectiveness with which (the maintenance and repair staff) did their work."
But he does make another important point: "Maintenance work was consid-
erably hampered because of the necessity of carrying spare parts for so many
different makes of trucks."

Captain William Greany also filed a final report. His official designation
was Statistical Officer, and he showed his mettle in his report. According
to Greany, the Convoy drove 3,251 miles in 62 days, or 58.1 miles per day
at an average of 6.01 miles per hour. The Convoy traversed "1,778 miles
or 54.7 percent of the mileage was over dirt roads, wheel paths, mountain
trails, desert sands and alkali flats. . .There were also encountered hundreds
of miles of mountain trails some of the most dangerous character with steep
grades, and numberous (sic) sharp turns, where a deviation from the wheel
paths meant destruction in the depths below."

According to his careful count, the Convoy damaged or destroyed eighty-
eight bridges or culverts, and stopped to repair or replace every one of them.
In addition, there had been "230 road accidents, that is, instances of road
failure and vehicles sinking in quicksand or mud, running off the road or
over embankments, overturning, or other mishaps due entirely to. . .appalling
traffic conditions."

The men of the Convoy reported for duty at new locations, according to
orders. Ike was granted leave and writes:

> I had four weeks with Mamie, our son, and her family. The Douds were
> ready for their annual trip to San Antonio to spend the winter. . .(We) joined
> them. . .We had no sooner left Denver than we encountered rain. Never ceasing
> rains. As we got into Oklahoma, all the roads were mud and we bogged down.
> There were moments when I thought neither the automobile, the bus, nor the

truck had any future whatever. Finally we got as far as Lawton. . .from there we could go no further. We stayed a full week, living in the hotel.

Ike also writes:

> That was the week of the World Series when Cincinnati of the National League met Chicago of the National League. . . .Mr. Doud and I (were) wondering why the great Chicago White Sox could not get going. . .We little dreamed that we were second-guessing an event that was to stand. . .as an all-time low for disloyalty and sellout of integrity. Out of the "Black Sox" scandal, I. . .began to form a caution that, at least subconsciously, stayed with me.

Looking back from our current vantage point, we of course know all that Ike couldn't have possibly foreseen. A little over a year later, the death of his beloved son, Icky, of scarlet fever at age three. The rapid proliferation of roads and vehicles, spurred on by the Convoy's heroics. World War II. Normandy. Global heroism. The White House. The interstate highway system and all of its manifold repercussions. It all seems so logically inevitable now, but in September of 1919 Ike was focused on being mudbound and stuck in an Oklahoma hotel room with his in-laws for a week. But a seed had been planted. Ike later wrote: "The trip had been difficult, tiring, and fun. I think that every officer on the Convoy had recommended in his report that efforts should be made to get our people interested in producing better roads."

He went on to expound on this:

> A third of a century later, after seeing the autobahns of modern Germany. . .I decided, as President, to put an emphasis on this kind of road building. . .This was one of the things that I felt deeply about, and I made a personal and absolute decision to see that the nation would benefit by it. The old Convoy had started me thinking about good, two-lane highways, but Germany had made me see the wisdom of broader ribbons across the land.

On my last day in San Francisco I arose well before sunrise and walked out from my hotel into the dunes by the Pacific. I found a good high place to sit facing the pounding ocean. In the darkness I could just make out two people down by the surf, perhaps fishing. A slender, tall woman jogged by and unleashed her retriever for a romp in the sand. I gazed down at the waves as the light slowly grew, and then turned around and faced back eastward, over the tops of the low buildings and the silhouette of the Dutch windmill in Golden Gate Park off to my left. I was thinking about all that I had seen over the past months of travel: the sights, the places, the people. Raj Rajkumar and his autonomous vehicles, Donna and her desert castle, Mel Gould and his roadside creations from rusted old junk. Dutch windmill heritage days. Apple butter days and the five-hole outhouse and the Studebaker wheelbarrow race. The dozens of once lovely but now crumbling small towns. Things in time also: the two little boys disappearing into the woods from their breakfast table, Henry Joy bogged down and fuming in Iowa gumbo, Shoeless Joe Jackson and the Black Sox, Ike's practical jokes out West. Dozens, hundreds of sensations all rattling around in my head, and I knew that I'd have to go back to my desk and somehow craft a sensible narrative out of the whole clattering hubbub of it all.

But for the moment I did not try to organize but instead just let it all roll over me, rolling like the Pacific waves right behind me. And so I sat there for a long time in the cool breeze and the gathering morning light, and I just watched as the sun slowly rose all across America.

CPSIA information can be obtained
at www.ICGtesting.com
Printed in the USA
BVHW041530251119
564681BV00002B/96/P

9 781457 570421